NARRATIVE AND

Also by Nick Lacey

Image and Representation

A-Level Exam Success Guide – Media Studies

NARRATIVE AND GENRE

Key Concepts in Media Studies

Nick Lacey

palgrave

Published by
PALGRAVE
Houndmills, Basingstoke, Hampshire RG21 6XS and
175 Fifth Avenue, New York, N. Y. 10010
Companies and representatives throughout the world

PALGRAVE is the new global academic imprint of
St. Martin's Press LLC Scholarly and Reference Division and
Palgrave Publishers Ltd (formerly Macmillan Press Ltd).

ISBN 0–333–65871–X hardcover
ISBN 0–333–65872–8 paperback

This book is printed on paper suitable for recycling and made from fully managed and sustained forest sources.

A catalogue record for this book is available from the British Library.

10 9 8 7 6 5 4
09 08 07 06 05 04 03

Editing and origination by
Aardvark Editorial, Mendham, Suffolk

Transferred to Digital Printing 2006

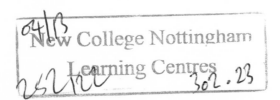

For Alex and Kate

CONTENTS

ACKNOWLEDGEMENTS

The author wishes to thank the following people for their assistance in writing this book: Kevin Atkins, Ian Bangay, Kirstie Barnes, Carl Bergin, Brian Bicat, Chris Bruce, Ian Croasdell, Yasmin Darnbrough, Jennifer Dawson, David Dredge, Catherine Gray, Ian Gray, Michael Greenwell, Kirsten Harrison, Martin Lees, Heather Mott, Ian Rutter, Roy Stafford, Chris Stephens, Norman Taylor, Aardvark Editorial and my wife, Kirsten. Thanks also to my students who have road-tested many of the ideas in this book. In addition, a big thank you to anyone who bought *Image and Representation*.

The author and publishers would like to thank the following for permission to reproduce copyright material:

BBC Worldwide Publishing for the front cover and broadcasting schedules from the *Radio Times*; Nicki Cox at *FHM* for the front cover of *FHM*, January 1998; Cliff Keys at Hitachi Europe for the Hitachi advertisement; the Kobal Collection and Image Select/Ann Ronan for the still from *Sunset Boulevard*; The National Magazine Company Ltd for the front cover of *Cosmopolitan*, January 1998; Ronald Grant Archive for stills from *Conan the Destroyer*, *The Fly*, *The Searchers* and *Lady from Shanghai* and for the *Bladerunner* poster and the picture of the cast of *NYPD Blue*; Tom Tomorrow for the cartoon 'Coming up next on the news...'.

INTRODUCTION

In course planning, 'common sense' often leads to teaching about one medium at a time... placing emphasis solely on the characteristics of only one set of practices... [which] ignores the fact that all individuals experience media as a set of interrelated and interacting systems. (Bowker, 1991, p. 5)

The structure of the series of books

The British Film Institute report Primary Media Education: Curriculum Statement, 'proposed six areas of knowledge and understanding as the basis for... curriculum development' (ibid.):

WHO is communicating, and why? WHAT TYPE of text is it? HOW is it produced? HOW do we know what it means? WHO receives it, and what sense do they make of it? HOW does it PRESENT its subject? (ibid., p. 6)

These 'signpost questions' lead to the following key concepts:

1. media agencies
2. media categories
3. media technologies
4. media languages
5. media audiences
6. media representations.

These key concepts inform the structure of this book, and two others on advanced Media Studies. By concentrating on these approaches to the subject I hope to give the student the basic skills they require for post-16 education, whether in their final years at school/college or in the first year of Media Studies degrees at

1

undergraduate level. It is intended that the books be used as a back-up to teacher/lecturer input.

There is an artificiality in splitting these concepts, for without technology there would be no media; without language we would not understand representation, and so on. However, for pedagogical purposes the categories are very useful.

The adaptation I have made follows the emphasis given by current syllabuses, but as it is dealing with key concepts of the subject, this book should be relevant to any future media syllabus that I can imagine. The adaptation is as follows:

1. media agencies – media institutions
2. media categories – genre
3. media technologies – remains as a category although is not dealt with separately, but in relation to each of the other categories – except in this volume because narrative and genre refers to how texts are *structured* while technology *mediates* this structure
4. media languages – image analysis and narrative
5. media audiences – audiences
6. media representations – representations.

I have paired the adapted concepts to illustrate clearly the interconnectedness of the categories without attempting to encompass the massive intellectual field of the subject in a single book. The three books are *Image and Representation* (Lacey, 1998), *Narrative and Genre* (Lacey, 2000) and *Media Institutions and Audiences* (forthcoming).

The structure of the book

Many students in post-16 education come to Media Studies with little or no previous experience of the subject. Although there is a plethora of books available, most of them are too academic for those who are still at school and some are too complex even for those who are doing a degree course.

Many text books have an implicit model of their audience as being an intellectually static individual. This text book differentiates between the pre- and post-16 student, a difference that represents not just 20 months of study but, for most, the rapid intellectual development of 16–18 year olds.

A consequence of this is that each of the key concepts is dealt with, first, at a basic level, appropriate for students at the beginning of the course. The following chapters introduce more advanced theories, such as ideology and semiotics, which are then applied to the concept. The book should form part of the structure of the (most common) two-year course, with more advanced chapters being used in the later stages. Be aware, though, that it is likely that most advanced level pre-university students will find at least some parts of this book difficult although undergraduates should be able to comprehend all.

For example, this book begins with a basic introduction to narrative theory. The third chapter deals with narrative voice, ideological narrative and alternative narrative systems. Similarly, the section on genre opens with a basic description of a number of case studies and is followed by more difficult concepts such as critiques of genre theory (Chapter 5).

The subject matter of Media Studies is the artefacts that influence us every day of our lives: advertising, movies, videotapes, CDs, the Internet and so on. It investigates how the media operate, what are their rules, conventions and ideological purpose, and what are the artefacts' meaning for us in the early years of the twenty-first century.

Unlike many subjects, Media Studies is exceptionally wide in its scope, without the narrow specialisation of which other qualifications are accused. Media Studies gives us a crucial understanding of our world. It should also be a lot of fun.

The examples I have used are a mixture of contemporary and classic (in the sense of being part of a canon) with an emphasis on film, which reflects my own interests and, in my experience, those of most students. However, these are not meant to supersede teachers' own preferences. Besides, students best understand the key concepts through discussion of their own experiences of media. Although this book can be read in isolation, it is also meant to complement the other volumes in the series. *Narrative and Genre* is the second book and you will find references to the first volume, *Image and Representation*; these are meant to indicate where further information of those key concepts (media language and representation) can be found. One exception to this is the chapter that deals with semiotics; readers are assumed to have, at least, a basic knowledge of the discipline (see Chapter 2 of *Image and Representation*).

One final note of caution. Although this text is obviously usable as a reference book, the later chapters do refer to material discussed earlier and this may cause confusion if sections are read in isolation.

NICK LACEY

Note on the use of examples

One of my pet hates is having people tell me narrative points in texts before I have seen or read them and I do not wish to spoil the narrative enjoyment of the reader. In many cases the 'giving away' of the end is not a problem because, through generic and narrative expectation, 'we know what is going to happen anyway'. I apologise now to any reader who hasn't seen, for example, *Star Wars* and may be frustrated by the fact I give the end away, but I'm sure you knew it anyway.

However, for some texts – like 'whodunits' – pleasure is experienced by the reader because they are ignorant of important facts. If I illustrate ideas using detective texts, I will endeavour not to give anything away in the main body of the text. Other texts, like *The Crying Game* (1992), have narrative 'shocks' within them which should not be revealed until the text allows it. For those who are not bothered about narrative knowledge, or those who have experienced the text referred to, then the full details will appear in Appendix 1 which is ordered alphabetically by title.

1

INTRODUCTION TO
NARRATIVE THEORY

AIMS OF THE CHAPTER

➤ To introduce the idea of narrative through a consideration of openings.

➤ To distinguish between 'story' and 'plot' and consider diegesis and time in narrative.

➤ To explain Todorov's theory and apply it to TV series (The X-Files) and serials (soap opera), and non-fiction texts.

➤ To explain Propp's theory and apply it to the films Se7en and Copycat.

➤ To describe Levi-Strauss's theory of binary oppositions, which is applied to newspaper stories, the reporting of the Gulf War and a Glasgow dustcart drivers' strike.

➤ To consider the ideological consequences of the narrative heroes and villains.

➤ To explain Barthes's narrative theory.

1.1 Introduction

While the term 'narrative' certainly is not as commonly used as 'story', most people know that it refers, in some way, to stories; in fact stories are endemic to our lives. Consider how many stories we experience on a daily basis; the texts may include the following:

- television programmes
- novels or short stories (read or written)
- a film (on television or in the cinema)
- advertisements
- news in newspapers or on television and radio
- via the Internet.

In addition, stories are not limited to texts. When you tell friends about something that has happened, it is unlikely that you only regale them with facts and figures; it is probable that you tell them the event in the form of a story. You were also almost certainly told stories by your parents from a very early age. Stories are not only a great influence upon our culture, anthropologists have yet to find a society in which storytelling was not important. Stories, it seems, are an inescapable part of human life.

However, this book is not called *Story and Genre* and our starting point should be a consideration of what exactly is narrative? As we shall see, narrative is such a powerful analytical tool that it is, arguably, an even more important key concept than genre.

Narrative has probably existed as long as human beings; it is likely that the stone-age artists who drew the 18,000-year-old cave paintings in the Ardèche, France, expected narratives to be woven around their images. Because narrative seems to be such a truly universal aspect of the human race, it is impossible to completely discuss relevance to our existence without dealing with wider discourses, such as psychology, psychiatry, sociology and religion, which are mainly beyond the scope of this text. From a Media Studies perspective, we shall begin by looking at definitions of narrative and, in order to do this, it is useful to consider the openings of a number of texts. Many of us experience our first story at a very young age, possibly beginning with the immortal phrase of countless fairy tales 'Once upon a time...'.

1.2 Once upon a time – openings

Exercise 1.1

Analyse the phrase 'Once upon a time...'

'Once' invites us into a narrative world which is set in the past; indeed, most narratives are recounted in the past tense (one exception is sports commentaries, which recount events as they happen). However, in fairy tales the world we are invited into is one that is very different from the world with which we are familiar. This 'past' is not the same as the one evoked in, say, historical narratives. The 'once' is 'upon a time'. As Berger says: 'It situates the story in the past *and* suggests that it takes place in a different world, one far

6

removed from that of the teller, listener, or reader' (my emphasis; Berger, 1997, p. 84). Normally, if a subject is 'upon' something we are referring to space (as in 'upon the table'); here it is 'upon' the fourth dimension, time. The effect of this is to suggest that the location of this narrative is not only in the past, but *literally* in another dimension, a world different from our own. The narrative function of this opening is to suggest that 'anything goes'; the normal rules of physics do not apply.

This dislocation of reality is peculiarly suited to the needs of young children as they do not have a fully developed world view. They may understand that 'what goes up must come down' but they do not know the laws of gravity so they can happily accept exceptions to the rule. Fairy tales, however, are not used to teach children about the physical laws that govern our existence; what they are used for will be suggested at the end of the chapter.

When we investigate Vladimir Propp's analysis of Russian folk tales, we shall see that fairy tales are not texts we necessarily 'grow out of' as we grow older. Despite its apparently futuristic setting, George Lucas's *Star Wars* (1977, RE: 1997), one of the biggest box office movies of all time, emphasises the fairy-tale origins of its narrative by opening with the classic 'once upon a time...' phrase.

Exercise 1.2

Write down what sort of things you expect to happen after the following openings (if you actually know what happens, then move on to the next opening).

(a) 'It was a bright cold day in April, and the clocks were striking thirteen.'

(b) 'The sweat wis lashing oafay Sick Boy; he wis trembling. Ah wis jist sitting thair, focusing oan the telly, tryin no tae notice the cunt. He wis bringing me doon. Ah tried tae keep ma attention oan the Jean-Claude Van Damme video.'

(c) Ext. street. day

Legs run along the pavement. They are Mark Renton's.

Just ahead of him is Spud. They are both belting along.

As they travel, various objects (pens, tapes, CDs, toiletries, ties, sunglasses, and so on) either fall or are discarded from inside their jackets.

They are pursued by two hard-looking Store Detectives in identical uniforms. The men are fast, but Renton and Spud maintain their lead.

Renton (voice-over)

> Choose life. Choose a job. Choose a career. Choose a family. Choose a fucking big television, choose washing machines, cars, compact disc players and electrical tin openers.

Suddenly, as Renton crosses a road. A car skids to a halt, inches from him.

In a moment of detachment he stops and looks at the shocked driver, then at Spud, who has continued running, then at the Two Men, who are now closing on him.

He smiles.

Openings are important because they are usually intended to grab and hold the attention of the receiver of the text. People may walk out of a movie or play that begins badly or boringly; many of us wouldn't bother finishing a novel that does not interest us from the start. So the effectiveness of the opening may well have an effect on the text's financial success: the opening must act as a narrative hook.

The 'opening' of a text is usually defined as more than the first sentence but even in such a small unit it is possible to distinguish some of the features that lead us into the narrative world. Take the opening of extract (a), George Orwell's novel *Nineteen Eighty-Four*: 'It was a bright cold day in April, and the clocks were striking thirteen' (Orwell, 1954, p. 5). What makes this sentence so intriguing is the fact that the clocks strike 'thirteen'. This immediately sets up a puzzle (an enigma, as we shall see later in the chapter): why thirteen? In 1949, when the novel was published, the answer was that Orwell was using it to help describe a future world with different rules – the world of 1984. I once read that Orwell had wanted to call his book *Nineteen Forty-Eight* but his publishers refused this title so he merely reversed the last two digits. What this emphasises is that, in common with many science fiction texts (considered in Chapter 4), Orwell was not writing about the future, but his present. The 1984 feature film version of the book highlighted this with very drab, post-Second World War settings.

Although *Image and Representation* dealt with understanding media language, it is worthwhile indulging in some textual analysis here because, of course, when we are trying to make sense of the opening of a text we are making a *reading*. As such everything is significant:

art is a system which is pure, no unit ever goes wasted, however long, however loose, however tenuous may be the thread connecting it to one of the levels of the story. (Barthes, 1977, pp. 89–90)

So in analysing texts it is useful to continually ask yourself questions; such as, what is the significance of the fact that it is April at the opening of *Nineteen Eighty-Four*?

Analyses of openings

April is associated with spring. Other famous references to the month in literature are Chaucer's General Prologue to *The Canterbury Tales* where April offers 'shoures sote' ('sweet showers') as an antidote to 'The droghte (dryness) of Marche'. By contrast, the opening of T.S. Eliot's *The Waste Land* (see Chapter 6 of *Image and Representation*) offers a subversive take on the month:

April is the cruellest month, breeding
Lilacs out of the dead land, mixing
Memory and desire, stirring
Dull roots with spring rain.
Winter kept us warm, covering
Earth in forgetful snow, feeding
A little life with dried tubers. (Eliot, 1974, p. 63)

In *Nineteen Eighty-Four* the fact that it is 'cold' suggests that Orwell's April is closer to Eliot's than Chaucer's, but the possibility of renewal is, at least, latent. However, as already stated, it is the time striking 'thirteen' that strikes a discordant note in this opening sentence. While this appears to be a reference to the twenty-four hour clock, it is couched in language unfamiliar to us: this world is not the same as our own. In addition, thirteen is often regarded as a fateful, or unlucky, number.

The first sentence of extract (b), Irvine Welsh's 1993 novel *Trainspotting*, uses similar techniques to get the reader interested: why is the sweat 'lashing oafay Sick Boy'? Who is Sick Boy and why is he sick? In addition, the use of working-class, Edinburgh dialect and crude language suggests a lowlife milieu, or setting. Although many writers (such as Dickens, Hardy and Lawrence) have used non-standard language for dialogue, it is unusual for it to be used in descriptive passages. Most of *Trainspotting* is written in the first person, and the use of Edinburgh dialect adds to the readers' sense of having direct access to the character's thoughts. Indeed, some sections (the 'Junk Dilemmas') are like a stream of consciousness (defined in Chapter 3). By contrast, the section 'The First Shag in Ages' is not only written in the third person, but is also in Standard English.

What has this got to do with the narrative of *Trainspotting*? In a carefully constructed novel, the opening will often contain, at least, the seeds of the themes that are to be articulated later. Although we can never be sure of this until we have experienced the whole text, if these 'seeds' are absent, reading the text can be very difficult. When we begin reading any text we engage in a process of prediction based on the clues offered. Most texts wish to orientate their audience quickly to the text and so will rapidly give audiences unambiguous signs about such things as:

- who is the hero and villain (using psychologically believable characters, or at least recognisable character types)
- a recognisable setting
- an understandable style
- a conventional narrative structure which includes cause–effect motivation.

All of the above can be subsumed under 'genre', which is the concept most readily mobilised by producers of texts to help audiences read their texts; indeed, audiences are usually informed *in advance* about the text's genre by marketing which includes a book's cover, a film's poster, a television programme's title sequence and so on. Once a genre has been established, most audiences have a 'ready made' framework with which to understand the text. Audiences' identification of the appropriate genre can vary in its difficulty: the latest action blockbuster from Hollywood virtually always offers us an 'off the shelf' framework, we know exactly what to expect; other texts may be offering a combination of genres and so audiences may take slightly longer to define the appropriate categories.

Exercise 1.3

What do you think will happen next and how did you arrive at this prediction?

'Too many strangers, that's the trouble in this yer one-eyed burg.' The hoarse, sneering voice rang out like a challenge, which indeed it was, and the speaker's bloodshot, savage glare roamed round the room as though daring those present to refute his statement. He was a big fellow, blue-shirted, with trousers stuffed into the tops of this high boots, and he wore two guns; a slouched hat partly shaded his bloated, unshaven face. (Strange, 1961, p. 7)

The extract is from a Western (*Sudden* by Oliver Strange) and the character described is clearly a 'bad guy': he sneers hoarsely; has bloodshot eyes; is savage; slouches (or at least his hat does); has a bloated and unshaven face. He is characterised as a bully. What happens next? He is 'taught a lesson' by the lean, clean-shaven hero. The opening paragraph sets up the first four pages of the novel and readers can experience the pleasure of, among other things, having their predictions proved right.

Non-genre texts, however, can be more difficult to 'get into' because the clues are likely to be more ambiguous: while generic texts usually offer, say, specific settings, non-genre texts can offer any setting. Despite this, it is almost certain that the non-generic setting will offer useful clues about the subject of the narrative. For example, *Pierrot le fou* (1965), directed by Jean-Luc Godard (see Chapter 3), starts in 'intellectual and sophisticated' Paris and finishes in the 'passionate and violent' south of France.

The most common style of media text is one that 'disguises' itself; the text's creator attempts to create an invisible window through which the text is read. While the openings by both Orwell and Strange are, stylistically, fairly neutral, Welsh's opening foregrounds itself and thereby becomes an important part of the text; as we shall see the use of Edinburgh dialect and accent helps create an 'authentic' naturalist milieu.

Narrative is, arguably, the most crucial hint offered to an audience: the structure of virtually all narratives, in the west at least, is the same and so is a very stable framework which will be described in this chapter.

Even though much of this reading of clues is conscious, the process of 'unconscious' reading – that which we do without thinking – still continues. Much of textual analysis in Media Studies is taken up with explaining this unconscious reading. For example, why are the characters in the opening of *Trainspotting* watching a Jean-Claude Van Damme video? A commutation test will help us understand the significance of the Belgian star to this particular narrative.

As Chapter 2 in *Image and Representation* showed, a commutation test is a useful way of ascertaining the meaning of a particular sign.

11

In brief, it consists of replacing the chosen sign with another from the same paradigm; in this instance the chosen sign is Jean-Claude Van Damme.

Jean-Claude Van Damme belongs to the paradigm of 'film star': by replacing the sign 'Jean-Claude Van Damme' with another sign from the 'film star' paradigm, we can assess what difference is made to the sentence. For instance:

'Ah tried tae keep ma attention oan the Tom Hanks video.'

Van Damme makes action movies (for example, *Universal Soldier*, 1992); Tom Hanks's films, by contrast, tend to be a lot 'softer' like the melodrama *Sleepless in Seattle* (1993). So it appears that it's important that the characters in *Trainspotting* are watching an action movie. Two connotations of action movies are that they are macho and undemanding. So, what if we used the paradigm 'action film star' rather than simply 'film star'?

'Ah tried tae keep ma attention oan the Sylvester Stallone video.'

Stallone has been associated with big budget, mainstream, Hollywood action movies, such as *Daylight* (1996) or *The Specialist* (1994). Van Damme, by contrast, is strictly a video star. Like Steven Seagal and Cynthia Rothrock, he has not (by 1999 at least) successfully 'crossed over' to mainstream films. Van Damme's movies, then, as well as being macho and undemanding, have lower budgets and are free from the pretence that often infects 'big budget' movies.

So what is the function of the 'Jean-Claude Van Damme' sign in the opening of *Trainspotting*? It is an economic piece of characterisation: it confirms the characters as lowlifes (the connotation of 'meathead' action movies as 'low culture') and emphasises the uncaring, typical masculine reaction to a friend's suffering (as does the word 'jist'). (There's no doubt that analysing an opening of a text is a lot easier if you know what happens in the rest of the text.)

A comparison between different versions of the same text is useful in showing how different media invite, or even necessitate, changes to the way the narrative is presented. The script of the opening of *Trainspotting* (extract c) cannot do full justice to the sequence as it appears in the film. The extract lasts 26 seconds and includes 13 shots, a very fast average of two seconds per shot. Throughout, the camera is usually moving at the same speed as Renton, adding to the dynamic quality already generated by the editing. As well as Renton's voice-over, the soundtrack also includes the opening of Iggy Pop's 'Lust for Life', a fast and rhythmic track which again helps drive forward the sequence.

In contrast to the novel's description of this sequence, film offers a plethora of visual signs which readers decode to make sense of the narrative. The performance of actors is crucial in this, their non-verbal communication tells us much about the character they play. For example, Ewan McGregor's (Renton) accent adds to the evocation of the lowlife Edinburgh milieu and the fact that he does not just 'smile', as directed by the screenplay (extract c), but actually laughs when hit by the car suggests that he is, at least slightly, mad. We can also, however, admire his sang-froid which indicates he is the character with whom we are, principally, invited to identify with.

Clothing is an important non-verbal cue: Renton is wearing old jeans, cheap running shoes, a T-shirt that reveals his belly. All this, when added to the fact that he is being chased through shoppers, suggests he is a criminal.

Although the film opening is clearly much more exciting than the novel this, obviously, does not mean that cinema is superior to literature; as we shall see in Chapter 3 there are some narrative techniques to which literature is ideally suited, and which cinema can only, rather pathetically, mimic.

So the openings of carefully constructed texts often contain hints of what is to follow and how they intend to engage their audiences. However, the opening of texts should not be confused with the opening of stories. The text may offer a beginning that is, for example, chronologically out of place with what follows; the chase that opens the screen version of *Trainspotting* occurs approximately halfway through the film (see the distinction between story and plot later in the chapter). But before we distinguish between the chronological structure of the text and the chronological structure of the narrative, we need to define more closely what is meant by narrative.

1.3 What is narrative?

The word derives from the Latin *narre*, which means 'to make known', so narratives frequently convey information. However, this is not on its own a sufficient definition: train timetables also give information but they are not narratives. What distinguishes narrative from other forms is that it presents information as a connected sequence of events. The most basic narratives are linear sequences which could be represented as A,B,C,D,E or 1,2,3,4,5. Moreover, this sequence is not random; it is structured logically. Most narratives structure their sequences causally: each event logically follows on from the previous one; each event causes the next one. A narrative therefore needs at least two connected events; one event is not a sequence. Narrative's emphasis on causality can also be demonstrated by using the discourse of linguistics.

Linguistics and narrative

Because narratives require at least two connected events, then, using linguistics, we could say that 'grammatically... the minimum requirements for a story are two clauses, whether these occur in a single complex sentence or two simple sentences' (Pope, 1995, p. 70). So the statement 'The king is dead' is not a narrative. Add another clause, 'and the queen has died of grief', then narrative exists. Although narrative can exist without any words at all, the fact that its structure is comparable to the structure of sentences is evidence of its universality. However, despite these similarities, a narrative cannot be reduced simply to being 'the sum of its sentences'.

Arguably, what makes narrative a key concept in Media Studies is its usefulness in looking at texts as a whole, particularly in demonstrating similarities between texts that appear completely different. So we need to take a step back and consider narrative in a wider sense.

As we have seen, the concept of sequence is crucial; without development there is no narrative. In order to describe this development accurately we need to define carefully and distinguish between two more concepts with very common names – the 'story' and the 'plot'.

Story and plot

Exercise 1.4

If you have seen the film Trainspotting, write a synopsis of the narrative.

Lacey's synopsis of Trainspotting

Renton is addicted to heroin, a state of affairs he is happy with. However, he makes the decision to 'get off' and prepares meticulously for the experience. Before he does so, however, he decided he needs one final shot.

He manages to purchase a suppository which he inserts. However, the constipation he is suffering from ends and he has to rush to the 'worst toilet in Scotland'. Here, his relief is short-lived as he realises the suppository has also gone down the toilet. He delves deep inside this shit-encrusted bowl and then climbs down the toilet. In a surreal sequence we see Renton diving deep in what looks like the sea; however the spot of light above situates the setting as the toilet bowl. Triumphantly Renton finds the suppository, climbs out of the toilet, reinserts the suppository and squelches on his way.

There follow a number of scenes which show Renton's 'day to day' existence; they include being picked up by Diane; being thrown out of her bedroom, after they have had sex, to sleep on the couch; and finding the next morning she is in fact an underage schoolgirl.

One of Renton's mates, Tommy (who is not addicted), finds that a video of himself and his girlfriend having sex has disappeared (in fact Renton took it). Worried that he's taken it back to the video shop by mistake, his girlfriend ends the relationship.

Two of Renton's mates, Sick Boy and Spud, also attempt to 'get off the skag'. However, after their mate Tommy attempts to take them on a walk in the Highlands, they decide to 'get back on'.

During one prolonged drug-taking session; a baby dies (cot death). Tommy, in his unhappiness at the end of his relationship with his girlfriend, starts taking heroin. Renton and Spud are caught shoplifting. Spud is sent to jail; Renton's sentence is suspended on condition he attends a rehabilitation programme.

However, Renton goes back onto heroin and suffers an overdose. After this, Renton's parents lock him in his bedroom and he is forced to undergo 'cold turkey'. This is successful and he decides to escape his past and get a job in London. He works as an estate agent and is doing well until one of his mates, the psychopath Begbie, arrives on the run from the police. Both return to Edinburgh for Tommy's funeral; he died from complications induced by AIDS.

While they are in Edinburgh, Begbie, Spud and Sick Boy persuade Renton to help them sell a large amount of heroin in London. Renton reluctantly agrees; he tries the heroin to make sure it is of high quality. The deal goes off successfully but, when they are celebrating, Begbie 'glasses' someone. During the following night Renton takes the £15,000 they have made and runs off, leaving Spud with some of the cash.

Your synopsis is probably different from mine. I left out a lot of detail, such as the scene in which Sick Boy and Renton discuss Sean Connery and shoot an air rifle at a dog which promptly savages its owner. However, the 'toilet scene' is described in some detail (because I find it hilarious). The synopsis could have been much shorter ('the tale of how a heroin addict makes a better life for himself') or longer. I also neglected the opening of the text which shows Renton and Spud being chased and caught after shoplifting.

What I have offered is a narrative synopsis that is structured as 'a chain of events in cause-effect relationships in time and space' (Bordwell and Thompson, 1993, p. 65). Although this cause–effect chain is common to both the story and the plot, they are distinct concepts as Bordwell and Thompson's (1993, p. 67) diagram shows.

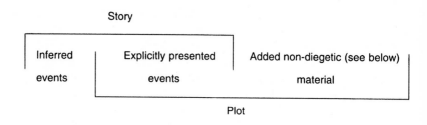

Figure 1.1

The plot is everything that the text explicitly presents. The story is the chronological order of all events explicitly presented *and* inferred by the text. For example, in *Star Wars* the plot starts with the Empire capturing Princess Leia and ends with the award ceremony where Luke Skywalker and his comrades are rewarded for their bravery. The story, however, includes more than this and includes Skywalker's father, a one-time Jedi Knight, even though he is already dead when the plot begins. Hollywood executives often refer to this background information, which explains characters' motivation, as the 'back-story'.

In *Trainspotting*, Renton's experiences on the toilet are part of the plot but his journey home afterwards is *not* because we are not shown it. The audience, however, *infers* that he has walked home; this journey is therefore part of the story. As Renton entered the toilet the words 'The worst   in Scotland' are superimposed upon the image of the toilet door (the sign 'toilet', which is on the door, fills the gap). We know the words are not actually on the door (unlike the word 'toilet'). These superimposed words are therefore part of the plot, but *not* the story because Renton would not know they were there.

Similarly, the title sequence and end-credits are also considered part of the plot because they are added to the text; but they are not part of the narrative world. In Media Studies, this narrative world is called the diegesis, discussed below, which is derived from the Greek for 'narration'.

Bordwell and Thompson (1993, p. 69) show how this distinction is useful in describing the narrative of detective fiction.

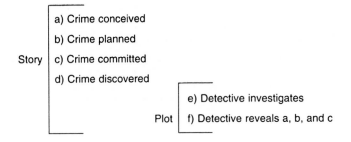

Figure 1.2

If this text is a 'whodunit', or 'murder mystery', and so it makes no sense for the plot to show the audience the crime being 'a' conceived, 'b' planned and 'c' committed because we would then know 'whodidit'. Indeed, the progress of the plot (e and f) consists of, in this case, the reconstruction of a, b and c. Commonly a, b, and c are revealed at the end by the detective to the assembled suspects ('It was the butler!'). However, if a, b and c are revealed in a flashback and *not* simply as a narration by the detective at the end (which Figure 1.2 above shows) then the plot changes (see Figure 1.3).

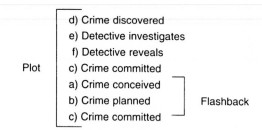

Figure 1.3

The story, however, remains as before 'a to f'. Indeed, in conventional narrative, stories must always be chronologically constructed otherwise they would be judged to violate the rules of our universe; they would destroy the rules of logical causality which define narrative. This is true even of time travel stories: the plot, like that of *The Terminator* (1984), may bounce between 1984 and 2029 but the story must be unravelled to begin in 1984 (I have not inferred any events before 1984 in *The Terminator*) and finish in 2029.

Victor Shklovsky was responsible for the original distinction between 'story' and 'plot'; his terms were *fabula* and *syuzhet*, which are sometimes translated as 'fable' and 'subject' (Todorov, 1988, p. 160). Todorov offers a way of distinguishing between these devices:

> the story is what has happened in life, the plot is the way the author presents it to us. The [story] corresponds to the reality evoked... the [plot] to the book itself, the narrative, to the literary devices the author employs. (ibid.)

As we shall see in Chapter 3, one of the most important 'devices' used by a text's creator (Todorov was referring solely to literature, we are dealing with media texts in general) is that of narrative voice. 'Story' and 'plot' can also be conceived of semiotically:

> **Plot** is *the narrative as it is read, seen or heard* from the first to the last word or image. That is, like a *signifier*, it is what the reader perceives.

Story is *the narrative in chronological order*, the abstract order of events as they follow each other. That is, like a *signified*, story is what the reader conceives or understands. (Thwaites *et al.*, 1994, p. 121)

If we carry Thwaite *et al.*'s analogy further then it is reasonable to call the resulting sign (which is created by the signifier and signified) to be the narrative itself.

Exercise 1.5

Choose any narrative text and distinguish between story and plot (if you're really ambitious, try either *Terminator* film).

Tomashevsky suggests that the plot can be seen as the aesthetic arrangement of ideas that the author wishes to bring to the attention of the reader (Lemon and Reis, 1965). Hence in 'whodunits' the important point is the revelation of the criminal's identity and so this occurs at the end of the plot otherwise audiences are less likely to read the rest of the story. Similarly, Renton's long walk home is not important and so does not appear in the plot.

Although all narrative texts consist of one plot, this may be made up of one or more subplots. Subplots are, basically, plots that feature secondary characters and are usually linked to the main narrative. In *The Full Monty* (1997) Gaz's relationship with his estranged wife and son is a subplot, as is Gerald's deception of his spouse; the main plot deals with the problems of unemployed men in desperate need for money.

Diegesis (narrative world)

The concept of diegesis helps us to distinguish between the world a text has created and any additional – non-diegetic – features. The easiest way to distinguish between the diegetic and non-diegetic is to consider what the characters in the narrative are able to perceive (see or hear in audio-visual texts) and what the audience perceives. Characters can only perceive diegetic material whereas the audience, obviously, can perceive everything a text has to offer, including non-diegetic material.

Table 1.1

Diegetic	Non-diegetic
filmed/video image or description	superimposed images (for example credits) or acknowledgements in novels
sound originating in world of text (a table falling over or music being played)	'added'* sound (music)
dialogue spoken by spoken onscreen or by characters who are part of the scene	voice-over

* Diegetic sound can also be added, dubbed, but remains diegetic because it, in the terms of the text, still originates in the narrative world.

The diegetic world will be created by the particular conventions of a form, medium or genre. Diegetic coherency is important because if there are discontinuities within the text, audiences may not 'believe' in the world that is being offered. One of the devices used to create a coherent diegesis is narrative voice, which will be dealt with in Chapter 3. Another device is the representation of time:

> In constructing the [text's] story out of its plot, the [audience] tries to put events in chronological *order* and to assign them some *duration* and *frequency*. We can look at each of these temporal factors separately. (Bordwell and Thompson, 1993, p. 70)

Temporal order

The story is simply the chronological order of events, which, as noted above, must always start at 'a'. The plot, however, can alter this order, something that Quentin Tarantino's first films delighted in doing. For instance in *Pulp Fiction* (1994) the plot's order of the film's 'chapters' is as follows:

(a) Prologue
(b) Vincent Vega and Marsellus Wallace's Wife
(c) The Gold Watch
(d) The Bonnie Situation
(e) Epilogue.

However this plot ordering (ignoring for the moment any pre-plot events inferred from the text, such as Vincent Vega's sojourn in Amsterdam) structures the story 'adebc':

(a) Prologue
(d) The Bonnie Situation
(e) Epilogue
(b) Vincent Vega and Marsellus Wallace's Wife
(c) The Gold Watch.

The Gold Watch also includes a tale that refers to events well before the beginning of the plot. Tarantino's directorial debut *Reservoir Dogs* (1992) has a similarly convoluted plot, as did his *script* for *True Romance* (directed by Tony Scott, 1993); the *film* version of *True Romance*, however, unravelled this and followed the *temporal order* of the story.

Temporal duration

Bordwell and Thompson, writing about film, describe three types of temporal duration: plot, story and screen; these, though, are applicable to all narrative media.

- *Plot duration* refers to the amount of time covered by the plot. A thousand plot years can pass in half a sentence (or in the split-second cut between the 'dawn of man' sequence and 2001 in *2001: A Space Odyssey*, 1968) or, by contrast, seconds can last for pages. The number of years covered in *Trainspotting* is not clearly indicated but we can infer that several years pass, enough time for Tommy to lose his girlfriend, take up heroin and die from an AIDS-related illness. The plot of *Se7en* (1995) covers eight days. In *The Nick of Time* (1995) the plot duration is in 'real-time'; that is the 89 minutes that the movie runs cover a continuous 89 minutes of the characters' lives. This 'real-time' representation is rare but was part of the realist project of naturalism which, in the nineteenth century, aimed to represent life 'second by second' (*Sekundenstil*). This was a philosophical and aesthetic project, whereas in *The Nick of Time* the conceit is used only to generate tension.
- *Story duration* is the amount of time covered by the story; this is usually more than plot duration. Any past events referred to are

part of the story's duration. If we knew nothing about the characters' lives before the beginning of the plot in *The Nick of Time* then plot and screen duration would have been identical.

• *Screen duration* is the amount of time it takes to show the film or television programme. *Trainspotting* runs for 93 minutes; *Se7en* for 127 minutes. A six-part 30-minute serial on television would take 180 minutes of screen time. You could apply the concept to novels by timing how long it takes to read a particular text, although it is doubtful whether this would be particularly informative; however, 'listening duration' is applicable to radio.

In some instances the plot can use the screen duration to override story time. Any slow-motion sequences will take longer to show than to happen. The use of montage to show an event repeatedly, such as when Megan Turner shoots the thief through a shop window in *Blue Steel* (1989) and Eisenstein's Odessa steps sequence in *Battleship Potemkin* (1926), has the same effect.

Of course authors are at liberty to do what they like with time: Martin Amis's *Time's Arrow* (1991) starts with the protagonist's death; the novel then follows the character's life backwards. In T.H. Whites' retelling of the Arthurian legend, *The Once and Future King*, most of the characters' lives progress forward in the usual way but Merlin and his owl are going backwards ('This is where I break my wing,' the owl says miserably, at one point).

Temporal frequency

The plot can alter a story's frequency in a number of ways: if an event is repeated numerous times in the story then it can be shown once, or a few times which signify that it has occurred for a longer duration. For example, if in a romance the couple go on a honeymoon tour then a few locations may be shown to suggest the whole length of their holiday.

Another alteration to the story, which involves frequency, can be a repetition of events. For example, in a 'whodunit' the denouement often consists of a flashback to the murder which was shown earlier (sometimes from a different point of view in order to give us the 'whole picture'). One of Stanley Kubrick's early films, *The Killing* (1956), showed the build-up to 'the killing' several times from the viewpoints of the participants. The fact that plot, in virtually all instances, manipulates the story suggests that the reader of texts has a significant role in the creation of a text; the reader has to piece together the story from the plot.

One of the prime ways in which readers understand texts is through our, usually implicit, knowledge of narrative structure. Among the most influential of recent work on narrative structure is that of Tzvetan Todorov although the roots go back to Aristotle and his Poetics.

1.4 Todorov and narrative structure

As we have seen, narratives must have clauses that are structured by causality. However, causality alone is not sufficient; few people would classify a conventional recipe as a narrative ('boil the egg for five minutes') although it both uses clauses and emphasises causality. In order to demonstrate this, try Exercise 1.6 on your own and, if possible, compare your version of the narrative with others.

.. Exercise 1.6 ,·.

Rearrange the images so they offer a narrative.

a.

b.

c.

d.

e.

f.

g.

h.

i.

Unless you have been deliberately perverse (and there's nothing wrong with that) it is likely that you have structured your narrative to have a beginning which is followed logically (causally) by a middle and finally an end. My suggestion would be a narrative entitled 'Kate and the Biscuit' d, c, g, h, f, i, b, e, a.

So narratives have a beginning, middle and an end. But so do recipes...

The beginning, middle, end and...?

Aristotle is usually credited with the first description of the 'three act' structure of dramatic texts (see his *On the Art of Poetry*, 1965). Lew Hunter gives a 'Broadway' version:

> In the first act you get your hero up a tree. The second act, you throw rocks at him. For the third act you let him down. (Hunter, 1994, p. 45)

This, too, is a very simple definition; in most narratives, simply reaching the end is not, on its own, fulfilling for the reader. Tzvetan Todorov showed that narrative is, in fact, a *causal transformation*; in other words, narratives have within them some form of logical change. This *transformation*, however, is not simply *any* change; the types of transformation that occur in conventional narrative tend to be very specific.

Todorov argued that the basis of conventional narrative structure consists of an initial situation (situation 1); a problem which disrupts this situation; a resolution of the problem which allows the reinstatement of the initial situation, perhaps with slight changes (situation 2). In the narrative for Exercise 1.6, the transformation was the movement of the child, whom we will call Kate, from being hungry (or at least desiring a biscuit) to being 'not hungry'. The middle bit was concerned with resolving the problem. It could schematically be described thus:

beginning > middle > end
situation 1 > problem > resolution (situation 2)
Kate playing > Kate hungry > Kate eats and then plays

Situation 2 is very similar to situation 1; the only difference is that the lack (of food) has been eradicated. Most narratives can be fitted into this very simple structure. In *Star Wars* (1977, RE: 1997) for instance, the narrative structure can be described as follows:

- *Initial situation*: a rebellion is being organised against the Empire;
- *Disruption*: the Death Star tries to crush the rebellion;
- *Resolution*: the Death Star is destroyed allowing the rebellion to continue.

In the novel *The Lord of the Flies*, by William Golding (1954):

- *Initial situation*: Boys being evacuated by air;
- *Disruption*: aircraft crashes and boy marooned on an island;
- *Resolution*: boys rescued to continue their journey.

In *The Full Monty* (1997):

- *Initial situation*: unemployed men with no future; for example, Gaz estranged from his son;
- *Disruption*: need for money; so Gaz can retain access to his son;
- *Resolution*: a successful striptease show providing money.

(However it is interesting to speculate about the future of the unemployed men; the fact that their problem has not been resolved is signified by the final shot's freeze-frame: if the film continued, this disruption would need to be resolved.)

Exercise 1.7

Choose three fictional texts and describe their narrative structure using the situation/problem/resolution model.

Narratives are not necessarily limited to fictional texts. Sporting events are often characterised as such. For example, a football team's situation at the start of a game is a certain position in the league; the opposition provides the problem; the resolution is the result that is likely to alter their league position (or their status in a cup competition). 'Friendly' matches, of course, have no such transformation which goes some way to explaining their lack of significance. We will consider some non-fiction narrative forms later.

As a rule, the narrative transformation also concerns the characters involved in the narratives; they, too, have changed as a result of the actions (usually their own) which resolved the problem. In 'Kate and the Biscuit' the child has discovered a way to get objects that are normally out of her reach, a solution she can apply to future problems. The narrative, simple as it is, concerns the learning experience of young children.

Another way of describing this simple beginning/middle/end structure is:

thesis > antithesis > synthesis

This description emphasises the transformational element of narratives. The initial situation (playing) is the thesis; this is opposed by the *anti*thesis, the lack of food, hunger that was spoiling the play. The obstacle was the table. Once the problem had been overcome, she could play again contentedly. However, the experience of the 'antithesis' had also transformed her; she had learned how to overcome her lack of height and was rewarded by 'non-hunger' (the synthesis).

Many very young children enjoy playing 'peek-a-boo', a variant of which was described by Freud as the *fort-da* game ('gone away-here'). Terry Eagleton has noted that:

> *Fort-da* is perhaps the shortest story we can imagine: an object is lost, and then recovered. But even the most complex narratives can be read as variants on this model: the pattern of classical narratives is that an original settlement is disrupted and ultimately restored. (Eagleton, 1983, p. 185)

This psychoanalytical perspective on narrative suggests, as did narrative's similarity to sentences, that narrative form is a defining characteristic of what it is to be human.

The 'beginning, middle and end' of a narrative are not *individual* elements of a narrative but are defined in *relationship* to each other: the beginning can only be defined by its position in relation to the middle and end. For example, we cannot be sure of the significance of events at the beginning of the plot until we know how they are going to be disrupted. Similarly, the disruption only occurs in order to be 'put right' at the end.

Todorov suggested a slightly more complicated description of narrative structure than the simple situation/problem/resolution structure. He posited five stages:

1. a state of equilibrium at the outset
2. a disruption of the equilibrium by some action
3. a recognition that there has been a disruption
4. an attempt to repair the disruption
5. a reinstatement of the equilibrium.

Our 'Kate and the Biscuit' narrative translates as follows:

1. Kate playing
2. Kate hungry (caused by the action of the hunger drive)

3. Kate stops playing as she desires food
4. Kate tries to get food and succeeds
5. Kate eats food and continues playing.

As Branigan says, Todorov showed how the changes:

> create an overall pattern or 'transformation' whereby [his] third stage is seen as the 'inverse' of the first and fifth stages, and the fourth stage the 'inverse' of the second (since it attempts to reverse the effects of the disruption). The five stages may be symbolised as follows: A, B, -A, -B, A. (Branigan, 1992, p. 5)

The narrative in 'self-contained' texts, ones that are not serial in character (see below), do not simply return us to the initial situation and so, although it spoils the symmetry somewhat, it is probably more accurate to symbolise the reinstatement of the equilibrium (stage 5) as A2 as this acknowledges a transformation has taken place.

Occasionally the resolution of a narrative problem can be seen by modern audiences to be somewhat unbelievable; the 'it was only a dream' conclusion used by many young children in their own attempts at narratives. A similar device – although it was not deemed to be unconvincing at the time – was used in medieval Mystery plays where the *deus ex machina* (an 'act of God') suddenly solves all the problems. Melodramas are sometimes concluded in a fashion that stretches credibility; however, this is often the point – see Chapter 4.

Exercise 1.8

Using the same three texts as in Exercise 1.7, use Todorov's categories to describe the narrative structure.

Television series – *The X-Files*

Despite what we have said about changes between opening and ending, there is one form of narrative, the series, where the second 'A' does return us exactly to the initial situation. The television series is a prime example of this narrative structure, which can be characterised as circular.

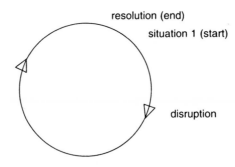

resolution (end)

situation 1 (start)

disruption

Figure 1.5   Narrative structure of series

It is essential that the programme ends as it began so that it can start again, from exactly the *same* point, the next week. In a series like *The X-Files*, Mulder and Scully investigate an unexplained event and, at the narrative's resolution, explain – to an extent – the 'unexplained' (the disruption). Next week they will do the same. *Star Trek*, which in the original 1960s serial was on a 'five year mission', must at the end of each episode (unless it is a two-parter) continue its quest, having overcome that week's disruption. An interesting point about *The X-Files* is that Mulder and Scully cannot ever fully resolve the narrative disruption because that would mean explaining the unexplainable thus destroying the basis of the series. For instance in *Dod Kalm* (series 2, episode 19):

> The last known position of the U.S.S. Argent was in the Norwegian equivalent of the Bermuda Triangle until a boatload of survivors is found. What particularly catches Mulder's inquisitive eye is that all of these sailors appear to have aged many decades in the course of days. (David Nattriss website)

In Todorov's terms the narrative is structured as follows:

1. a state of equilibrium at the outset – Mulder and Scully await mission
2. a disruption of the equilibrium by some action – US Navy ship detected adrift off Norway
3. a recognition that there has been a disruption – Mulder and Scully despatched and

4. an attempt to repair the disruption – attempt to discover why most of crew have died of old age but become 'infected' themselves, Mulder, in particular, near death
5. a reinstatement of the equilibrium – Scully, using Mulder's notes, finds an antidote and both are able to return home ready for their next mission.

Note that the disruption switches from trying to discover *why* the people on board the stricken vessel have aged, to preventing Mulder and Scully from ageing. If the attempt to discover why ageing occurred had been successful, the main characters would have been able to explain the 'unexplainable'. If they had done this then the sense of reality that the programme is careful to cultivate, through the use of 'actual' stories and the documentary-style specification of time and place, would have been dispelled. The explanation of the unexplainable belongs to the genre of horror (and possibly science fiction). Part of the appeal of *The X-Files*, and associated programmes such as *Dark Skies*, is to 'conspiracy theorists' who believe that government agencies (particularly in USA) are withholding information about such things as contact with aliens. Central to the conspiracy theory is Area 51, a US military site which is rumoured to house a UFO that crash landed in the 1950s. This area made an appearance in the biggest box office movie of 1996, *Independence Day*.

Frederic Jameson (1992) has suggested that the appeal of 'conspiracy theory' narratives lies in the audience's alienation from the modern world. If an individual feels powerless, and has difficulty in understanding what is 'going on in the world', then a 'conspiracy' is a simple way of explaining her or his ignorance. Jameson deals with a number of films in the 1970s, such as *The Parallax View* (1974), *The Conversation* (1974) and *All the President's Men* (1976), which portrayed the paranoia engendered by political systems that appear to be unaccountable to the populace. More recently, 'paranoid movies' seem to have made a comeback; including *The Game* and *L.A. Confidential* (both 1997), *The Truman Show*, *The X-Files*, *Enemy of the State*, *The Spanish Prisoner* (all 1998) and *The Matrix* (1999).

In the 'Dod Kalm' episode of *The X-Files* a, neat, narrative sleight of hand allows for a resolution. Mulder and Scully are saved, without having to explain the ageing. Of course, if the programme attempted this narrative 'cheat' in every episode, it is unlikely it would have been so popular.

Although each episode in a series ends with the same situation with which it began, there are occasional developments. For instance, a character may be written out of the series (maybe for contractual reasons) and so they will not appear next week. In one of the early episodes of *Star Trek – The Next Generation* a central character, the security officer Tasha Yar, is killed. The effect is quite shocking because there can be no return to the opening equilibrium at the end of the episode.

After the first episode of a series there is usually no need to re-establish the initial situation in each subsequent episode; the producers can assume the audience has a familiarity with the equilibrium. This means that Todorov's step 2 (and almost invariably 3) occurs at the opening of the plot. It is a frequent convention of US series that these happen even before the credit sequence; the hope being that audiences are 'hooked' into the programme at an early stage and will watch to the end to discover the resolution (audiences know, of course, that the disruption will be successfully resolved). Once the problem has been set out, the broadcasters feel safe enough to risk an advertisement break; this is something terrestrial viewers in Britain would find surprising. In series, then, it is likely that 50 minutes of screen duration will consist of the first three minutes, or so, covering steps 2 and 3 and then 44 minutes attempting to repair the disruption leaving approximately three minutes for the resolution. This is an example of how institutional factors can influence the creation of a text.

Slightly unconventionally, *The X-Files* offered narrative development throughout each series. Mulder, for instance, appeared to be getting closer to the identity of the 'smoking man' – until the latter's demise – who, if he had been found, could have offered an explanation of events. For those who are not conspiracy theorists this explanation would have been an impossibility because the programme's use of a realist aesthetic (the documentary-style signification of time and place) means that it can only deal in the rational and alien visitations have not (yet) been proven. More importantly, discovering the truth behind the stories would deprive *The X-Files* of its narrative disruption: without the unexplained there are no X-Files. The science fiction genre, to which it can be argued that *The X-Files*, at least partly, belongs, is dealt with in Chapter 4.

The serial

Care should be taken to distinguish the television *series* from the *serial*. Like series, serials also have numerous episodes; however, although they may have numerous subplots, they normally deal with *one* overarching narrative which runs through *all* the episodes. A characteristic of serials is that episodes conclude with a cliffhanger, an immediate problem the hero must overcome, in the next episode, in order to reach the ultimate resolution.

The serial is a form that has thrived on television and has its recent origins in Victorian Britain where novels were often published in instalments. Both Charles Dickens, in his own weekly publication, *Household Words*, and Thomas Hardy serialised their novels. This was a practice that only became economically viable with the evolution of a sizeable 'reading public'; before the nineteenth century illiteracy would have been too high. Recently, Stephen King's novel *The Green Mile* (1996) was published in six parts, each volume retailed at £1.99 in the UK.

Richard Dyer has noted:

It's clear humans have always loved seriality. Bards, jongleurs, griots and yarnspinners (not to mention parents and nurses) have all long known the value of leaving their listeners wanting more, or playing on the mix of repetition and anticipation, and indeed of the anticipation of repetition, that underpins serial pleasure. However, it is only under capitalism that seriality became a reigning principle of cultural production. (Dyer, 1997, p. 14)

Dyer also notes that 'Serial killing is often taken to be the crime of our age' (ibid.); a theme that will be taken up later in the chapter with a consideration of the narrative structure of *Se7en*.

Eco – see below – has shown how capitalism has exploited seriality. The importance of repetition as a fundamental human learning device was brought home by the phenomenal success of *Teletubbies*. This is, possibly, the first television programme that not only *seeks* to address the 18-month-old but also actually *does* so. These bizarre creatures (Laa Laa, Po, Dipsy and Tinky Winky) have faces with simple features and speech that uses the phonemes that babies must practise in order to form words. They constantly repeat actions, much to the delight of their target audience, and (the programme's cult status suggests) many more. Unsurprisingly, the Teletubbies exist in a fairy-tale location: 'over the hill and far away'.

In the early days of cinema, the Saturday matinée serial narratives, showing the exploits of characters such as Buck Rogers and Flash Gordon, were very popular. Feature films could be produced as serials, for example Mickey Rooney's thirteen 'Andy Hardy' musicals. The cinema serial both took advantage of the fact that audiences tended to go weekly and encouraged the trend, giving the public a weekly reason for cinema-going: to find out how the hero survived the cliffhanger.

'Classic' serials are often seen as a hallmark of 'quality' television. These are usually adaptations of pre-twentieth-century novels whose length militates against a short, one-off drama adaptation. Although it is possible to make film versions of long novels, clearly the greater screen duration available in the serial format potentially allows more of the original material to be used. The 1963 British film version of Henry Fielding's 874-page novel *Tom Jones*, published in 1749, has screen duration of 131 minutes compared to the 1997 BBC television version which had five episodes of nearly 60 minutes each. Since the BBC's *Middlemarch*, in 1994, the classic serial has experienced a renaissance in British television. The adaptation of *Pride and Prejudice* created such a great sensation that even the repeats merited a *Radio Times* cover for 'sex symbol' Darcy (see Figure 1.6).

Richard Dyer has also suggested that, with reference to the 'classic' serial *The Jewel in the Crown*, first broadcast in 1984, seriality can contribute to the passive representation of women:

> It is not just the place of women in the serial's narrative – at once typical, yet marginal and helpless before events – that constructs a notion of white femininity as inaction. It is also the organization of the narrative. Two aspects of serial form are relevant here. The first is the handling of sequence, the second is the connections made across the length of the serial. (Dyer, 1996, p. 234)

Dyer goes on to show how inaction is created by sequence: the 'classic' serial has a slow pace; the narrative has very little drive, despite the chronological ordering of scenes, because the emphasis is on talk and looking backwards; unusually *The Jewel in the Crown* did not liberally use cliffhangers to keep audiences watching across breaks, thereby encouraging a sense of stasis. In addition, the very conscious, melodramatic (see Chapter 4), use of symbols emphasises the impotence of white characters.

Figure 1.6   'Sex symbol' Darcy

The advantage to television and radio companies of serials is clear: by withholding the narrative resolution, audiences are encouraged to watch all the episodes and thus increase ratings. The risks are equally obvious: if a serial is a big 'turn off', the broadcaster may be left with hours of unwatched airtime. This is one of the reasons why serials are less popular with broadcasters than series. Another reason is their expense: series can use the same expensive setting for each new episode; serials are more likely to demand numerous settings, and/or more characters, and so bigger casts, in order to maintain audience interest.

With the exception of state-funded organisations such as the BBC, most broadcasters are funded by selling advertising airtime and/or subscription. Hence there is a pressure to generate large numbers of the 'right' sort of audience (those who can afford to buy the products and services advertised). Series can do this just as readily as serials without demanding audience loyalty every episode.

Umberto Eco has examined how seriality mimics 'industrial-like' production in the cultural industries and offers definitions of the different types of repetition:

- *The Retake*: sequels, and on some occasions prequels; a successful text is resurrected by showing what happens to the characters after the plot of the original finishes. Prequels may be considered as the plotting of the story *before* the plot of the first text began; for instance *Star Wars*: Episode 1 – *The Phantom Menace* released 22 years after the first film.
- *The Remake*: successful texts can be remade (though this is certainly *not* likely to happen in literature). Contemporary Hollywood is voracious in its appetite for remakes, whether they be from film or television. Some of the remakes released in 1998 were: *Lost in Space, City of Angels, Godzilla, The Avengers, Dr Dolittle, The X-Files, The Mask of Zorro, The Rugrats Movie, Psycho, You've Got Mail, Mighty Joe Young; Payback* and *The Out-of-Towners* appeared in 1999.
- *The Series*: dealt with above.
- *The Saga*: typically North American, with the focus on large families and their lives across generations.

Exercise 1.9

Choose one day's schedules from a listings magazine and total the number of series and serials (excluding soap operas). Which predominates?

Soap opera

Soap opera is an example of an exceptional type of serial and is enormously popular. Brown listed eight generic characteristics of soap opera:

1. serial form which resists narrative closure
2. multiple characters and plots
3. use of time which parallels actual time and implies that the action continues to take place whether we watch it or not
4. abrupt segmentation between parts
5. emphasis on dialogue, problem solving, and intimate conversation
6. male characters who are 'sensitive men'
7. female characters who are often professional and otherwise powerful in the world outside the home
8. the home, or some other place which functions as a home, as the setting for the show. (Brown, 1987, p. 4)

It should be noted that point 3 probably only applies to the country of origin. For example, episodes of *Neighbours* broadcast outside Australia do not correspond to 'actual' time; for example a Christmas episode can be broadcast any time of year.

We shall return to soap operas as genre in Chapter 5; for our purposes, the first four of Brown's points all refer to the soap's narrative. Although soap operas are series, they have a distinctive, and possibly unique, narrative structure. A major reason for this is that they are, potentially, never-ending. Although, of course, soaps do die (*Peyton Place*, *Dallas* and *Crossroads*, for example), they are narratively unique in that they *could* go on forever. *Coronation Street* (Granada), *The Archers* (Radio 4) and *Neighbours* (Grundy Television) could be still playing as the 'last trumpet' blows and the universe winds down in entropic doom. Soaps are able to do this because they do not centre their narratives on one, or two, main characters; instead they follow the lives of several characters in a particular setting with a multi-stranded narrative structure. The number of strands varies between soaps, and between episodes of the same soap, but there are usually around half a dozen different narratives occurring at once. Some of these narratives may begin and end in one episode; others will continue for several episodes or even years. In the popular British soap opera *EastEnders*, Mark Fowler was diagnosed as being HIV positive; there are two possible resolutions to this narrative problem: death or cure (of course it could simply be bypassed by avoiding the transition to 'full blown AIDS'). Several years have passed since this diagnosis and the problem can be reactivated any time the producer wishes.

Although conventional series may also use more than one narrative strand, they are usually linked together. In soaps, however, some strands will be related to others while some are completely separate. For example, *Coronation Street*, which was first broadcast in 1960, is among the top-rated programmes on British television with audiences of nearly 20 million per episode; in a two-week period in February 1996 there were 13 narrative strands in progress.

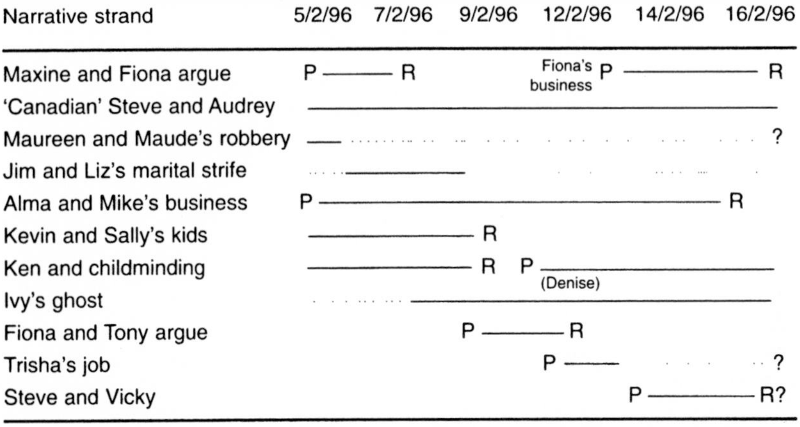

Narrative strand	5/2/96	7/2/96	9/2/96	12/2/96	14/2/96	16/2/96
Maxine and Fiona argue	P ——— R			Fiona's P ——————— R business		
'Canadian' Steve and Audrey	————————————————————————					
Maureen and Maude's robbery	—— .... ?					
Jim and Liz's marital strife	.. ... ———————			. . . .		
Alma and Mike's business	P ——————————————————— R					
Kevin and Sally's kids	——————— R					
Ken and childminding	——————— R P ————————————			(Denise)		
Ivy's ghost	. . . . ———————————————					
Fiona and Tony argue	P ——— R					
Trisha's job	P —— . . . ?					
Steve and Vicky	P ——————— R?					

P = problem; R = resolution; .... = strand not active in episode; ? = status not certain – this could be a result of one of three things: the strand will be resolved in a later episode; the strand has been left unresolved (unlikely); or I've managed to miss the resolution when watching the episodes, because the telephone rang (likely).

Figure 1.7   Narrative strands in *Coronation Street*

In any one episode some narrative strands are active while others lie dormant: a character who goes on holiday for a week is unlikely to be seen for a week. This could also be caused by actors having 'time off'.

Figure 1.7 clearly shows one of the ways soaps maintain their popularity is through constantly resolving narrative strands while creating new ones; indeed, it is highly unlikely that there would be any point where everything, however temporarily, is resolved. While it is possible that one or two narrative strands may not be resolved across the entire existence of a soap (a family feud maybe), most narrative strands are resolved to be replaced by new ones.

Although soaps are serials, they differ slightly from conventional serials in the way they use time:

> serials... use a set of unresolved narrative puzzles to carry viewers across the time gap from one episode to another but the length of the fictional time which is deemed to have passed between episodes depends on the

demands of the narrative: it may be a minute, a month, a year; it may be no time at all if the following episode returns to the moment of drama on which the preceding episode ended. (Geraghty, 1991, p. 10)

However, many soaps give the impression that they reflect real time and the same number of days pass between episodes for both the audience and characters. So although the audience 'visit', say *Coronation Street*, for 26 minutes three times a week (plot), the characters' lives (their stories) continue when viewers are not watching.

From the description of the narrative strands in *Coronation Street*, it is also clear that soap narratives are driven by conflicts in relationships.

Soaps are full of talk, of gossip. We generally learn of action by report rather than see it occur. The action is largely in the cutting, the quick-bite scenes which frame both the story and the time in which it takes place. Soaps move through time but they also suspend it to suggest simultaneity, or actions taking place at exactly the same time. (Watson, 1998, p. 135)

Like series, soaps use the same setting and a regular cast of characters, thus avoiding the expense of numerous locations and characters that serials are prone to incurring. See also Chapter 5 for a consideration of gender and the soap opera genre.

Narrative and non-fiction

It has already been noted how narratives are endemic in our lives, we even tell each other stories about real events. It is one of the strengths of Todorov's narrative theory is that it is also applicable to non-fiction texts. What follows is a brief consideration of how we can apply his theory to newspapers and music.

- *Newspapers* Journalists usually construct their reports as narratives. For instance, the first paragraph of the lead story in *The Times*, 6 December 1997:

A three-hour-old baby was snatched from her cot at her sleeping mother's side in a hospital maternity ward yesterday by a woman who managed to evade its elaborate security system.

This narrative was constructed as:

1. a state of equilibrium – mother and child in hospital
2. a disruption of the equilibrium by some action – a woman 'snatches' child
3. a recognition that there has been a disruption – it is noticed that child is missing
4. an attempt to repair the disruption – the report described this as:

> Police cordoned off the area around the building, a helicopter searched overhead and officers with tracker dogs scoured the grounds

5. a reinstatement of the equilibrium.

Point 5 was not included in the newspaper story. This is often the case because news stories, like all narratives, are created by a disruption but unlike most fiction, this disruption is not necessarily resolved. This is why the negative character of news is so often remarked upon (the 'negativity' news value). Fortunately the resolution appeared the following day when the baby was found unharmed, demonstrating another news value, the inheritance factor; once a story has hit the headlines it is defined as news and is likely to be continued to be reported.

The fact that news stories are structured as narratives also explains why some news events can get very little coverage. Industrial disputes, for instance, will fit comfortably into the equilibrium (normal working) and disruption (the strike) model. However, if the dispute is long-running there is likely to be less and less to report after the disruption; 'the dispute continues' is not, on its own, news. Only significant events, those which appear to be leading to a resolution, are likely to be reported. In news terms, until there is a resolution, the dispute may be forgotten. One of the results of this is that there is an under-reporting of trends.

However, as Len Masterman has pointed out, there is a perspective that suggests that news is *not* structured narratively. Although individual stories, whether they are in newspapers or broadcast, are narratives, the texts taken as a whole are not. If an edition of *The Times*, or the complete broadcast of a news programme, is assessed then it can be seen that:

They do not follow a linear progression. They are fragmented. They don't 'add up' or help us to interpret the world as a whole. In that sense their function is the antithesis of most narratives. (Masterman, 1985, p. 182)

The news thus becomes a fragmented collection of stories that have no links. Although newspapers tend to group stories together, such as foreign news, and broadcasters may sometimes place stories with similar subjects together, *links* between them are eschewed. So stories about, say, crime and poverty are dealt with separately even though there is a connection between them. The result of this is that audiences are not assisted in seeing society as a whole and the world is represented as an inexplicable place; as a Biff cartoon puts it:

Figure 1.4

It may be an interesting exercise to take every news story from a broadcast and try to cast them *all* into a narrative.

- *Music* It can be quite straightforward to look at the narrative structure of certain song lyrics, or of musical forms – such as opera – which offer stories, but thinking about the narrative of the music itself, one of the most abstract of the popular arts, is more problematic. However, if we investigate music of the 'classical' era (roughly 1750–early 1800s), we can see how Todorov's model operates:

> The essential factor is the key scheme, the creation of tension by modulation away from the tonic and the resolution of tension by returning to the tonic. (Grout, 1962, p. 420)

Most western music is tonal, which means it follows certain key structures. So a piece that begins in, say, C major will end in C major. If it remains in the same key throughout, it is likely to sound monotonous (much like a narrative without a problem) so the home key will modulate into, for instance, G major (the dominant). This helps set up a conflict in the music as our ear will expect the piece to end in the home key. If the idea of conflict, or disruption, in music bemuses you then listen to Beethoven's 5th Symphony where the conflict is so great that 54 bars of C 'are needed to ground the extreme tension of that immense work' (Rosen, 1971, p. 72). It is beyond the scope of this publication to deal with musical theory but it is clear that the structure of tonal music is analogous to Todorov's narrative structure.

The most influential form of 'classical' music was the Sonata form which structured reams of instrumental (usually piano) music, chamber music and symphonies. This form consists of an Exposition, Development and Recapitulation where the musical material of the exposition is developed in the following section; the recapitulation restates the original material but in a developed form. This is also similar to Todorov's ideas where the narrative's conclusion returns us to a stable situation, like one-off dramas, which is a slightly changed (A1) initial situation:

- *Initial situation*: exposition
- *Disruption*: development
- *Resolution*: recapitulation.

Anthony Storr also draws parallels between music and narrative form, although his focus is slightly narrower:

> Hero myths typically involve the protagonist leaving home, setting out on adventures, slaying a dragon or accomplishing other feats, winning a bride, and then returning home in triumph. Sonata form also celebrates a journey toward a new union between elements which were originally contrasted. The end of the piece is usually indicated by a return 'home' to the tonic; most commonly to the major triad, less commonly to the minor. (Storr, 1992, p. 82)

The analogy between musical form and narrative structure also applies to pop music. Most pop music consists of simple chord progressions which are repeated. The different chords can produce tension that is then resolved with the return to the 'home chord'. These progressions are useful in defining the particular genre to which the music belongs.

Even texts that are apparently narrativeless, such as quiz and game shows, can conform, albeit loosely, to Todorov's structure. Quiz and game shows start with an initial situation – the game – and a problem to be resolved: 'who is going to win?' Often this is presented dramatically: 'one of the families will be driving home in this family saloon' (*Family Fortunes*). A show of this kind without a winner would be like a narrative without a resolution. However, the tone of these shows, which are usually 'light entertainment', means that even the loser usually wins some sort of consolation prize.

Although Todorov's theory is useful in defining types of text it 'does not represent directly the actual processing of the narrative by a perceiver but only its conceptual or logical form after it has been interpreted' (Branigan, 1992, p. 5). This returns us to the distinction between story and plot: we only completely understand the initial situation, disruption and resolution, and their relationships to one another, at the narrative's *completion*. Todorov's theory describes the *story* that we understand by observing the *plot*. Everything within a text is intended to contribute towards narrative development; there is little or no redundancy – see the consideration of *Copycat* later in the chapter.

Todorov suggests that there is, basically, one narrative *structure* for most narrative texts. It is also possible to isolate an abstract of recurring stories and it is arguable that *all* narrative texts deal with, at least, one of the following abstracts:

- *the quest*: where the hero is sent, by the old king, to challenge evil (the villain) and thereby save the king's daughter whom he will later marry. In this quest a magician will give the hero a magic object that enables him to succeed in the quest. A classic British quest narrative is the Arthurian legend that deals with the search for the Holy Grail (see Chapter 2). The quest story is also central to fairy tales.
- *redemption*: a story where the central character sins but redeems her or himself by self-sacrifice; for example, Christ redeems humanity through his death in the Bible story. Oedipus (in Sophocles' *King Oedipus*) plucks out his eyes to atone for his, inadvertent, sins of patricide and incest.
- *journey to another world*: in Greek mythology this 'other' world was usually Hades, the world of the dead. Orpheus charmed his way, with his lyre, to Hades in order to bring his wife back from the dead.
- *the beast transformed by love*: classically with 'the Beauty of the Beast'; also, tragically, in *Frankenstein* (see Chapter 4) because the monster realises that he cannot be loved.
- *the solving of riddles*: Grimm's fairy tales often deal with riddles but this form is most commonly found in crime texts.
- *the 'biter-bit'*: 'the worm turns', a story where the oppressed rise up and throw off the tyrants. George Orwell's *Nineteen Eighty-Four* uses this story but it concludes (like a serial) with the initial situation little changed and so the protagonist, therefore, has failed.
- *the stranger saviour*: the stranger comes to town and acts as a catalyst for the residents to overcome their fear. Clint Eastwood has often played this character, often named 'the stranger' in 'spaghetti Westerns' and parodies of that 'genre' he directed in the 1970s.
- *the rise and fall*: a family's, or empire's, rise to power and subsequent decline in their, or its, fortunes. For example, Isaac Asimov's original *Foundation* trilogy.

Remember, these are *abstracts* and therefore offer a very general description of narrative content.

Exercise 1.10

Think of examples for each of the above story abstracts and, if you can remember them, examples of fairy stories that also reflect the abstracts.

Fairy tales figure very strongly in the work of the other great eastern European narrative theorist, Vladimir Propp. He, like Todorov, also defined narrative structure; unsurprisingly there are similarities between the two theories.

1.5 Propp's narrative functions

Vladimir Propp's *Morphology of the Russian Folktale* was first published in 1928 but it was not until 1958, when an English translation became available and the intellectual climate of the following decade was conducive to his ideas, that the book's importance was recognised in the west. Propp's premise was that it was a mistake to try and categorise all folktales, or indeed narratives, by their content because the task is far too large. He endeavoured to show how folktales are linked by a common structure, and this structure can be applied to any old or, theoretically, new folktale. As 1960s academics found, using Propp's ideas was not only useful when delving into the arcane world of Russian folktales; they apply to many – some argued all – narrative texts as well.

The first part of this section will describe Propp's structure of narratives and how characters operate in this structure; his ideas will then be applied to a variety of media texts. The proper test for any theory, of course, is whether it adds to our understanding of texts.

Propp's functions

We are used to considering the importance of character in fictional texts; for instance, our education in literature often focuses upon character studies that try to work out what makes a character 'tick'. Propp, however, is not interested in the psychological motivation of individual characters but what their *function* is in the narrative. Propp conceptualised these functions in two ways: the actions of the characters in the story and the *consequences* of these actions for the story.

Propp concluded there is a maximum of 31 functions in folktales and, although it is not necessary for a tale to include all the functions, the ones that do appear are always in the given order. The table below is an adaptation from Arthur Asa Berger's book *Narratives in Popular Culture, Media, and Everyday Life* (1997).

Table 1.2

Function			Description
	α	initial situation	Members of family are introduced; hero is introduced.
1.	β	absentation	One of the members of the family absents him- or herself.
2.	γ	interdiction	Interdiction addressed to hero (can be reversed).
3.	δ	violation	Interdiction is violated.
4.	ε	reconnaissance	Villain makes attempt to get information.
5.	ξ	delivery	Villain gets information about victim.
6.	η	trickery	Villain tries to deceive victim.
7.	θ	complicity	Victim is deceived.
8.	A	villainy	Villain causes harm to a member of the family; or
	a	lack	Member of the family lacks something, desires something.
9.	B	mediation	Misfortune made known; hero is dispatched.
10.	C	counteraction	Hero (seeker) agrees to counteraction.
11.	↑	departure	Hero leaves home.
12.	D	lst donor function	Hero tested, receives magical agent or helper.
13.	E	hero's reaction	Hero reacts to agent or donor.
14.	F	receipt of agent	Hero acquires use of magical agent.
15.	G	spatial change	Hero led to object of search.
16.	H	struggle	Hero and villain join in direct combat.
17.	J	branding	Hero is branded.
18.	I	victory	Villain is defeated.
19.	K	liquidation	Initial misfortune or lack is liquidated.
20.	↓	return	Hero returns.
21.	Pr	pursuit, chase	Hero is pursued.
22.	Rs	rescue	Hero is rescued from pursuit.
23.	O	unrecognized arrival	Hero, unrecognized, arrives home or elsewhere.
24.	L	unfounded claims	False hero presents unfounded claims.
25.	M	difficult task	Difficult task is proposed to hero.
26.	N	solution	Task is resolved.
27.	R	recognition	Hero is recognized.
28.	Ex	exposure	False hero or villain is exposed.
29.	T	transfiguration	Hero is given a new appearance.
30.	U	punishment	Villain is punished.
31.	W	wedding	Hero is married, ascends the throne.

NB: 1–7 Preparation; 8–10 Complication; 11–15 Transference; 16–19 Struggle; 20–26 Return; 27–31 Recognition

Our first definition of narrative suggested that at least two clauses are required; these clauses can be seen as Propp's functions:

Propp divided the overall composition of the tales into a set of MOVES, consisting of several functions strung together which represent a distinct line of action. (Stam *et al.*, 1992, p. 81)

Propp noted that the first seven functions are a preparation and that many narratives start at function eight where the disruption occurs. Unsurprisingly, Propp's structure is quite readily comparable to Todorov's:

1. a state of equilibrium at the outset – '0'–8;
2. a disruption of the equilibrium by some action – 8;
3. a recognition that there has been a disruption – 9;
4. an attempt to repair the disruption – 10–17;
5. a reinstatement of the equilibrium – 18–31.

It is interesting to note that most narratives climax with the defeat of the villain, function 18, and this is conventionally followed by punishment (which may occur in the defeat if the villain is destroyed) and the hero's heterosexual union with saved 'heroine'. Functions 20–29 are therefore rarely used but this does not invalidate Propp's theory for, as he stated, not all the functions need be present.

Clearly Propp's description needs adapting to contemporary narratives. For example, 'magical agents' only appear in certain genres (science fiction, fantasy or horror) and it is rare for contemporary plots to conclude with a wedding. However, the function of 'magical agents' is not necessarily caused their *magic*, it is their usefulness in helping the hero affect a transition. For example, in the James Bond movies the hero often extricates himself from an 'impossible' situation by using a gadget supplied to him by Q.

It should be noticed that each function develops logically from the previous function. As we saw in our initial definition, causality is crucial to narrative development. In most narratives it is the characters who initiate, and respond to, actions so it follows that these functions should be distributed among the text's characters. Propp termed these characters 'spheres of action', which is a useful way of avoiding confusing 'characters as narrative functions' with 'characters as psychological entities'.

Exercise 1.11

Choose any narrative with which you are very familiar and list the number of functions that occur within it. Are they in Propp's order? You will probably have to re-read the narrative in order to answer the question.

Although contemporary texts may not often conclude with weddings (one recent exception – albeit ironically – is *Clueless*, 1995) they usually do end with a heterosexual couple cementing their relationship. Because many family units are now not based around a married couple, this lack of emphasis on weddings is acceptable today. We have already noted how contemporary Hollywood often exemplifies Todorov's ideas; it also has its own 'version' of Propp.

In 1985 Christopher Vogler, a story analyst working for Disney, produced a memo which he later expanded into a book, *The Winter's Journey*. In it he described the twelve steps of the hero's journey and it, reportedly, became very influential in Hollywood. The twelve steps below are applied to *Star Wars*.

Table 1.3

Step	Star Wars
1. Ordinary world	Restless teenager Luke Skywalker is bored with life on the remote farm where he lives with his uncle and aunt.
2. Call to adventure	Luke accidentally finds the beautiful Princess Leia's desperate plea for help, addressed to Obi-Wan Kenobi, and stored in the droid R2D2.
3. Refusal of the call	Luke seeks out Obi-Wan but doesn't dare take up the challenge, saying that his uncle and aunt need him.
4. Meeting the mentor	Luke finally puts himself in the hands of Obi-Wan and begins to learn about the Force.
5. Crossing the first threshold	Luke takes up the challenge when Imperial troops barbecue (*sic*) his uncle and aunt.
6. Tests, allies, enemies	Luke and Obi-Wan head for a spaceport bar, meet up with Han Solo and the Wookie and make a bitter enemy of Jabba the Hut.
7. Approach to the inmost cave	Luke and company have a series of adventures that culminate in an attempt to break the Princess out of the Death Star.
8. Supreme ordeal	The ordeal is made up of a series of adventures in the Death Star, including a near-death experience in garbage compactor.

Table 1.3 (continued)

Step	Star Wars
9. Reward (seizing the sword)	Luke and company escape with the Princess and the information needed to destroy the Death Star, but not without the sacrifice of Obi-Wan.
10. Road back	The worst (*sic*) is not yet over: the Death Star, moving within range of the rebel base, still has to be destroyed.
11. Resurrection	Luke trusts the Force and destroys the Death Star by sacrificing an old part of his personality, his dependence on machines.
12. Return with elixir	Luke and friends are decorated as heroes, in front of a large crowd. Luke's internal elixir is his new self-knowledge and control of the Force.

Source: Widdicombe, 1994, p. 10

Vogler was influenced by the ideas of Joseph Campbell, an American mythologist, hence the references to swords and elixirs.

Exercise 1.12

Compare Vogler's 'steps' to Propp's 'functions'; can you relate the steps to the functions and do they follow the same order?

My suggestion is that all but three of the functions are comparable and both steps and functions follow the same order.

Table 1.4

Step		Function
1. Ordinary world		Initial situation
2. Call to adventure	9.	Mediation
4. Meeting the mentor	12.	1st donor function
5. Crossing the first threshold	13.	Hero's reaction
6. Tests, allies, enemies	15.	Spatial change
7. Approach to the inmost cave	16.	Struggle
8. Supreme ordeal	17.	Branding
11. resurrection	18.	Victory *and* 19. Liquidation
12. return with elixir	20.	Hero returns

These missing steps, however, do fit in order: '3 Refusal of the call' comes between Propp's functions 9 and 10 while '9 Reward (seizing the sword)' and '10 Road back' fit between 17 and 18. How many contemporary, or even 'classical', Hollywood films fit this pattern?

Exercise 1.13

Apply Vogler's steps to three films you know well.

This extremely formulaic approach to narrative is one of the reasons 1990s Hollywood, which relies upon a consistent supply of high concept, blockbuster movies to remain financially viable at the box office, has been criticised; after all, Vogler's steps are even more limited than Propp's functions.

Spheres of action

Propp contended that there are seven 'spheres of action', or narrative functions: villain; donor; helper; princess (and father); dispatcher; hero (seeker or victim); false hero. Each of these 'characters' has a specific role in the development of the narrative; the villain, for instance, is responsible for the narrative disruption and the hero for the resolution. The seven spheres of action are:

- The *villain* who creates the narrative complication.
- The *donor* gives the hero something, it may be an object, information or advice, which helps in resolution of the narrative.
- The *helper* aids the hero in the task of restoring equilibrium.
- The *princess* is usually the character most threatened by the villain and has to be saved, at the climax, by the hero. The *father's* (who in fairy tales was often the king) role is usually to give the princess away to the hero at the narrative's conclusion.
- The *dispatcher* sends the hero on her or his task (who can also be the princess's father).
- The *hero*, usually male, is the agent who restores the narrative equilibrium, often by embarking upon a quest (or search), saves the princess and wins her 'hand'. Propp distinguishes between the 'victim hero', who is the centre of the villain's attentions, and the 'seeker hero', who aids others who are the villain's victims. The hero is invariably the text's protagonist or central character

and is usually sent on his (the hero's usually male) quest by his community.

- The *false hero* appears to be good but is revealed, at the narrative's end, to have been bad (this sphere of action occurs in functions 24 and 28 which, as has been noted, does not occur often).

Characters can fulfil more than one 'sphere of action' and 'spheres of action' can be made up of more than one character; so a princess may also be a helper and a text may have several villains. Table 1.5 shows where the characters fit within Propp's overall schema.

Table 1.5

Type of character (sphere of action)	Functions (see Table 1.2)
villain	A, H, Pr
donor	D, F
helper	G, K, Rs, N, T
princess (and father)	M, J, Ex, U, W
dispatcher	B
hero	C, E, W
false hero	C, E, L

Source: Berger, 1997, p. 27

Exercise 1.14

Using the same narrative as in the previous exercise, isolate the spheres of action.

Does Propp's theory account for all narratives? Academics seem to be sceptical, although there have been a number of Proppian analyses that have worked well: see Peter Wollen's (1976) analysis of *North By Northwest* and John Fiske (1987) on television series and serials. However, David Bordwell has concluded, with regard to film, that:

[Proppian] analyses have failed through distortion, omission, unconstrained associations, and theoretical inadequacy. There is at present no sound reason to conclude that films share an underlying structure with folktales, or that film studies' version of Propp's method can reveal the structure underlying a narrative film. (Bordwell, 1988, p. 16)

Of course you should come to your own conclusion: does the application of Propp's theories add to your understanding of individual texts? It should also be noted that mainstream texts can eschew narrative drive. For example, *The Thin Red Line* (directed by Terrence Malick, 1998) ran for three hours and consisted of, roughly, three sections of equal length: the preparation; the battle; the aftermath. In narrative terms the resolution of conflict occurs in the battle, however the film runs for another hour afterwards. In addition, although it does have a central character (Witt), the film focuses on a number of individuals and does not offer Proppian villains in a conventional sense. Despite this, the film did respectable box-office business. In the early 1970s, New Hollywood produced numerous films that had 'downbeat' endings: for example, *The Last Picture Show* (1971) and *The Conversation* (1974). In the last 25 years, however, much of Hollywood product can be characterised as being high concept which invariably offers a happy ending and simplifies narrative to such a degree that it is little more than a hook to hang, among other things, the special effects (see also section 5.4).

It could be that Propp's theories are only useful in suggesting similarities between narratives rather than giving particular insights into individual texts. My own view is that both Todorov and Propp have described very *general* and conventional narrative structures and the application of Propp's ideas to particular narratives can, on occasions, be very revealing. What follows offers some examples of how narrative analysis helps illuminate a text's meaning.

Applying narrative theory

Chapter 5 of *Image and Representation* discussed how gender was represented in *Blue Steel* (1990), *Thelma and Louise* (1991) and, in Chapter 6, the *Terminator* movies. These films have been lauded as offering positive, dynamic representations of women (although reservations have been expressed about *Terminator 2: Judgment Day*, 1991). However, an analysis of them in *narrative* terms shows that, although the women take on the hero 'sphere of action' in these films (except in *T2*), they are cast in the form of a 'victim hero'. While there are examples of female 'seeker heroes', such as Ripley in *Aliens* and MJ Monahan in *Copycat* (dealt with later in the chapter), it may be significant that films lauded for putting women at the centre of the narrative, also cast them as victims. Men, too, can be 'victim heroes' but it would be interesting to compare, across a large number of texts, what percentage of 'seeker heroes' are male compared with the percentage of female 'victim heroes'.

Earlier in the chapter seriality was related to serial killing which itself is a popular subject:

1. serial killing featured strongly in Granada television's *Prime Suspect*, staring Helen Mirren, which was both serial – each narrative had a number of episodes – and series (there were five separate productions)
2. there are numerous fictional serial killers (for example, Thomas Harris's Hannibal Lecter novels, Philip Kerr's *A Philosophical Investigation* – see section 1.7)
3. television documentaries, books and part-works (publications published weekly in parts) often show a morbid fascination with serial killers (particular the 'Rippers', Jack and Yorkshire)
4. serial killing has appeared in many films (see Withall, 1996).

This fascination may, as Dyer suggests, simply be a reflection of humankind's obsession with seriality; it may also reflect a particularly morbid sensibility that mirrors the *Zeitgeist* of the twentieth century. One of the most surprising box-office hits of recent years was 1995's *Se7en*. If you have not seen this movie, or *Copycat*, you should skip the next section as it is primarily illustrative material and it will spoil the films if you do decide to see them. Of course the best course of action would be to see the films and then read the following.

Se7en

Exercise 1.15

If you have seen Se7en, apply, as best you can, Propp's 31 functions to the film; if you cannot do this (through intellectual incapability or lassitude), decide which characters fulfil the narrative functions and apply Todorov's structure to the film.

Character	Actor	Narrative function?
Mills	Brad Pitt	
Somerset	Morgan Freeman	
Tracy	Gwyneth Paltrow	
John Doe	Kevin Spacey	
Police Captain	John C. McGinley	

Se7en , directed by David Fincher, is, literally, a very dark movie; a neo-*noir* which offers a bleak, and some have argued reactionary (Taubin, 1996), view of humanity. Despite the bad reviews it received from many North American critics it was the top box-office movie for five weeks (movies rarely stay top for more than one or two weeks) and grossed over $100 million. The film was similarly successful in Europe.

A narrative analysis does not give us a complete picture of how *Se7en* seeks to disturb its audience; for instance, this form of analysis simply registers the deaths as 'murders' and does not consider how they are, in different ways, grotesque. Despite the limitations, a narrative analysis is useful in showing how the film creates some of its disturbing effects.

1. a state of equilibrium at the outset – a rookie cop arrives in a crime-ridden city to take over from a retiring cop
2. a disruption of the equilibrium by some action – the first murder
3. a recognition that there has been a disruption – the realisation that this is the work of a serial killer (Murder in general is not the disruption; in the pre-credit sequence we see Somerset at the scene of a homicide demonstrating that this is a part of everyday life. It is the seriality (the first of seven) that makes the 'Gluttony' murder a disruption.)
4. an attempt to repair the disruption – cops seek the killer
5. a reinstatement of the equilibrium – the killer is killed and *the hero is damned*.

Using Propp's 31 functions shows the film to be, apparently, very traditional in its structure:

Function		Description
α	initial situation	Members of family are introduced; hero is introduced.

Mills (the 'victim hero') joins Somerset (donor and helper) at the scene of a crime.

1. β	absentation	One of the members of the family absents him or herself.

Strictly speaking Somerset does not absent himself, however we do learn that he is to retire (this is an example of what Bordwell criticises as 'distortion').

2. γ	interdiction	Interdiction addressed to hero (can be reversed).

Somerset instructs Mills to do as he says.

5. ξ	delivery	Villain gets information about victim.

TITLE SEQUENCE: Doe has already planned his murders and carried one out.

8. A	villainy	Villain causes harm to a member of the family.

The first murder (Gluttony). The family is 'urban society' (which both Mills and Somerset are members of) because we are all potential victims; the killer needs to be captured before 'he strikes again'. Unlike most serial killers, Doe's victims are not solely women. He chooses 'sinners' regardless of their social status: both rich and poor are victims.

Crucially, the post-title sequence scene shows Mills with his wife (they are the final two 'innocent' victims) who have moved to the city because Mills feels he can 'do good'; however Tracy, a schoolteacher, only sees inner-city deprivation and desperation. Passing trains constantly rattle their home; they have been duped by an estate agent.

9. B	mediation	Misfortune made known; hero is dispatched.

Mills receives a call forcing him to leave his wife; he arrives at the first murder scene. The cut to the scene of the murder, from the bedroom, shows Mills standing, hangdog, in the pouring rain holding two cups of coffee, he looks anything but a hero.

10. C	counteraction	Hero (seeker) agrees to counteraction.

Somerset does not want this investigation to be his last; Mills is keen to take on the case. Somerset, at this point, appears to be the 'seeker hero' (although our knowledge of Hollywood's use of stars makes this unlikely).

Function	Description
11. ↑ departure	Hero leaves home.

Mills begins his quest for the murderer; his impotence is emphasised by the fact that his first 'port of call' is the second murder scene (Greed) where muttered comments are made by uniformed police officers about his inexperience.

12. D lst donor function or helper.	Hero tested, receives magical agent

Mills receives information that resulted from research that Somerset had undertaken on the Seven Deadly Sins.

13. E hero's reaction	Hero reacts to agent or donor.

Mills tries to understand the literature of the Seven Deadly Sins (he reads digests of Dante's Inferno).

14. F receipt of agent	Hero acquires use of magical agent.

Using Mills's inadvertent suggestion, Somerset uses the FBI's illegal monitoring of library usage to find more information which allows them to find where John Doe lives.

15. G spatial change	Hero led to object of search.

Mills and Somerset finds Doe's apartment.

16. H struggle	Hero and villain join in direct combat.

Mills chases Doe.

17. J branding	Hero is branded.

Mills is knocked unconscious by Doe; his face bleeds profusely.

18. I victory	Villain is defeated.

Doe gives himself up.

Up to this point, as we have seen, the narrative structure of *Se7en* has been highly conventional. But the villain giving himself up undercuts the moment when audiences expect the hero to triumph. This offers an enigma (see section 1.7): why has he given himself up? When Doe crows that he would never have been captured, Mills can only lamely retort that 'they would have done and nearly did'.

Function	Description
19. K liquidation	Initial misfortune or lack is liquidated.

Although it appears that the 'initial misfortune' (the serial killings) has been liquidated – how can Doe murder anybody in custody? – there are the sixth and seventh killings to be revealed and completed.

Function	Description
20. ↓ return	Hero returns.

Mills was dispatched from his home, however he does not return there; he does not yet know that he has no 'home' because his wife has been murdered.

Function	Description
25. M difficult task	Difficult task is proposed to hero.

The task proposed to Mills is to follow Doe's instructions or a plea of insanity will be entered and Doe will get 'off lightly'.

Function	Description
26. N solution	Task is resolved.

The instructions are followed but it is the villain's task (that the hero should make him the seventh victim) which is resolved. By killing Doe (whose sin is Envy) Mills (Wrath) condemns himself (to Hell in Biblical terms; to, at worst imprisonment, at best thrown out of the police, in secular terms).

Function	Description
27. R recognition	Hero is recognised.

There can be no recognition of Mills. His tragedy is great because he was an idealist (contrasted with Somerset's 'worldly wise' cynic) who felt 'he could make a difference'. He did not.

Function	Description
30. U punishment	Villain is punished.

The villain has been punished, with his death, however it is something he desires so it can hardly be called a punishment. Chaos takes over at this point: the director, having filmed the shooting in close-up offers us the relief of an extreme long shot of the scene from the circling helicopter. We hear the monitoring member of the SWAT team plead: 'Somebody call somebody, somebody call somebody...' In addition...

Function	Description
31. W wedding	Hero is married, ascends the throne.

...there can be no marriage for the hero and he descends (to Hell). He is offered help from the members of his immediate family, the police; 'whatever he needs', says Somerset.

This Proppian analysis suggests that the disturbing nature of *Se7en* is, at least in part, created by its subversion of narrative expectation. Although the villain is punished, a crucial aspect of narrative resolution, it is a punishment he desires. The nature of Doe's crime are such that 'capital punishment' may seem appropriate but the film – through the sympathetic, intellectual and moral Somerset – makes it clear that this is wrong. The executioner, whether it be society or Mills, is condemned by the act. In the climactic scene Somerset paces impotently, calls Mills by his Christian name for the first time (the men's habit of only using their surnames was a point made by Tracy when Somerset came to dinner) and tries to convince the hero not to act. But the hero is a man of action and not a man of thought (he struggled with the literary references that Somerset supplied as part of his donor function, 'faggot poetry' he called them). The resolution is bleak, terrifying, disturbing and only saved from complete nihilism by Somerset's statement that 'he'll be around' (that is, not retiring).

Ultimately Mills is the (victim) hero although, like the 'seeker hero' he does embark on a quest. The princesses are the murder victims who stand in for the ills of contemporary urban society. The princess is society and the milieu of the film, typically *film noir* (see Chapter 4), is exceptionally bleak: it is constantly raining, the low-key lighting helps create a suffocating *mise-en-scène* imbued with brown shades:

> The print 'was processed through silver retention, a seldom-used method whereby the silver that's leeched out during the conventional processing is rebonded. Silver retention produced more luminosity in the light tones and more density in the darks. (Taubin, 1996, p. 24).

However, although serial killing is often considered the crime of modern society, it is not simply a text about the ills of contemporary American society (the city is not identified, but a yellow cab suggests New York as a possible location). Somerset's research into the 'Seven Deadly Sins' shows violent illustrations from Dante's *Inferno* which are cross-cut with Mills studying photographs of the first murder. The editing of this scene also emphasises the similarity of Mills' and Somerset's quest for knowledge (who is the murderer?), this is further highlighted by the use of music. When Somerset enters a grand, Gothic library, peopled only by security guards who are playing cards, he expresses amazement that all they can do is gamble when surrounded by so much culture. One of the guards says 'I'll show you culture' and plays a recording of Bach's third orchestral suite. At this point the music is obviously diegetic; however, what follows is a montage (presumably covering hours) of Somerset's research. Once time has passed, signified by a dissolve, the music becomes non-diegetic (as it continues in an unbroken

·flow). Similarly, when Somerset's search is intercut with Mills's study of photographs, the apparent appearance of Bach's *Suite* in Mills's apartment is also non-diegetic (unless he happened to be playing the piece at the same time). Although the characters are very different (the man of thought and man of action), this scene, and a crucial conversation in a bar after the harrowing interrogation of the unwitting perpetrator of the Lust murder, suggests that Mills is a younger version of Somerset.

It is implied that violence is endemic to human society; humanity is the princess. We, the audience, too, are the princesses who need saving. Mills, in killing Doe, merely condemns us to further suffering; no redemption is offered, only hope that the 'man of thought', who stays on, can help us. Somerset quotes Hemingway in voice-over (the only time this typically *film noir* device is used in the film): 'The world is a fine place and worth fighting for... I agree with the second part.' In fact this hope was:

> desired by the studio, intended to give some crumb of Hollywood comfort in a film so extraordinarily un-American in its pessimism. (Dyer, 1999, p. 77)

Umberto Eco, among others, has suggested that the detective genre is the narrative form *par excellence*. Bordwell and Thompson's analysis of the genre, in Figure 1.2, when applied to *Se7en* shows how the narrative structure of the quest is made explicit:

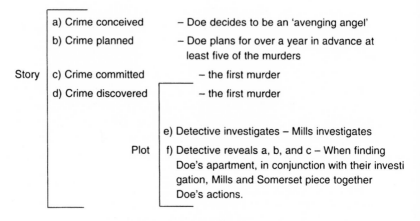

Figure 1.8   Story and plot of *Se7en*

Although the detectives do make a lot of progress in working out Doe's story they are denied the opportunity to restore order; their quest fails. This contrasts with the usual denouement of detective fiction where the discourse of 'law and order' is represented by the detective's triumph. It is interesting to speculate why such a film, which offers a conclusion of 'and hell continued' rather than 'happy ever after', did so well at the box office. If it was because audiences perceived Doe's execution as a happy ending, and not an act that condemns Mills, then society is indeed in trouble. Richard Dyer (1999a) has suggested that the (Racinean) classical purity of the narrative structure offers an incredibly satisfying ending despite the terror engendered.

Although the lack of a conventional resolution is obvious, analysing *Se7en* using Propp's structure allows us to pinpoint the moment of disturbance (function 18) and how what follows is the reverse of most narrative structures. It is, I suspect, this inversion that gives the film its subversive grip. It should be noted that this subversion exists in what is, in many ways, a high concept film which is not usually associated with alternative 'ways of seeing'.

In the analysis of *Se7en* it was noted, on a number of occasions, how important moments are often 'set up' earlier in the text; for instance the poignancy of Somerset addressing Mills by his first name during the climax was made clear because Tracy had pointed out their typically male use of surname. This is an example of narrative economy; little, or nothing, is redundant, virtually everything contributes to the development of the narrative.

Narrative economy in *Copycat*

To continue the theme of serial killing let us consider narrative economy in *Copycat*, released like *Se7en* in 1995. Conventional texts usually attempt to reduce narrative redundancy to a minimum; this is particularly true of feature films because their narratives are usually tightly compressed to fit in a sub-two hour screen duration. So it is important that everything that is shown should, in some way, contribute to narrative progress.

This is even true of character development; for example, in the scene which introduces the hero (cop MJ Monahan played by Holly Hunter) we see her on a training exercise with her male, and subordinate, partner (Ruben). He goes for the bloody kill; she seeks to disable. Later Monahan disables a man, with a crack shot, who is threatening Ruben, however the man recovers and Ruben is fatally wounded. Monahan realises that her partner was killed because, although she successfully disabled the assailant, she was not prepared for the rapid recovery. In the climactic scene Monahan again disables the 'bad guy' but is this time ready for him to recover and she shoots again, this time to kill.

Another example of how scenes early in a plot can prefigure climactic moments is when serial-killer expert Helen Hudson (Sigourney Weaver) tries to leave her apartment to get a newspaper which has fallen a few metres short of her doorway. In this scene we find out that she suffers from, what appears to be, vertigo whenever she is stressed or tries to leave her apartment. This scene introduces both Hudson's incapacity and, later, explains why she cannot escape an assailant. This economy of development is based on action and is one of the reasons why some critics, who value psychological development over action, deride popular cinema.

In an early scene in *The Rock*, a big hit in 1996, the central character is shown being reluctant to use an antidote because he has to inject himself in the heart; at the climax of the film he, of course, must do this. Stephen Heath describes this as 'the narrative... striv[ing] to gather up the elements it puts forward in order with them to go forward *evidently*' (Heath, 1981, p. 134). Everything is intended to be *of use*.

However, this is not to say that *everything* in a conventional text always contributes towards narrative progress. There is a scene, early in *Copycat*, where a cop interviews a 'loony' who claims he is the serial killer. This does not progress the narrative, it is treated as a joke; although, possibly, the presence of the actual killer in the background – presumably waiting to be interviewed – indicates police inefficiency. As Heath says:

> The narrative cannot contain *everything*... the narrative film can only seek to maintain a tight balance between the photographic image as a reproduction of reality and the narrative as the sense, the intelligibility, of that reality. (ibid., pp. 134–5)

In addition, the style of high concept films can militate against narrative flow with the use of slick images that, while they look good, do not actually contribute anything to the movement of the plot.

Copycat was chosen not only because, like *Se7en*, it is a recent 'serial killer'/*noir* movie, but also because it deals with gender in an unconventional, and interesting, fashion. *Copycat* is particularly interesting because its 'hero' and 'helper' are both female; although, typically, women are also the princesses:

> *Copycat's* opening scene has Helen underline in her lecture the fact that serial killers are overwhelmingly male and white. This moment counters two of the mainstays of serial-killer movies. First, it insists that the killers are (in all other respects) typical white men, not exceptional monsters; second, it is a woman who demonstrates this, with all the authority of expertise. (Dyer, 1996, p. 17)

At the film's climax the killer is closing in on Hudson and she is trapped on a roof. Her response: laughter. Even though she has overcome her 'vertigo', and can now live her life again, she laughs at the irony of the situation because it seems she is about to be murdered. In addition, it was one serial killer that made her 'ill' and it is another who cures her. Her laughter is, as Dyer says, 'female derision', which unmans the killer, confusing him enough to allow MJ to deliver the *coup de grâce*.

> Why does Helen laugh? Perhaps a kind of hysteria, or relief that now her life of anxiety will be ended. But also perhaps because she see the profound absurdity of the seriousness with which men take serial killing. (ibid., p. 17)

Although this brief analysis is rooted in narrative theory – female hero and helper – it also demonstrates that narrative alone is not sufficient in analysing texts. Clearly we are drifting into the concept of 'representation' when we are considering gender in this movie.

In Chapter 5 we will consider why certain genres are popular at a particular time. The 1990s has seen a number of popular 'serial killer' movies; hits include *The Silence of the Lambs* (1991), *Basic Instinct* (1992) as well as *Se7en*. Dreamworks' marketing chief has stated that:

> People everywhere are intrigued by [them]. There is... a morbid fascination with people who carry out multiple murders. It's more than horrific. You get into the psychology of 'Why?' (Broeske, 1998, p. 12)

The title of Propp's book, *Morphology of the Russian Folk Tale*, suggests that we should not be dogmatic in the application of his ideas; 'morph', after all, means 'shape'. When we describe the shape of an object, or idea, we normally deal in generalities; if we wanted to be accurate, we would measure the dimensions. If we paraphrase Propp as offering the 'shape of narratives', this dissipates the sense of prescriptiveness that sometimes accrues to the use of his theories. We are free to apply them to find what they tell us about texts without the pressure to determine whether all texts fit a particular pattern.

Arthur Asa Berger neatly sidesteps this problem by suggesting that Propp, and indeed it follows Todorov, are applicable to 'popular culture genres':

> Modern popular culture genres can be thought of as involving variations, modifications, camouflaged versions, and so forth of what Propp called [folk] tales. A large number of the functions that Propp found in his Russian fairy tales can also be found in contemporary spy stories, science fiction, soap operas, westerns, and the like. (Berger, 1992, pp. 21–2)

We shall consider the implications of this apparent 'universality' of narrative for popular culture texts in Chapter 3. However, there is no reason to assume that popular culture genre texts will always follow conventional narrative patterns; one way of assessing whether they do is to apply the theories to any popular television programmes, big box-office movies or bestselling books: see Appendix 2.

1.6 Levi-Strauss and binary oppositions

As we have seen, both Todorov's and Propp's ideas about narrative emphasise the resolution of conflict. Both of their models derive from structuralism, a discourse that looks at 'systems, relations and forms – the structures – that make meaning possible in any cultural activity or artefact' (O'Sullivan et al., 1994, p. 302). One of the most influential structuralists was Ferdinand de Saussure, who demonstrated that signs, whether they be words or images, do not have any intrinsic meaning because they are arbitrary in nature. This means that a sign's meaning is derived from its context (syntagmatic dimension) and the group (paradigm) to which it belongs. As Thwaites put it:

> a sign... works through a system of *differences* (from what it isn't), rather than of identity (with itself). It means something not because it has some fixed identity, but because it is different from other signs. We could put that in a succinct but paradoxical form by saying that what a sign is due to what it isn't. (Thwaites et al., 1994, p. 32)

In brief, the consequences of this are that we only understand language by using a system of oppositions, the most extreme of which is a 'binary opposition'. For example, we cannot conceive of 'good' if we do not understand 'evil', 'black' without 'white' and so on (for a full explanation of this see Chapter 2 of *Image and Representation*). Claude Levi-Strauss, a French structural anthropologist, theorised that binary oppositions formed the basis of humanity's attempts to understand reality through the creation of myths and he demonstrated how:

> myths... were used to deal with the contradictions in experience, [and] explain the apparently inexplicable, and to justify the inevitable. Within myths, contradictions and inequities which could not be resolved in the real world were resolved symbolically. (Turner, 1993, p. 72)

So myth is an 'anxiety-reducing mechanism that deals with unresolvable contradictions in a culture and provides imaginative ways of living with them' (Fiske, 1987, pp. 131–2). Narratives, too, have deep structures that consist of binary oppositions and, in the context of this book, we are interested in how these oppositions are articulated by narratives. Binary oppositions are obviously applicable to narrative because stories are structured by the attempt to resolve conflict, characterised by the *opposition* between the hero and villain. By considering binary oppositions, Berger (1997) showed how it was possible to adapt Propp's 'spheres of action'.

Table 1.6

Good	Bad
Heroes	Villains
Helpers	Henchmen
Princesses (love objects	Sirens (sexual objects)
Magicians (good magic)	Sorcerers (evil magic)
Donors of magic objects	Preventer/hinderers of donors
Dispatchers of heroes	Captors of heroes
Seekers	Avoiders
Seeming villains who are good	False heroes/heroines who are evil

Source: Berger, 1997, p. 44

It follows from these antinomies that the basic actions of characters in narrative should also be categorisable as oppositions.

Table 1.7

Good		Bad
Cooperate	versus	Compete
Help	versus	Hinder
Escape	versus	Imprison
Defend	versus	Attack
Initiate	versus	Respond
Uncover	versus	Disguise
Reveal	versus	Pretend
Love	versus	Hate and lust
Unravel	versus	Mystify
Pursue	versus	Evade
Search for	versus	Evade
Tell truth	versus	Lie
Allow	versus	Prohibit
Question	versus	Answer
Rescue	versus	Endanger
Protect	versus	Threaten
Punish	versus	Suffer
Dispatch	versus	Summon
Allow	versus	Interdict
Retain	versus	Lose

Source: adapted from Berger, 1997, p. 43

NB. Although Berger did not explicitly state this, the categories can be, loosely, defined as 'good' and 'bad'. I have therefore reversed the oppositions 'uncover', 'reveal' and 'punish' as they are more likely to be the actions of the hero.

While audiences are used to considering narrative as a linear, cause–effect chain, these oppositions are less obvious. Berger's point in identifying these oppositions is to demonstrate that:

> When we follow the exploits of characters, we see and interpret everything they do in terms of bipolar oppositions (generally not recognised or brought to awareness by the reader) that give any action meaning. (Berger, 1997, p. 43)

One of the ways these opposites manifest themselves is through the looks of the hero and villain; that is, heroes are, invariably, good looking and villains are often ugly. How does the articulation of these opposites fit in with the myth-making potential of narratives? The answer is to be found in the *relationship* between the opposites:

> One element in a binary opposition is often *privileged* over the other. This means that binary oppositions are also *hierarchies* (*sic*), with one half dominating the other. The second term often comes to represent merely the absence of the first. This has the effect of devaluing the second element. (Moon, 1992, p. 3)

In narratives, the hero, invariably, dominates the villain at the conclusion; one part of the opposition is shown to be superior to the other. So, in mythical terms, the hero represents the triumph of what society (ideologically) holds to be good; whereas in the 'real world' good does not always or, maybe, even usually, win. Conventional narratives show us a successful struggle against opposing forces; whereas in life our struggles (for example to court a person we desire or to pass our exams) are never foregone conclusions, there is always uncertainty. This guarantee of success is part of the function of entertainment.

One way of isolating a text's binary oppositions is to consider what theme is being articulated. For example, in the Penguin Passnotes edition on William Golding's *The Lord of the Flies* the section on 'Themes' opens:

> In this story, a group of English schoolboys gradually turn into a tribe of 'savages'. We see a process in which the veneer of civilization is slowly stripped away until only the most primitive of human energies – fear and violence or what Golding calls the capacity for evil – are left. (Hanscombe, 1986, p. 61)

This novel articulates the oppositions of nature:culture, or savagery:civilisation, represented by the villain, Jack, and the hero, Ralph. *The Lord of the Flies* has a conventional ending, with the hero triumphing; the text's preferred reading is that savagery is wrong. However, it is clear that much of what is 'evil' in Jack, also exists in Ralph and much of the power of the book comes from, what might be called, this 'unresolved resolution'.

In fictional texts the definitions of the hero and villain are often straightforward; however there are texts where this process is less straightforward.

Binary oppositions in the news

Exercise 1.16

Isolate the villain of the following versions of the same news story.

Blood transfusion centres appealed for emergency donors yesterday after more than a tenth of the nation's blood stock was discarded because of contamination fears.

Operations were cancelled yesterday and thousands of pints of blood are to be dumped after a fault was found in packs imported from Australia. (*The Times*, 1 July, 1995)

Health officials sought to cut costs by buying the Australian-made blood bags whose faults have led to more than a tenth of the country's blood supply being destroyed, it emerged last night. (*Guardian*, 1 July, 1995)

In the *Guardian's* story the narrative disruption is caused by faulty blood bags which are a consequence of cost cutting; in *The Times* the emphasis is simply on the fault. These emphases are also indicated by the headlines:

Cost cut led to blood alert

Plea for 5,000 donors as blood is dumped

By identifying the narrative villain we can isolate the ideological basis of a text. Both of these stories, like all news stories, are presented as factual. However, the politically liberal *Guardian* identifies the villain as the cost-cutting assault on a public service; *The Times*, which is conservative, chooses not to emphasise this angle because it was pro cost-cutting in the public services. Unsurprisingly, these newspapers present a story, using narrative, in such a way as to promote their own agendas.

During the Gulf War of 1991, and for many years after, the western media constantly placed Saddam Hussain in the villain 'sphere of action'; the reporting in some Arab countries, however, had Iraq's leader fulfil the hero function. Similarly, in the 'Serbian war' of 1999, the Serb's President Milosevic was the villain for NATO countries but the hero 'locally'. Before any reader derides the 'other side's' reporting as biased, think about whether 'our' reporting may not also be skewed.

These oppositions structure the whole way such events will be reported. For instance, during the Gulf War, the *Guardian* listed the way the war was being reported in the British press.

Table 1.8

West	Iraq
We have	*They have*
Reporting guidelines	Censorship
Press briefings	Propaganda
Our boys are...	*Theirs are...*
Professional	Brainwashed
Lion-hearts	Paper tigers
Cautious	Cowardly
Confident	Desperate

Source: Guardian, 23 January 1991

Concepts such as 'loyalty' (us) were placed in opposition with 'blindly obedient' (them); however, it is arguable that these are not oppositions at all. This definition of the west as good and Iraq as evil, personified by the President of USA, George Bush, and Saddam Hussain, created the framework for virtually all reporting of the war leading to the following disturbing oppositions.

Table 1.9

We	They
Our missiles cause...	*Their missiles cause...*
Collateral damage	Civilian casualties
We...	*They...*
Precision bomb	Fire wildly at anything in the skies
George Bush is...	*Saddam Hussain is...*
At peace with himself	Demented
Resolute	Defiant
Statesmanlike	An evil tyrant
Assured	A crackpot monster

Source: Guardian, 23 January 1991

It is exceptionally unlikely that the actual events of the war fitted neatly into these oppositions: reality is never so straightforward. The oppositions were used to frame the narrative of the events and so privilege the west over Iraq. Broadcast news in Britain, however, is supposed to be 'impartial and balanced'.

The same oppositions appeared again in 1999: the Serbs were described as perpetuating 'atrocities' whereas the NATO bombs and missiles, which inadvertently killed civilians, 'inflicted collateral damage'.

As we have seen, without narrative conflict there is no story and so something must be identified as the villain. In stories about, for example, natural disasters, this is not a problem; but how do news editors decide who is the villain in other stories?

During the 1970s, the Glasgow Media Group analysed the neutrality of British broadcasting institutions and found there was a definite bias against, among others, trade unionists and the Greenham Common women (anti-nuclear weapon protesters). One of the Group's case studies was the coverage of the Glasgow dustcart drivers' strike of 1975 which was caused by poor pay compared to HGV drivers; the dustcart drivers received £32.50 a week compared with the lowest rate of £37.00 a week for an HGV driver in road haulage. The strike was reported as follows:

> The news established that the story of the Glasgow dustcart drivers was about the piling up of uncollected rubbish, the eventual official declaration of a health hazard, and the calling in of troops to break the strike and clear the rotting refuse. (Eldridge, 1993, p. 284)

In narrative terms, then, the disruption was the piling of uncollected rubbish, which was caused by the dustcart drivers, who were therefore the villains of the piece:

> The most remarkable feature of this coverage was that the workers who had apparently caused all this never appeared on the screen to explain their actions. (ibid.)

Despite the fact that broadcast news must show itself to be impartial, the 'villains' of the story could never present their case to the public at large; as the Group's findings showed this *partiality* was endemic. No doubt their version would have portrayed the employers (the Glasgow Corporation) as the villain because it was their offer of poor pay that caused the disruption and in this scenario, the dustcart drivers would be the princesses. However, in the news report, the general public fulfilled this function and the army (strikebreakers) were the heroes.

Exercise 1.17

Analyse the narrative structure of the first three stories of a news broadcast. Consider if there are other ways of casting heroes and villain; do these alternatives show any bias within the actual report?

The decision of who should take on the role of the villain is ideological; that is, it reflects certain values. One of the Glasgow Media Group's conclusions was that the so-called unbiased broadcast news coverage was consistently on the side of the Establishment. During the Cold War, Russians (and Communists in general) were stock villains in western texts, whether the texts were fictional or news, documentary or current affairs. An analysis of the James Bond movie villains can give an indication of the political status quo of their eras.

During the 1930s and 40s, oriental types often took the villain role; for example the Emperor Ming in the *Flash Gordon* serials which reflected the perceived threat, to the west, of the Far East. The absence, in the 1930s at least, of many examples of 'Nazis as villains' suggests an ambivalence towards fascism which now seems puzzling. The 'Hays' code of cinema censorship, which was formulated in the 1920s, explicitly stated that villains must be punished; the 'law of compensating value' meant sinners always had to pay.

Similarly, who takes the hero function is equally ideological. We have already considered the fact that the preponderance of male heroes is indicative of patriarchal society. Ethnicity is also important, the hero of North American movies is invariably a white, Anglo-Saxon, Protestant (WASP).

Exercise 1.18

List as many film stars as you can and categorise them in terms of race and gender. What conclusions do you draw?

Adrian Tilley (1991) offers some useful signpost questions that help define what the process of the narrative has created. He suggests that we compare the opening and ending and ask:

1. what has changed in the world of the story?
2. what has been transformed?
3. what has been added or lost in the process?
4. how have the characters' relative positions of power and status changed?

The answers to these questions are likely to reveal the narrative's ideological basis.

1.7 Barthes's narrative codes

Roland Barthes defined realist texts as those which efface their own production (discussed in Chapter 6 of *Image and Representation*) and showed how:

> The 'texture' of the realist text is... created by the interweaving of different *codes*, each less important in itself than for the way in which they are combined. (Cook, 1985, p. 238c)

Here we will focus, specifically, on the role of narrative codes in this combination which creates an impression of reality. Because a realist text *cannot* formally be verified by reference to the 'real world', realism must be derived from the interaction between the text's own internal logic and its reference to other texts, its intertextuality. 'Intertextuality' refers to the text's references to other texts because a sign's *referent* is not the 'real world'.

In his analysis of Balzac's novella *Sarrasine*, Barthes concentrated on how the 'internal logic' is structured by the narrative. Barthes's codes describe how the audience becomes a writer-reader because they, in effect, (re)create the narrative. The audience (de)code a text's 'internal logic' by understanding the following narrative codes:

- *Hermeneutic, or enigma code*: 'all the units whose function it is to articulate in various ways a question, its response, and the variety of chance events which can either formulate the question or delay its answer; or even constitute an enigma and lead to its solution' (Barthes, 1990, p. 17) (certainly Barthes is not concerned with making life easy for *his* audience).

Narratives 'capture' their audiences by making them want to know what is going to happen next. This code both sets puzzles and resolves them. Imagine a narrative resolution where all the puzzles set within a text are not answered; it is likely that such a narrative would be unsatisfying to most (some texts, however, like the film *Last Year in Marienbad*, 1961, purposefully seem to consist of unresolved narrative codes). It is the delay between the proposition and the resolution of the code that motivates audiences to continue their 'reading'; it is the 'motor of the narrative'. Hermeneutics is the philosophical tradition of interpretation, however, in the Barthesian sense:

> the function of the hermeneutic code is to delay revelation, to dodge the moment of truth by setting up obstacles, stoppages, deviations... delaying final disclosure until the ultimate moment. (Stam *et al.*, 1992, p. 192)

In *Se7en* one of the enigmas posed is the motivation of the serial killer; in *Copycat*, we are offered, for some time, the generic enigma of 'whoisdoingit'? Titles are often enigma codes: 'Seven' what? 'Copying' what? The latter is particular sinister as 'copycat' is a phrase used by children.

- *Semic code*: the way in which characters, objects and settings take on particular meanings. For example, Propp's 'spheres of action' are individualised into a character by their codes of speech, clothing, gesture (although they can be stereotypes). In *Se7en*, Somerset wears the 'traditional' garb of a detective, trench coat and trilby. The red dress worn by Helen Hudson, the criminal psychologist specialising in serial killers, at the beginning of *Copycat* signifies her self-confidence and, in Freudian terms, her sexual assertiveness. These are determined by the needs of the culture in which the narrative is produced rather than narrative function. In western society there appears to be a need that the central characters are physically attractive and the villains are often less than physically perfect (signifying degeneracy). Iconography can act as a semic code, a 'ray gun' is likely to connote 'science fiction' and the setting of Transylvania is likely to suggest vampires.

- *Symbolic code*: codes which signify Levi-Strauss's binary oppositions (such as good:evil; male:female; youth:adult) and/or Freudian symbols.

The symbolic code maps out the fields of antitheses in which culture articulates meaning through the differential representation of symbolic

73

identities so that the oppositions appear natural, inevitable and non-linguistic. (Stam *et al.*, 1992, p. 196)

One of the most frequently articulated oppositions is gender. For example, in *Once Were Warriors* (1994) this opposition is explicitly presented in the opening sequence with images of men body-building and a woman reading a story to children. Gender roles form a very important part of the narrative, although not always conventionally. The sequence also shows a woman swigging out of a bottle of beer in a masculine fashion.

In *Se7en*, the drab and hostile city streets, generic to *film noir*, set up an opposition with country. However, *Se7en* undermines this opposition at the film's conclusion by offering a countryside that is desert-like and straddled by high-tension towers. So, despite the fact the sun is shining for the first time in the film, the environment is a suitable terrain for the terrible actions of the conclusion. The symbolic code helps the audience understand the oppositions that the narrative will be articulating.

- *Proairetic, or action, code*: the codes of behaviour that we under-stand, not in relation to behaviour in the 'real world' but from experience of other narratives. They are often used as a shorthand way of advancing action: a cop readying a gun signifies trouble ahead. When Somerset is paged, during his discussion with Tracy, he stands up to leave; this is an action code for his journey to his destination.

Action codes also determine whether it is appropriate to show an action. For example, if a character goes to sleep there is no need to show them 'falling asleep', the preparation is sufficient. These codes are also related to censorship: for non-adult material sexual inter-course can be signified by a couple getting into bed; for adult mate-rial it is appropriate to show the 'full monty'. Similarly, sex between characters is likely to be portrayed differently depending upon the genre, for example romance and pornography.

- *Cultural, or referential, codes*: these codes refer not to the text's narrative but to outside the text. The outside, however, is not reality but 'a common stock of a culture as it is expressed in the 'already written' knowledges of morality politics, art, history, psychology, and so on' (Fiske, 1987, p. 143). Stam suggests 'in practice, it is often difficult to separate the semic codes from Barthes' ...cultural codes' (Stam *et al.*, 1992, p. 195).

In *Se7en*, the cultural references to the 'art' of *film noir* are important in making sense of the text. Somerset's research into the Seven Deadly Sins leads him to the works of Chaucer and Dante who are, culturally, highly valued. These codes can be absolutely crucial in the reading of alternative texts; for example, it is only possible to make sense of *Memories of Underdevelopment (Memorias de subdesarrollo*, directed by Tomas Gutierrez Alea, 1968) with reference to the history of the Cuban revolution. The associations engendered by the cultural code function in a similar way to the connotations of the 'semic' code.

Use of Barthes's narrative codes

We saw in the quote from Barthes, at the beginning of the section, that he can be a very difficult read. While most Media Studies textbooks refer to the codes, actual applications of them to texts are exceptionally thin on the ground (see Lesage, 1985). So what use are they? In *S/Z* Barthes spends approximately 170 pages analysing a 33-page story; it is impressive (in terms of work and in the analysis) and mad. Barely a sentence passes without the presence of a code, which of course shows how important narrative is in constructing a text, but the weight of detail can end up deadening the experience of the text. However, I suggest the codes are useful as a shorthand way of describing how texts are working. For instance, the opening of Philip Kerr's novel *The Philosophical Investigation*:

> The unfortunate victim, twenty-five-year-old Mary Woolnoth, was found naked in the basement of the offices of the Mylae Shipping Company in Jermyn Street, where she had worked for three years as a receptionist, her face beaten in with a claw hammer. (Kerr, 1993, p. 1)

The Philosophical Investigation. Like most titles, an enigma: 'investigation' suggests a crime novel, but 'philosophical'? Connotations of academia suggests a crime novel set in a university (although this is not the case).

'The unfortunate victim...' symbolic code evoking the binary opposition of good:evil. For there to be a victim there needs to be a villain who the hero must overcome.

'...twenty-five-year-old Mary Woolnoth, was found naked...' semic code, a young female and naked woman is likely to have been sexually attacked; she is a conventional victim.

'in the basement of the offices of the Mylae Shipping Company in Jermyn Street...' cultural code as the victim's and company's name refers to T.S. Eliot's *The Waste Land*:

> To where Saint Mary Woolnoth kept the hours
> With a dead sound on the final stroke of nine.
> There I saw one I knew, and stopped him, crying: 'Stetson!
> 'You who were with me in the ships at Mylae!
> 'That corpse you planted last year in your garden... (Eliot, 1974, p. 65)

The reference helps set the tone of the novel which is a bleak view of the future.

'...where she had worked for three years as a receptionist, her face beaten in with a claw hammer.' Action and enigma codes: she has been violently murdered, suggesting a psychopathic villain, and sets up the central enigma, assuming this to be of the crime genre which the title and opening sentence suggests (another cultural code): who is the murderer and will the hero track him (killers are usually male) down? This also illustrates that more than one code can exist within any particular unit of meaning.

I think the above does suggest how referring to the code in any analysis can help with a concise description of the way the text is creating meaning. By identifying the codes you are immediately pointing out the constructedness of the text, a crucial point in Media Studies. Also, by considering which code is present in any unit of meaning, which Barthes calls *lexias*, our attention is focused upon the narrative element of a text; this avoids the trap of only dealing with narrative from a macro-perspective (Todorov, Propp and Levi-Strauss). Barthes's codes do serve an important function as they show us that:

> the illusion of realism in a narrative is founded on the integrated func-
> tioning of five levels of codes, all of which work together to suggest what
> seems to be the Meaning (often signalled by the denouement) and all of

which suggest other previously established cultural meanings beyond themselves. (Lesage, 1985, p. 479)

Narrative does not deal with reality at all but strives to create an illusion of reality by referring to other sign systems.

How important do you think that narratives are to our lives? Where would you place narrative on a scale of one to ten? In his 'hierarchy of needs', Maslow suggested that human beings' most basic needs are physiological (food, water, shelter, sex and so on); above this are safety needs (for example security); next are love needs which are followed by the need for esteem (both self-esteem and esteem from others); on top of the hierarchy sits the need for self-actualisation (a sense of fulfilment in one's own life).

Clearly, in Maslow's terms narrative is not particularly important (unless one's ambition, and need for self-actualisation, is to create or read narratives); however, narrative is not only something that we experience when listening, reading or watching stories, it is also, as we have seen, a way of seeing that is fundamental to the under-standing of human existence. Berger, drawing upon the work of Bettelheim (1976) and Luthi (1984), demonstrated that fairy tales have a particular function:

A child may become anxious when hearing a particular story, but once he or she becomes acquainted with fairy tales in general, the troubling aspects of these stories tend to disappear and the reassuring aspects become more dominant. The original anxiety the child feels turns into pleasure based on facing and mastering that anxiety... Anxiety is gener-ated and then relieved, leading to feelings of mastery. (Berger, 1997, p. 91)

As I hope we have seen in this chapter, adult narratives are also anxiety-reducing devices: the reassuring resolutions, where good invariably triumphs over evil, offer stable reference points that are absent from most people's existence.

2

A HISTORY
OF NARRATIVE

AIMS OF THE CHAPTER

➤ To offer a history of narrative with reference to:

- *The Epic of Gilgamesh*
- Aristotle's theory of art
- the oral tradition
- *Le Morte D'Arthur* (*The Death of Arthur*)
- Shakespeare
- the novel
- romanticism
- modernism
- postmodernism.

➤ By doing so, to assess the social functions of narrative and how technology influences the production of narrative texts.

2.1 Introduction

It was suggested in Chapter 1 that narrative structure appears to be common to all cultures. One way of testing the truth of this statement is to assess whether narratives from texts created in the past are structured, narratively, like modern ones. As was shown in Chapter 4 of *Image and Representation*, the conventions that have governed the production of images have varied throughout history because the modes of representation are ideologically determined. If narrative structure is also ideologically influenced, it will vary through time and theorists cannot claim they have isolated universal structures.

However, we shall soon see that narrative structure has been fairly constant throughout history and the main purpose of this chapter is to consider:

1. the different social functions of narrative
2. how technology affects the production of narrative texts.

On a cautionary note, what follows is no more than a précis; it is beyond the scope of this text to indulge in the sort of narrative analysis performed, in the last chapter, on *Se7en*. Rather the chapter is, in part, intended to complement the 'history of western images' which appeared in *Image and Representation*; once again I have to emphasise my cultural 'blindness' as my knowledge of non-western narratives is severely limited.

2.2 *The Epic of Gilgamesh*

In trying to answer the question of whether narrative is a social construct, like realism, or an expression of a 'universal' structure, it is useful to look at *The Epic of Gilgamesh*. This is the world's oldest known narrative; it is believed to date from 2000BC. The fullest version of the text that exists, although it is still incomplete, once belonged to the library of the Assyrian king Ashurbanipal, who ruled between 668 and 627BC. There is no historical evidence for the actual events narrated in the poems, but it is believed that Gilgamesh was a real person who ruled Uruk during the first part of the third millennium BC.

The first part of the poem, 'The Coming of Enkidu', seems to contradict the theories we considered in Chapter 1. Gilgamesh, who we expect to be the hero, is tyrannical in nature:

> Gilgamesh the king is about to celebrate marriage with the Queen of Love, and he still demands to be first [that is, 'have sex'] with the bride, the king to be first and the husband to follow. (*Epic of Gilgamesh*, 1960, p. 68)

However, it soon transpires that this is because of Gilgamesh's existence as half-man, half-god and not through any inherent villainy. In order to curb his excesses, the gods send Enkidu to be his friend and helper. They then embark upon a series of adventures, all characterised by conflict which the hero and helper overcome, albeit in ways that are unconventional to modern audiences. For example:

> Like a raging bull... the watchman of the woods turned full of threaten-ings, he cried out... He nodded his head and shook it, menacing Gilgamesh; and on him he fastened his eye, the eye of death. Then Gilgamesh called to Shamash and his tears were flowing. (ibid., p. 81)

Shamash, a god, then proceeds to save Gilgamesh by summoning a variety of winds. Later, when Gilgamesh refuses to marry a god, a divine bull is sent by the jilted deity to destroy the king, but the two friends kill the 'animal'. In addition to these conflicts, there is refer-ence to an apocalyptic flood, an event which has reappeared many times in narratives, including the Bible and J.G. Ballard's science fiction novel *The Drowned World* (1965). Towards the end of the epic Gilgamesh tries to find out how to cheat death in order to resurrect Enkidu, who was killed in revenge for destruction of the bull, an event which has elements in common with a number of Greek myths and is an example of both the 'quest' and 'journey to another world' narratives. After the 'fantastic' journey he finds the plant that will renew youth, only to lose it immediately.

The synoptic extracts above all deal with conflict, which we have seen is endemic in modern narratives, that must be ended to create a narrative resolution. All, that is, except the last one which dealt with death; however, we would not expect this to be resolved as one fact of life that cannot (yet) be overcome is death. Despite its great age, and some very clear differences to modern forms, Todorov's description of narrative structure does describe the construction of the Babylonian narrative and Proppian functions are identifiable. Because *The Epic of Gilgamesh* is so old, this is strong evidence for the argument that conventional narrative is a universal, rather than an ideological, structure. However, it may simply mean that this struc-ture is simply an *extremely* enduring one; we cannot be certain that in one hundred years our narratives will still be the same.

Looking backwards, we shall see that conventional narrative structure changes very little through history but, in contrast, the way the narrative *form* is expressed evolves radically.

2.3 Aristotle's theory of art

Aristotle's *Poetics* remains one of the most influential texts about aesthetics. Aristotle contrasted poetry with history, privileging poetry because it deals with Platonic types rather than the specificities of history; he defined theatrical genres as 'comedy' and 'tragedy' and poetic genres as 'epic' or 'ballad'. For our purposes, it is most fruitful to focus on tragedy, the function of which, Aristotle concluded, was to 'purify' the emotions of the audience. This purification refers to the sense of satisfaction engendered by the resolution of the disruption at the end of a play, film or other text; an experience that will be familiar to many. This purging of emotion was called a 'catharsis'.

One of the ways in which catharsis is produced is by identification with characters in the text; it is likely that most of us will identify with the hero although it is possible to identify with other 'spheres of action'. While in our real lives our struggle to succeed sometimes fails, by identifying with a hero we can 'take part', for a while, in a successful struggle. This helps purge ourselves of everyday frustration and forms part of Aristotle's catharsis.

Aristotle's definition of the function of conventional narrative, and its catharsis, is by no means an out-dated concept. In one of the many 'how to write a screenplay' books, Lew Hunter shows Hollywood, too, seeks 'catharsis':

> Aristotle was the first to put the storyteller's trade tricks down on paper[2] the contemporary Act One, the beginning, is *the situation*. The idea. Why you call people to their neighbourhood multiplex. Act Two, the middle, is *the complications*. The plot must thicken. Cause and effect. Push and shove. The third act, the end, is *the conclusion*. The climax. The catharsis. The wrap-up. (Hunter, 1994, p. 20)

Aristotle described tragedy as a form (in the terms of traditional literary criticism, a genre) that inverts the conventional narrative pattern:

> The perfect [tragic] plot... must have a single... issue; the change in the hero's fortunes must be not from misery to happiness, but on the contrary from happiness to misery; and the cause of it must lie not in any depravity, but in some great error on his part. (trans. Ingram Bywater, Bratchell, 1990, p. 21)

In Aristotlean tragedy, the narrative disruption is caused not by the actions of the villain but by those of the hero. For example, in Sophocles' *King Oedipus*, Oedipus makes several mistakes; including unknowingly killing his father and marrying his mother. When he finds out what has happened, he breaks into his mother's/wife's bedroom (the following extract is not for the faint-hearted):

> CHORUS: We saw a knotted pendulum, a noose,
> A strangled woman swinging before our eyes.
> The King saw too, and with heart-rending groans
> Untied the rope, and laid her on the ground.
> But worse was yet to see. Her dress was pinned
> With golden brooches, which the King snatched out
> And thrust, from full arm's length, into his eyes –
> Eyes that should see no longer his shame, his guilt,
> No longer see those they should never have seen,
> Nor see, unseeing, those he had longed to see,
> Henceforth seeing nothing but night. (Sophocles, 1947, p. 61)

(In Freudian terms the 'plucking out of eyes' represents castration.)

In Greek tragedy, the hero makes his errors because the gods intervene in mortals' lives. In Shakespearean tragedy, they result from flaws in the hero's personality (Hamlet's indecision; Othello's jealousy). So the narrative disruption is directly caused by the hero; in Proppian terms – in terms of its function in the narrative – the hero in a way takes on the role of the villain. Oedipus kills his father; Hamlet spends the whole play *not* acting heroically, until it is too late, to solve the disruption caused by his father's death. The hero is a 'victim hero', a victim of himself. This does not mean that the *character* (not the 'sphere of action') of the villain cannot also exist and influence events: for example, in *Othello*, Iago persuades Othello of his wife's unfaithfulness. Although the hero must eventually be punished for his (tragic heroes are usually male) actions, invariably by death, he is not evil. This is the essence of tragedy; the unnecessary death of a good person. However, Todorov's 'equilibrium' is restored at the text's close.

2.4 The oral tradition

The ability to read words is seen as of paramount importance in our society and it is difficult to imagine a time when narratives could only be transmitted orally. The oral tradition, which survived long after the invention of writing, now seems a long way off:

> We are no longer linked to our past by an oral tradition which implies direct contact with others (storytellers, priest, wise men, or elders), but by books amassed in libraries, books from which we endeavour – with extreme difficulty – to form a picture of their authors. (Levi-Strauss, 1968, p. 366)

As we shall see in Chapter 3, we are able to form a picture of a text's author by decoding the addresser from the text. In the oral tradition, however, the addresser would be a combination of the text *and* the bard; that is, the addresser would be a combination of the spoken words and the actual performance. The sender would be the actual individual 'playing' the role of the bard.

The oral tradition clearly involves 'live' performances: audiences have a different relationship to a text if they are present at a performance rather than being distanced by technology (written text, television, cinema and so on). For instance, at live events audiences can participate in the performances, sometimes in a controlled way (as in pantomime's shouted 'behind you!'), sometimes in less organised ways (throwing tomatoes in disgust). However, although the bards are dead, their function may still be with us: according to Fiske and Hartley (1978), television as a medium tries to fulfil the 'bardic' function by using the oral mode to communicate to its audience. This view has been taken up by other commentators:

> [Kosloff] observes that television often seems to want to compensate for the fact that it is an industrial and impersonal mass medium. Television, she argues, in its discourse, seeks to 'personalise the impersonal' through its use of on-screen presenters, or off-screen continuity announcers. (Tolson, 1996, p. 42)

It is fascinating to think that the most influential medium of the twentieth century is closely related to such an ancient mode of representation.

Beowulf

Exercise 2.1

Read the Anglo-Saxon poem *Beowulf*.

The oldest surviving piece of English literature is *Beowulf* and it forms part of the oral tradition. However, even if you do not read *Beowulf*, you may be familiar with the poem through adaptations for children (for example, Sutcliff, 1961, and Keeping and Crossly-Holland, 1982) and a recent film version. *Beowulf*, as an oral poem, is meant to be performed, sung or spoken to an audience. As in Homer's Greek epics, the power of the spoken word helps convey the narrative ideas; take the alliterative force of the opening:

> Attend!
> We have heard of the thriving of the throne of Denmark,
> how the folk-kings flourished in former days,
> how those royal athelings earned that glory.
>
> Was it not *Scyld Shefing* that shook the halls,
> took mead-benches, taught encroaching
> foes to fear him – who, found in childhood,
> lacked clothing? Yet he lived and prospered,
> grew in strength and stature under the heavens
> until the clans settled in the sea-coasts neighbouring
> over the whale-road all must obey him
> and give tribute. He was a good king! (translated by Michael Alexander, 1973, p. 51)

This passage seems to cry out to be recited in a declamatory style. However there is no reason why it should not also be spoken differently; using a commutation text we might be able to ascertain the effect of a rendition in a completely different manner, say by the camp Julian Clary or the acerbic Denis Leary. The test also demonstrates how much the addressee, of a performed *Beowulf*, would depend upon the bard's style of performance.

Texts in the oral, bardic, tradition often used a rhyme scheme to help performers memorise the text; the use of a consistent rhythm also helps recall. The need for specific metres, such as the dactylic hexameter (a stressed syllable followed by two unstressed, six times per line) of Greek and Latin epic poetry, explains the use of standard epic similes and metaphors – they help fill lines with the required number of syllables.

Beowulf recounts the eponymous hero's battle, first with Grendel and Grendel's mother and then, after he has been crowned king of the Geats, with the dragon. The poem falls easily into conventional narrative structure: the monsters are the villains; Wiglaf, the only Geat brave enough to assist Beowulf in his final, fatal and successful confrontation with the dragon, is a helper. However, *Beowulf* is also different from modern narrative:

> [The] habit of regarding everything in the narrative as if it had already happened and the results were only too well-known is typical of traditional poetry: we are told the results of all three monster-fights not only in advance but several times afterwards as well. (Alexander, 1973, p. 43)

This use of narrative repetition would be deemed madness by today's Hollywood executives who, in the words of Samuel Goldwyn, try to start their movies with an earthquake and build up to a climax. In the oral tradition repetitions are common and help audiences remember what has happened earlier in the narrative; in a live, oral, performance, audiences cannot 'flick' back to remind themselves of events and they do not have visual memory to aid them (cinema's images or theatre's actions). While contemporary conventional narrative is characterised by an economy, which eschews such redundancy, repetition is necessary in the oral mode. In addition, the fact that oral literature is *performed* is likely to encourage the creation of flamboyant, if redundant, passages; such as the exchanges, in *Beowulf*, between Wulfgar and the coastguard which the poet hoped the audience would enjoy. What may seem flat and irrelevant in written literature could, in the mouth of a talented performer, become an exciting, virtuoso passage.

When villains in a narrative are human, the plot will usually involve conflict *between* individuals or communities. In *Beowulf*, the villain function is taken by monsters; this allows the narrative to concentrate more on the *nature* of community. The failure of the Geats to come to their elderly king's aid, when he takes on the dragon, leads to the loss their leader. After Beowulf's death, a messenger foretells the end of the Geats now that their great leader is dead. If they had supported their leader, all would have been well: the moral of the tale seems to be 'the next time the leader asks for assistance, help him'. As always, there are ideological implications to this: do as you are told; be obedient to authority.

Fiske and Hartley suggested the following oppositions for oral and literate modes of exposition (see Table 2.1).

These *oppositions*, however, do not mean that narrative structure cannot be the same as these modes. It does not matter to the 'situation/disruption/resolution' pattern whether the narrative is spoken, written or acted.

Table 2.1

Oral modes	Literate modes
dramatic	narrative
episodic	sequential
mosaic	linear
dynamic	static
active	artifact
concrete	abstract
ephemeral	permanent
social	individual
metaphorical	metonymic
rhetorical	logical
dialectical	univocal/'consistent'

Source: Fiske and Hartley, 1978, pp. 124–5

In modern society the oral mode is virtually dead. However, although contemporary Hollywood films are not likely to include such virtuoso displays by a narrator, many movies have been made as 'star vehicles'; films in which the star's performance is more important than the narrative. The plots of Elvis Presley's movies, for instance, are merely excuses for the performance of songs; early Hollywood musicals, too, also often included vaudeville stars who contributed virtuoso turns; the film *Private Parts* (1997) was built around the talent of Howard Stern.

2.5 *Le Morte D'Arthur (The Death of Arthur)*

Beowulf is about the myth of community, which in later years was sometimes defined as 'nationhood'. One of the most potent myths of English nationalism is the tale of King Arthur. Modern readers often find Sir Thomas Malory's episodic, 'prose romance' version of the Arthurian legend quite difficult to read. One reason is the unfamiliarity of language; however, more important to our purposes, difficulties are also caused because Malory dispenses with the (bourgeois) need to situate scenes clearly in narrative space and time:

Then Ulfius was glad, and rode on more than a pace till that he came to King Uther Pendragon, and told him he had met with Merlin.
'Where is he?' said the king.
'Sir,' said Ulfius, 'he will not dwell long.'
Therewithal Ulfius was ware where Merlin stood at the porch of the pavilion's door. And then Merlin was bound to come to the king. When King Uther saw him, he said he was welcome. (Malory, 1969, Book 1, Chapter 2, p. 11)

The only description present is what is necessary for the story; the creation of a (in our terms) convincing diegesis is deemed superfluous. Compare the above with a more modern rendering of the legend which uses the novel form:

'Have some mustard,' said the magician, when they had got to the kidneys.
   The mustard-pot got up and walked over to his plate on its silver legs that waddled like the owl's. Then it uncurled its handles and one handle lifted its lid with exaggerated courtesy while the other helped him to a generous spoonful.
   'Oh, I love the mustard-pot!' cried the Wart. 'Wherever did you get it?'
   At this the pot beamed all over its face and began to strut a bit, but Merlyn rapped it on the head with a teaspoon, so that it sat down and shut up at once. (White, 1962, p. 31)

White's description allows us to conceptualise the space and time ('waddled over to his plate') in which the events of the narrative are occurring. As we shall see in the consideration of the novel, 'realism' is the form's defining characteristic.
   Although the style of Malory's rendition is much more old-fashioned than T.H. White's, he was, in fact, undertaking, for his day, a sophisticated and modern project:

by unravelling the complex cycles which appealed to medieval taste into single tales, by playing down symbolic patterns in favour of emotion and motive, and by paring the theological elaborations of (source material) so as to accentuate the mystical force of the Grail appearances, he ensured the continuing appeal of the Arthurian story to modern tastes. (Daiches, 1971, p. 345)

We have seen, in our consideration of Barthes's narrative codes, how a convincing diegesis is created by audiences decoding a text's 'internal logic'. Clearly the codes Malory used are different to contemporary codes; for example, the 'enigma' code is absent because pre-Renaissance texts had no 'interest' in motivating audiences through curiosity. Similarly, it is inevitable that the other codes should be culture-specific and so their meaning should change across the centuries.

Despite the differences from modern narratives, Todorov's structure is apparent: Malory translated and adapted Arthurian stories which told the tales – probably both fabricated and real – of how the legendary King fought off the disruptive, invading, hordes of Saxons and Irish thereby maintaining the existence of Britain as a nation.

The extent to how much we are familiar with a particular era's mode of narrative expression is determined by how much texts from the past are part of contemporary culture. There is no doubt, in English-speaking societies, that the codes of Elizabethan times, primarily through familiarity with the work of William Shakespeare, are the most known from the distant past.

2.6 Shakespeare

Shakespeare is regularly described as the greatest writer in the English language; his works are regarded as unique and the themes they deal with are thought to be universal. This may be true, but Shakespeare was also a product of his time. In common with his contemporaries and antecedents, he used many existing narratives as his source material. The major reason novelty, the new, was eschewed in Shakespeare's time was the prevailing feudal view of the world:

> Chaucer, Spenser, Shakespeare, and Milton, for instance... like the writers of Greece and Rome, habitually used traditional plot; and who did so, in the last analysis, because they accepted the general premise of their times that, since Nature is essentially complete and unchanging, its records, whether scriptural, legendary, or historical, constitute a definitive repertoire of human experience. (Watt, 1972, p. 15)

For example, the main source of *Othello* was 'the seventh story in the third decade of the *Jecatommithi* of Giraldi Cinthio, published in Venice in 1566' (Ridley, 1989, p. xv). As was normal in his day, Shakespeare structured his play into five acts that in narrative terms fit the 'situation, disruption and resolution' pattern. The narrative structure is conventional and could be characterised, in *Othello*, as such:

1. a state of equilibrium at the outset – Venetian society approves of Othello's inter-racial marriage to Desdemona
2. a disruption of the equilibrium by some action – Iago attempts to convince Othello that his wife has been unfaithful
3. a recognition that there has been a disruption – Othello believes Iago
4. an attempt to repair the disruption – Othello determines to kill his wife
5. a reinstatement of the equilibrium – Desdemona is murdered by her husband who then kills himself.

There is no 'fairy tale' ending to *Othello* because it is a tragedy. While all these intrigues have been going on Othello has been despatched from Venice to Cyprus and subdued a rebellion... all in three days! In keeping with the current ideological worldview, the detailed realities of place and time, as we understand them, had little importance in Shakespeare's plays. The belief was that 'the truth about existence can be fully unfolded in the space of a day as in the space of a lifetime' (ibid. pp. 24–5). One consequence of this is the modern audience's confusion when faced with the time-schemes in Shakespeare's plays.

The lack of a modern sense of time also reveals itself in Shakespeare's sense of history: that is, he did not have one that we understand. At the time, history was not seen as being a linear development from the past to the present; all history was simply there, 'en masse' so to speak. As Watt points out, the term 'anachronism' did not appear until 30 years after the Bard's death.

2.7 The novel

Texts in Shakespeare's era recycled the old because, it was believed, there could be nothing new. Then came the novel. Chapter 6 of *Image and Representation* dealt with the rise of capitalism and the individualist bourgeois ideology, and how these were reflected in the rise of the novel. With the novel, the universals of feudal ideology were rejected in favour of:

> the total subordination of plot to the pattern of the autobiographical (and this) is as defiant an assertion of the primacy of individual experience in the novel as 'cogito ergo sum' was in philosophy. (ibid., p. 15)

One of the first novels, Daniel Defoe's *Robinson Crusoe* (1719), purports to be an autobiography. Indeed, it is prefaced by a note that:

> The editor believes the thing to be a just history of fact; neither is there any appearance of fiction in it. (Defoe, 1985, p. 25)

One reason for this assertion was that the powerful Puritans, who had closed theatres in the seventeenth century, disliked fiction; the presentation of a text as 'real' was one way of avoiding being victimised by their bigotry.

The novel soon became, and remains, one of the most influential forms of western civilisation. Even though television is arguably the dominant communications medium of the twentieth century, we still attach more importance to teaching our children to read fictional narratives in print than we do to teaching them to read visual and aural images (a central task of Media Studies).

The novel epitomises the bourgeois realist aesthetic in its insistence that searching for truth is the pursuit of the individual; conflict in narratives is caused by, and resolved by, individual actions. As a form, the novel is exceptionally elastic and does encompass non-conventional narratives. The novel's emphasis on subjectivity was stretched even further with the rise of Romanticism.

2.8 Romanticism

> Oh there is blessing in this gentle breeze
> That blows from the green fields and from the clouds
> And from the sky: it beats against my cheek,
> And seems half-conscious of the joy it gives.
> O welcome Messenger! O welcome Friend!
> (Wordsworth, 1970, p. 1)

The extract is the opening lines of Wordsworth's massive poem, *The Prelude*, subtitled 'Growth of a Poet's Mind'. Its egocentricity is characteristic of the romantics' emphasis upon subjectivity. In narrative terms the poem deals with a young boy whose interaction with Nature, at first, terrifies him (the disruption). However, later in life he comes to appreciate the religious significance of the countryside (resolution).

Not all romantic poets were so enraptured by Nature that they forget about the realities of the 'real' world: Lord Byron was politically active and Percy Bysshe Shelley (the husband of Mary Shelley, author of *Frankenstein*, see Chapter 4) wrote about the 'Peterloo massacre' where a parliamentary reform meeting of 60,000 people was dispersed by the 15th Hussars, leaving 11 people dead and 400 injured.

In England, romanticism was a reaction against the dominant ideological view of the time which considered that unless anything had 'economic value' it was worthless. Art, by its nature, tends not to be practically useful and so artists took refuge in a new aesthetics, that of the 'poetic':

> The assumption that there was an unchanging object known as 'art', or an isolatable experience called 'beauty' or the 'aesthetic', was largely a product of the... alienation of art from social life... (Eagleton, 1983, p. 21)

The romantics defined art as objects of beauty; indeed another romantic poet, Keats, characterised aesthetics as 'truth and beauty':

> Beauty is truth, truth beauty, – that is all
> Ye know on earth, and all ye need to know.
> ('Ode to a Grecian Urn', Keats, 1966, p. 129)

Although this definition of art (or at least of 'high art') is conventional now, it is worth noting that it was originally radical because it opposed the dominant ideology. The social conditions that launched the romantics' radicalism have been described by Terry Eagleton:

> In England, a crassly philistine Utilitarianism [was] rapidly becoming the dominant ideology of the industrial middle class, fetishizing fact, reducing human relations to market exchanges and dismissing art as unprofitable ornamentation. The callous disciplines of early industrial capitalism uproot[ed] whole communities convert[ed] human life into wage-slavery, enforce[d] an alienating labour-process on the newly formed working class and [understood] nothing which [could not] be transformed into a commodity on the open market. As the working class [responded] with militant protest to this oppression... the English state react[ed] with brutal political repressiveness which convert[ed] England, during part of the Romantic period, into what [was] in effect a police state. (Eagleton, 1983, p. 19)

It was against this sort of exploitation that nostalgia arose for the agrarian past and, in part, explains why the romantic poets embraced nature. Although the romantic era is mostly associated with poetry, there were important novelists of the era; Walter Scott wrote many historical novels that also looked backward to feudal times. There are also clear romantic elements in his work despite the fact that he professed to dislike Wordsworth and the other 'Lake poets'. For example, in *The Heart of Midlothian* (1818) he showed:

> An interest in the peasant, as a symbol of a more spontaneous way of life, close to nature... (Phelps, 1979, p. 187)

By the time of Scott, the novel form reached its 'mature' development, one that used conventional narrative structure. The next development, modernism, would start to 'shake' the foundations of the thesis/antithesis/synthesis pattern.

2.9 Modernism

Modernism is seen often as a response to the ruptures in society caused by the First World War and the major scientific developments such as Einstein's formulation of quantum mechanics. Modernism is a self-reflexive form, so-called because texts draw attention to themselves as *texts*. In conventional narrative we expect event to follow event in a logical fashion towards the resolution. In the modernist novel, non-events can also feature, for example in Franz Kafka's *The Trial* (*Der Prozess*, 1925) Josef K. is arrested – an obvious disruption – in the novel's opening sentence:

> Someone must have been spreading lies about Josef K. for without having done anything wrong he was arrested one morning. (Kafka, 1977, p. 17)

K. spends the novel attempting to find out what he has been charged with but is confronted by a labyrinthine bureaucracy; he is, in effect, attempting to resolve the disruption. However, we *never* get to the event that promised to resolve the narrative conflict, the trial.

Modernists also often keep an ironic distance between the narrator and her or his characters: Thomas Mann, in *Death in Venice* (1912), didactically articulates the opposing impulses of the Dionysiac and the Apollonian (one pleasure-seeking, the other privileging the intellect) and does not seek audience identification with the central character; in *Ulysses* (1922), James Joyce offers a multiplicity of voices which can offer only an unstable reality.

From a narrative point of view, modernism also eschews the need for a realist setting. In Samuel Beckett's seminal *Waiting for Godot* (1955) the two protagonists, Estragon and Vladimir, spend the entire play waiting on 'a country road [with] a tree'; time is signified by the appearance and disappearance of a moon. Essentially, the setting is unimportant and psychological motivations are not apparent because the diegesis is not realistic. The promised resolution of Godot's arrival never occurs, so narrative convention is broken, although narrative *tension* is still engendered because the audience *expects* Godot to appear. The play is polysemic, it invites many readings, and this plurality is engendered partly by the lack of narrative closure. Narrative closure is a way of anchoring the preferred reading, audiences have to work hard to find a preferred reading in *Waiting for Godot*; indeed there probably is not one. To many the play suggests that life is meaningless; however, this may simply be another way of saying that texts without narrative closure are meaningless. We are so used to conventional narrative structure, that we expect meaning to be created by closure. Narrative – which in most texts strives to be conventional – is the perfect form with which to subvert audience expectation, a common modernist aim.

In cinema, the first modernists were 1920s Soviet film-makers, such as Sergei Eisenstein and Dziga Vertov. It was not until the late 1960s, with the experiments of Jean-Luc Godard (see section 3.5 – *Pierrot le fou*), that modernist cinema got a significantly large audience in the west.

2.10 Postmodernism

One of the major problems with postmodernism is the difficulty in defining it. This is not surprising since postmodernism:

> is committed to modes of thinking and representation which emphasize fragmentations, discontinuities and incommensurable aspects of a given object, from intellectual systems to architecture. (O'Sullivan *et al.*, 1994, p. 234)

Strinati (1997) offered a more concrete way of looking at the concept by describing five features.

The breakdown of the distinction between culture and society

Art was once believed to reflect reality and cultural artefacts would be understood with reference to this reality. In postmodern society, however, the opposite is true: we make sense of *reality* with reference to media texts. For example, there is an increasing tendency for newspapers to accompany factual stories with film stills: the *Guardian* illustrated a report about the British government speeding-up the regeneration of former coalfields with a still from the film *Brassed Off*. This breakdown between what is cultural (mediated) and real is evident at sporting events where large video screens now offer immediate slow-motion replays of significant events to the spectators; it is as if the 'live' experience is no longer complete without the intervention of a medium.

In addition, the relationship between popular culture and consumerism, and hence the economy, is increasingly blurred. Advertising heavily influences our 'buying choices' and, particularly for young people, branding is important in creating a personal identity (the right make of trainers; ownership of a Playstation and so on).

An emphasis on style at the expense of substance and content

Because postmodernism does not deal with the way texts, or artefacts, refer to reality, postmodern texts can only deal in surfaces. So because we are, for example, strongly influenced by branding when making buying choices, the label becomes more important than the product and the packaging more important than the contents. In media texts this can manifest itself as intertextuality, where texts make their meaning through reference to other texts. Take the '*Cape Fear*' episode of the *The Simpsons*: in one short extract students, studying the programme, picked out references to: Quentin Tarantino (surf music on Bart's radio); *Edward Scissorshands* and *Nightmare on Elm Street* (Flanders' trimming and his 'gloves'); prison movies ('Sideshow' Bob and his cellmate); *Taxi Driver* ('Sideshow' Bob talking to himself in the mirror); *Night of the Hunter* (Bob has 'hate' written on his knuckles). When the students were asked what all this meant the response was (rightly) one of silence. Postmodernism is not about content, it is only concerned with its own eclecticism.

Pop videos are often characterised as the postmodern form *par excellence* because it does not usually matter what images we are seeing, all that matters is that is *looks* good.

The breakdown of the distinction between high culture (art) and popular culture

The artificial status between what is defined as 'high art' and 'mass culture' is no longer tenable, except for traditionalists. The certainties of the established canon are lost, although critics like Harold Bloom argue vociferously against this. A result of this is that everything is 'up for grabs' and eclecticism is the defining aesthetic because there are no absolute standards, all is relative. This book, for instance, references both 'great works of literature' as well as soap operas.

Confusions over space and time

With the growth of satellite communications in the 1960s the idea of the 'global village' evolved. Marshall McLuhan suggested that, with the advancement of technology, the transferral of information would accelerate and so the meaning of information would change. One of the consequences of this acceleration is the way national boundaries are transcended, events the other side of the world (indeed, from other worlds) can be relayed to us 'live'.

> Because of the speed and scope of modern mass communications, because of the relative ease and rapidity with which people and information can travel, time and space become less stable and comprehensible, more confused, more incoherent, more disunified. (Strinati, 1997, p. 424)

For example, in *Wuthering Heights* (1847) Cathy's father takes several days to make the return journey to Liverpool from the Yorkshire Dales (which would now take less than three hours on a motorway). Liverpool, however, was not simply a place 70-odd miles distant from Wuthering Heights, it was also an exotic location. At the time Liverpool was a thriving port, and therefore a gateway to the rest of the world, so it was an ideal place to find the sinister (Other) Heathcliff. In postmodern society it is less easy to create exotic locations as the mass media, television in particular, have given us access to (what appears to be) the rest of the world. It is as if we can see everywhere, at almost any time, from the comfort of our homes.

Postmodern society, then, is characterised by 'instantaneity' which makes it difficult for individuals to set events in their context; it is as if everything is 'here and now'.

The decline of the meta-narratives

Because postmodernism does not accept the notion of a reality independent of culture, it does not believe that there are absolute ways
('meta-narratives') of explaining reality. These meta-narratives are
necessarily cultural and so are part of our reality; they therefore
cannot 'step back' and explain reality. So meta-narratives, whether
they be Christianity's *The Bible*, Marxists' *Das Kapital* or physicists'
'theory of everything' (TOE), cannot offer *absolute* knowledge.

Postmodernist texts

One of the ways in which postmodern 'fragmentation' is emphasised is through a melange of references that are not rooted in any
particular time and space. A 1990s film version of *Romeo and Juliet*
(directed by Baz Luhrmann, 1996) uses Shakespeare's sixteenth
century verse but gives it a modern setting. However, the setting is
not quite the reality we know, in science fiction terms it could be
described as an alternative world:

> *Romeo and Juliet* is set in a 'constructed' world, one that is different enough
> from a 'real' one to allow for different ways of being and knowing, but
> with enough similarities to permit understanding. (Arroyo, 1997, p. 6)

It is not only the setting that is unusual, Luhrmann's style is
explicitly postmodern. For example, the fight between the Capulets
and Montagues, which opens the film, is shot as a 'spaghetti'
Western complete with: absurd camera angles; the gunman as
poseur; slow-motion; a spectacularly over-the-top conflagration. In
other scenes, Lady Capulet moves as if she is in a speeded-up
'silent' movie and Friar Lawrence appears to administer for some
New Age religion. This collection of disparate elements is a feature
of postmodernism and is one of the reasons the 'movement' is
sometimes criticised as being ahistorical:

> Constructing a world which combines the real with the imagined, the past
> with the present, results in a depiction of a sense of time and space which
> is quasi-mythic.
> Fredric Jameson has argued that this is typical of the dehistoricising
> effects of postmodern culture. But one could counter-argue that what he
> calls dehistoricising can be a means of making past conventions of story
> telling understandable in the present context. (ibid., p. 8)

Arroyo's argument is intriguing; Luhrmann's version of Shake-speare's play was a comparatively big hit (over $45 million at the North American box office) and so, clearly, 'spoke' to modern audiences, particularly the core cinema audience of 16–25-year-olds. Luhrmann's eclecticism may have helped the audience make sense of the poetry. For instance:

- the prologue is a television news report, complete with the typical speech inflections of the anchor
- the clothing of the Montagues and Capulets represents them as contemporary gangs
- the emphasised ethnicity, particularly in the Hispanic Capulets, of the warring groups allows the sense of family loyalty to resonate clearly
- Mercutio as a drag queen and 1970s disco diva contextualises the character's flamboyant eccentricities

and so on.

Luhrmann's *Romeo and Juliet* is well worth seeing as it is an exceptionally rich and cinematic text. It does not, however, have a post-modern narrative.

Postmodernism in narratives can, arguably, manifest itself in structures that relate not only to the text's diegesis but also to the act of storytelling in the 'real world'. The first novel of Paul Auster's *The New York Trilogy, City of Glass* (1985), has an opening paragraph that asks the following question:

> In the beginning, there was simply the event and its consequences. Whether it might have turned out differently, or whether it was all prede-termined with the first word that came from the stranger's mouth, is not the question. The question is the story itself, and whether or not it means something is not the story to tell. (Auster, 1987, p. 3)

Postmodernism's preoccupation with the status of the text, and its relationship to reality, is immediately to the fore. Near the end, another question is asked:

> The last sentence of the red notebook reads: 'What will happen when there are no more pages in the red notebook?' (ibid., p. 131)

Clearly, a narrative must end when the text ends; the last page is a material way of guaranteeing a conclusion. However, conventional texts must offer the audience narrative closure before the text terminates. The postmodern text can deal with this expectation self-consciously, just as it deals with genre in a playful fashion. Auster's novel is cast as 'hard-boiled detective story' (defined in Chapter 4) with the typical setting of the city:

> New York was an inexhaustible space, a labyrinth of endless steps, and no matter how far he walked, no matter how well he came to know its neighbourhoods and streets, it always left him with the feeling of being lost. Lost, not only in the city, but within himself as well. (ibid., pp. 3–4)

The narrative focuses on a detective novelist, Quinn, who is mistaken for a private detective, called Paul Auster (the text, confusingly, refers to reality as Auster is the author who had used the pseudonym Paul Quinn early in his career). Despite the confusion, Quinn takes on Auster's case which concerns a mentally ill man – Peter Stillman – who, his wife believes, is under threat from his father; Stillman's father has just been released from prison. If the scenario is identifiably hard-boiled (Stillman's wife also seduces Quinn) then the narrative development is, in conventional terms, unrecognisable. One of the 'enigma' codes in the novel concerns the father's (if it is the father, his identity is not certain) random ramblings around the city. Quinn (as Auster) discovers the ramblings represent letters that spell 'THE TOWER OF BABEL'. Before the Tower was constructed humanity had one language and when:

> Noah's descendants wandered to the plain of Shinar (Babylonia)... they perfected the techniques for monumental brick architecture and built the renowned tower of Babel. Building the tower (was) interpreted as an act of arrogance, and human history is here understood to take a decisive turn from a common thread to many strands as God descends to confuse human speech and scatter the people all over the earth. (Metzger and Logan, 1993, p. 71)

The investigation, then, appears to be concerned with language rather than any threat to Peter Stillman: the novel's words are about the search for words and therefore meaning (the legend of the Tower of Babel can be seen as a metaphor for semiotics – see Chapter 2 of *Image and Representation*). Detective fiction traditionally deals with the unmasking, by the plot, of the story. However, if the prey is words there can be nothing to unmask because, as semiotics suggests, the meaning of words is arbitrary, there is nothing 'beneath' language.

Postmodernism also places the reader in a *self-conscious* position as the (re)creator of the texts she or he is experiencing. Similarly, the central concern of postmodernist media texts is less to do with the traditional objective of 'knowing' (epistemology) and more to do with 'being' (ontology). The reader is not simply using information to create the text, he or she is interacting with the text in 'referencing spotting', almost as if it were a quiz.

What do we learn from the narrative of *City of Glass*? Probably 'nothing': there is no absolute meaning in the world because communication is based on language; it then follows that there can be no meaning in a novel because it uses words. While most narratives articulate mythical ideas about, say, good and evil, postmodern narrative has itself as its subject.

Some postmodernists have suggested that we are at the 'end of history' as we have dispensed with the primacy of reality; our reality is now only understood with reference to culture. I think this viewpoint fails to realise that postmodernism is simply another 'way of seeing' and will be superseded. It is more likely that postmodernism is not the end of history but is *about* the end of history. Postmodernism cannot look forward, it only looks back so when the next 'paradigm shift' in artistic expression occurs, postmodernism will not see it.

This section has only dealt with the notion of postmodernism as an aesthetic construct; it can also be linked directly to the current state of capitalism:

> Post-modernism is the cultural form of the current moment of late capitalism just as realism was the privileged artistic form of the first state of capitalist industrialist development and modernism corresponded to the economic moment of imperialism and monopoly capitalism. (MacCabe, 1992, p. xii)

The link between (capitalist) media institutions and postmodernist media texts will be investigated in *Media Institutions and Audiences*.

3

THEORY OF NARRATIVE 2

AIMS OF THE CHAPTER

➤ To liken narrative to semiotic structures and show how audiences use narrative to make sense of texts.

➤ To briefly consider Chatman's distinction between story and discourse.

➤ To investigate various types of narrative voices, including:
  - dramatised
  - undramatised
  - observers
  - narrative agents
  - telling versus showing.

➤ To investigate the notion of ideological narratives with reference to *The Searchers*.

➤ To exam of alternative narrative systems with reference to *Pierrot le fou* and documentary.

3.1 Introduction

As was outlined in the Introduction, this textbook is differentiated; that means it covers the key concepts more than once but at different levels of difficulty. Chapter 1 gave all the narrative theory that is required at advanced level Media Studies and much of it at undergraduate level; this chapter outlines, for those who are interested, areas of narrative study that are intellectually even more demanding. However, it is not the intention of this text to delve into the more esoteric areas of narrative theory. Todorov's elucidation of his theory, for example, looks more like a mathematical formula; he describes the minimum narrative sequence as:

X–A+	(X)$_{\text{OPT}}$ Y >	Y$_a$ >	XA
initial situation	desire	modification	end

Todorov, and many other structuralists, was attempting to isolate the universal structures of literature and, it follows, language. This is useful in that:

> The advantage must lie in the extent to which such analysis loosens the anaesthetic grip that fiction has on us, as members of a society committed for so long to 'literary' modes of perception. It forces us to look again at stories, and to recognize them for what they are: particular uses of language, or rather of that derivative of language, writing. (Hawkes, 1977, p. 99)

Much of the criticism surrounding narrative theory concerns its lack of concern with content; for structuralists it often does not matter *who* the villain, or hero, is or what events occur in the narrative. What structuralists attempt to do is offer a grammatical analysis of narrative that tries to demonstrate the universality of narrative. In Media Studies, however, it is crucial that students be concerned with content and not solely with form.

3.2 More advanced narrative theory

As we found in Chapter 1, narrative is distinguishable from other forms of knowledge in that it presents information as a connected sequence of events and that it, therefore, needs at least two connected events. From a semiotic point of view (see Chapter 2 of *Image and Representation*), narrative, which must exist in time, is to be found in the diachronic (horizontal) dimension; the same is true, incidentally, of genre. Narrative, as a structure, actually foregrounds time; there is no point in dealing with narrative *flow* synchronically (vertically), it only makes sense diachronically. Narrative movement is a syntagmatic combination of events; like a menu (starter–main course–dessert), its structure, as a *story*, is very rigid and, as such, usually follows Todorov's five points:

1. a state of equilibrium at the outset
2. a disruption of the equilibrium by some action
3. a recognition that there has been a disruption
4. an attempt to repair the disruption
5. a reinstatement of the equilibrium.

Propp, too, emphasised the syntagmatic element of narrative; Levi-Strauss, on the other hand, focused on narrative as a paradigm:

> The hypothetical paradigmatic matrix is typically one in which polar oppositions such as life/death, male/female are mediated. (Dundes, 1968, p. xii)

Although it is obvious that narrative has a linear flow, Levi-Strauss's point is that the 'latent' content is more important than the 'manifest'.

Despite the fact that a story's structure is rigid, that of narrative *plot* is not; the order of the story can be 'mixed up'. Thwaites *et al.* (1994) have shown how the plot and story are analogous to the constituents of a (semiotic) sign:

> **Plot** is the *narrative as it is read, seen or heard* from the first to the last word or image. That is, like a signifier, it is what the reader perceives.

> **Story** is *the narrative in chronological order*, the abstract order of events as they follow each other. That is, like a *signified*, story is what the reader conceives or understands. (Thwaites *et al.*, 1994, p. 121)

Although narrative progress is necessarily diachronic, this does not mean that we cannot construct narrative from a synchronic text. For example, we can usually create a narrative using any still image from a film by adding our own diachronic dimension based on the cues in the picture. Similarly, still images in advertisements often imply a narrative which the audience is expected to decode in order to make the preferred reading. In this instance, narrative allows the codes contained in the advertisement to 'come alive' by coordinating the sign systems, present in the text, in three ways:

1. It offers a **time frame** over which the signified connotations and myths will come into play.
2. It reinforces a network of social meanings by transforming events into *actions* performed by **characters**...

3. It adds to the enjoyment of a story – through the use of characters and forecast of their actions – to the text's signs. (ibid., pp. 114–15)

We use narrative to add the diachronic dimension to a synchronic image. This helps us to *understand* narrative texts and it can also help us understand our experience of the world. As was considered at the beginning of Chapter 1, we also use narrative to *represent* experience. To complicate things further:

> More specifically, narrative is a way of organizing spatial and temporal data into a cause–effect chain of events with a beginning, middle, and end that embodies a judgment about the nature of the events as well as demonstrates how it is possible to know, and hence to narrate, the events. (Branigan, 1992, p. 3)

This was demonstrated in Chapter 1 (section 1.6): narrative is ideologically constructed through the decision ('judgment') of who is the 'hero' and who the 'villain'.

Narratives do not exist only in texts, they need readers to (re)create them. Because narrative exists in time, the reader, using the cause–effect structure, engages in two forms of prediction in order to make sense of the text:

> *existents*, which assert the existence of something... and *processes*, which stipulate a change or process under a causal formula. Typical existents are characters and settings while typical processes are actions of persons and forces of nature. (ibid., p. 5)

Lew Hunter describes how the similar concepts of 'vertical and linear stories' (*not* to be confused with synchrony and diachrony) are used in Hollywood script conferences: vertical narratives focus on character and linear narratives on plot (although it is likely that the characters, as *spheres of action*, do still motivate plot). The films of Woody Allen from the last 25 years, for example, emphasise character (as does melodrama – see Chapter 4) whereas in action films, for example, character development is often limited. Whether a text is 'vertical' or 'horizontal', emphasises 'existents' or 'processes', has no affect on narrative structure which conforms, usually, to Todorov's syntagmatic pattern.

103

Applying narrative to still advertisements

The Hitachi advertisement, see Figure 3.1, uses narrative to sell the product, the Hitachi VT-FX770. However, partly because the image is still, there is no obvious narrative in the text; it can only exist once the reader has added the diachronic dimension to what is a synchronic image.

Figure 3.1

Exercise 3.1

Apply the three ways, listed above, by which still advertisements can 'come alive', Try also applying a cause–effect chain and Branigan's distinction between *existents* and *processes*.

The advertisement is attempting to sell the Hitachi VT-FX770 through its unique selling proposition (u.s.p) which is the machine's ability to 'remember' what is recorded on a videocassette. The character in the advertisement does not have this product and so must rely upon his memory which, confronted with stacks of apparently unlabelled videocassettes, is failing him. This failure of memory is signified by the expression of his face and the finger placed on his temple. So his narrative problem is not knowing which tape it is he wants to watch; the disruption, unsurprisingly, can be resolved by the purchase of the VT-FX770.

This is a straightforward analysis of the advertisement; however, what the above does not consider is *how* the reader created the advertisement's narrative. Narratives need time frames (because it consists of a cause–effect chain) and so by adding a diachronic dimension we can imagine the character attempting to find, and probably failing to do so, a video. The synchronic moment, captured in the advertisement, leads to (causes) a failure to find the video which, in turn, leads him to the purchase of the Hitachi VCR.

The appearance of a character in the image is important; he is the narrative agent who tries to choose a videotape to view. However, at the captured moment, he cannot do this; he needs help. In this scenario the VT-FX770 becomes a 'helper'; the man the (potential) 'hero' who must make the choice of videocassette (and buy the product). He and the setting form the narrative's *existents*. The choice of a young male in this role is important: youth is associated with being 'up-to-date' (the product is new) and men, stereotypically, are more interested in entertainment technology (as distinct from kitchen technology) than women. The advert suggests that this person, who also happens to be 'good looking', is the addressee; the target audience for new videocassette recorders.

The advertisement's setting is slightly ambiguous. The wooden floor connotes chicness and therefore expense (desirable qualities that associate themselves with the product) and, along with the presence of videocassettes, suggest the man's front room. However, the *mise-en-scène* is not naturalistic: videocassettes are not normally stacked like that and the extreme high-angle shot gives the advertisement an expressionist feel. It is as if the dominating, and precarious, stacks of cassettes are an expression of the man's confused mind (finger on temple). The setting then, creates an environment of confusion which, the text suggests, will be solved by the purchase of the product.

In my view, the third point ('enjoyment') is not applicable to this advertisement; although this is probably a consequence of my particular reading. In the Nokia advertisement, featured in *Image and Representation* and showing an attractive young woman using a mobile phone, pleasure was available in speculating about who she was talking to and – to heterosexual male eyes at least – ogling her beauty.

All that remains, the addresser hopes, is for the cause–effect chain to be completed; the *process* of buying the VT-FX770. The preferred reading is that the purchase is the right thing to do as it will solve our problems. In addition, it will give the buyer the hero function in a real narrative: once the product has been bought the problem of managing videocassettes will disappear for(happy)ever after; or at least until the next product innovation.

Another way of conceiving narrative is Chatman's (1978) distinction between story and discourse.

Story and discourse

In this model, narrative consists of the *story*, which is elaborated by the plot, *and* the way the story is told, its *discourse* which includes the address to the audience and any background information they can be assumed to have.

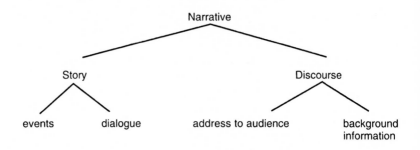

Figure 3.2   Chatman's story and discourse

Different media can obviously tell the same story, but the way that story is told will be influenced by the form of the medium. Chatman's schema is useful when considering how a text is adapted for another medium. In Chapter 1 of *Image and Representation* the consideration of the 'contact' between addresser and addressee focused on the formal characteristics of different media; for example radio aural and television audio-visual.

In addition to this, each medium has institutional aspects that will influence the 'discourse'. For instance, the institution of cinema (or 'cinematic apparatus' as it is sometimes called) means that film stories are experienced in a communal setting, which can be very important for certain genres such as comedies. And anyone who goes to see the cult movie *The Rocky Horror Picture Show* (1975) will gain much from the experience if they have the 'background information' of how and when to participate. Films, in the cinema, are also experienced in the dark and, hopefully, in warmth and comfort; this imbues a state of hypersensitivity into the audience. Whereas television watching is often characterised by numerous interruptions, poor picture quality and interference from other light sources. Unlike cinema, which offers a very closed narrative, television:

> Has a more dispersed narrational form: it is extensive rather than sequential. Its characteristic mode is not one of final closure or totalising vision; rather, it offers a continuous refiguration of events. (Ellis, 1992, p. 147)

While this may sound as if television dispenses with Todorovian closure, Ellis is referring to the medium as a whole and not specific texts. As we saw in Chapter 1, seriality is very important to television; in series, situations will be resolved only to be disturbed again in the next episode. Television offers a multiplicity of narrative voices; cinema, usually, offers the one of the main feature.

The formal variables of different media also have a great deal of influence in *how* a narrative is told through the construction of narrative voice.

3.3 Narrative voice

All narrative texts have a narrator: 'someone' must be 'speaking' in order for the audience to 'hear'. At a basic level we may say this narrator is the text's author. However, as was demonstrated in

Chapter 3 of *Image and Representation*, the text's author (the sender) is not necessarily the same as the text's addresser:

> The addresser and addressee are the sender and receiver of the *message as structured by the communication*. Texts have implicit addressees: this book, for example, clearly has Media Studies students as its target audience, and you assume that the addresser – me – is a person qualified to write such a text.
>
> The actual *receiver* and *sender* of the text, however, may be completely different. There is nothing to stop a one-year-old picking up this book and dribbling all over it, and it is possible I don't know what I'm writing about. In addition, while there is one addressee of this book (a person interested in and/or studying Media Studies) it has, hopefully, many thousands of receivers who have bought or been given the book. Of course there is only, basically, one sender. (Lacey, 1998, p. 79)

So although an author can obviously create a narration they are not the narrator. Even though the author John Fowles appeared as the narrator *in The French Lieutenant's Woman* (1977), he (the sender) must be distinguished from his fictional self, because Fowles does *not* exist in a novel (the addresser). Anyway, in Media Studies we are not particularly interested in the author as a person; a concern that can lead to the 'art as autobiography' type of criticism favoured by some literary and music critics. Media Studies' interest in the addresser can be for pragmatic reasons: it is unlikely we can ever get to know the author but we are able to decode the addressee because she or he (it?) is in the text. This is not, however, to decry the role of institutions in the creation of a text. There is, for example, what Noel Burch (1980/81) called the institutional mode of representation which, in classical Hollywood cinema, consisted of:

> conventions of *mise-en-scène*, framing, and in particular of editing, by means of which coherent narrative space and time are set up and fictional characters individuated in ways which both engage, and are imperceptible to, the spectator. (Kuhn, 1985, p. 208)

However, as our focus is here on narrative, we will focus solely on the addresser (which, in any case, will be influenced by the producing institution); issues of institution will be dealt with in *Media Institutions and Audiences*.

Wayne C. Booth describes, using the discourse of literary criticism, the difference between the sender and addresser:

Even the novel in which no narrator is dramatized creates an implicit picture of an author who stands behind the scenes, whether as stage manager, as puppeteer, or an indifferent God... This implied author is always distinct from the 'real man [*sic*]'. (Booth, 1961, p. 151)

So it follows, of course, that the same author (sender) can write many books that have different narrators (addressers). While the sender *implies* an addresser, we – as an audience – can only *infer* who this might be. In a text, in which the reader accepts the preferred reading, it is quite possible that the implied and inferred addresser are very similar, if not the same. While a text's *overall* narrator is the addresser, there is, usually, at least one other narrator present; these appear in various forms and have been described by Booth. Although his focus is on literature, his conclusions are readily applicable to any narrative text whether it be fiction or non-fiction. He suggests, for instance, that the common distinction made between first ('I') and third ('he' or 'she') narrative voice is not particularly useful. He believes that the difference between *dramatised* and *undramatised* narrators is a more fruitful perspective; however, it should be noted that the idea of a 'narrative *voice*' is necessarily a metaphor.

Dramatised narrator

The dramatised narrator is a character through whom the narration passes; this may be in the first-person but can also be through a 'third-person' reflector where we are given a particular character's point of view. The dramatised narrator is comparatively rare in audio-visual texts, although films (particularly *films noir*) and television drama can do this by employing a voice-over narration which is usually spoken by the hero. Otherwise the narrator in audio-visual texts is created by a combination of the *mise-en-scène* and editing (this is probably one of the reasons why the director is often considered to be an *auteur* because she or he is considered to be responsible for these elements). There are even films that are wholly shot from the point of view of the central character; for example, *The Lady in the Lake* (1947), a *film noir* directed by its star, George Montgomery (whom we only see on two occasions).

Postmodernist texts often deal with the role of the narrator in a self-conscious fashion. The French film directed by Jacques Audiard, *Un héros très discret* (*A Self-Made Hero*, 1995) opens with a dramatised narrator, the central character Albert Dehousse, looking into the camera and declaring he wants to tell the audience a story. This is the story of his life and how he fabricated tales of being a Resistance hero; at the end, in the same shot as the opening, he asks the audience 'how have I done'? For a narrative that is about making up stories this is rather provocative because it suggests even the film's story has been made up; which of course it has. This postmodern preoccupation with the constructed nature of texts reached an 'absurd' conclusion in *The Usual Suspects* (1995) (see Appendix 1). The point these postmodern texts appear to be making, as we saw in Chapter 2, is that nothing is true, everything is a narrative.

Even if there is a dramatised narrator, we must be aware of the narrator beyond: the addresser. In some texts, the dramatised narrator is palpably unreliable; for example the meaning of the *film noir Detour* 'depends on the fact that Al is incapable of providing the impartial account of the action which convention leads us to expect in first-person narratives' (Britton, 1994, p. 174). So although Al is the voice-over narrator of *Detour*, 'beyond' him is the addresser, the 'overall narrator', who undermines his version of events with the *mise-en-scène* (see Appendix 1 regarding *Basic Instinct* (1992) and Chapter 4 for a consideration of *film noir*). It may be useful in such circumstances to distinguish between the diegetic narrator, in this case Al, and the non-diegetic narrator. Take Emily Brontë's *Wuthering Heights* (published in 1847) which starts off straightforwardly enough:

> 1801. –
> I have just returned from a visit to my landlord – the solitary neighbour that I shall be troubled with. (Brontë, 1978, p. 3).

The novel then 'flashes-back' to 1777, then goes forward to 1801, then backwards again and so on; it does not go beyond 1801 until the end of the novel. The 'I' of the extract is Lockwood who discovers the history of the central characters, Cathy and Heathliff, from numerous other narrative voices including: Cathy (in her diary); Nelly Dean, the housekeeper; Heathcliff; Isabella (in a letter). All the competing voices, however, are filtered through Lockwood who, as the opening sentence suggests, is a misanthropist (Figure 3.3).

This potential for distance between the dramatised narrator and the actual narrator, or addressee, applies to all narrative texts. This distance is evident in *Wuthering Heights* because of the unpleasantness of Lockwood's character; there is little sense that we are meant to identify with him:

Lockwood (his name signifies closure, tightness, repression) dare not admit Heathcliff and Cathy into his world, i.e. (since he is narrator) into the world of the novel. (Jackson, 1981, p. 129).

Lockwood cannot cope with the passion unleashed at Wuthering Heights and he is afraid of what the central characters represent; however, there is no sense that we, as addressees, are invited to join in his condemnation of Heathcliff and Cathy. The events are portrayed as tragedy, which means the narrator is, at least, more sympathetic than the consciousness (Lockwood's) through which the narration is filtered. The addresser can, in this instance, be characterised as 'Emily Brontë' – the addresser – who, like the fictional characters, is a creation of the text; but not as Emily Brontë, the flesh and blood human being – the sender – who wrote the novel.

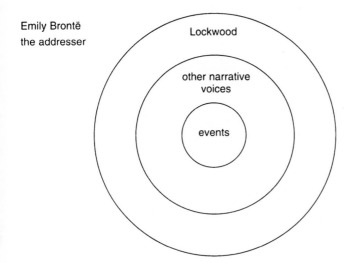

Figure 3.3   Narrative voices in *Wuthering Heights*

To pinpoint how this preferred reading, offering sympathy for Heathcliff and Cathy, is created is beyond the scope of this book; however, it is likely that Nelly Dean's narration is instrumental in this because she evinced at least some understanding of the protagonists' plight.

The multiplicity of narrative voices in the novel also helps create the sense of 'other-worldliness' that possesses the central characters. At the end of the novel Cathy and Heathcliff are left 'exorcised by (being confined) to their own vampiric relationship: they are mere restless spirits drifting around the abandoned enclosure of the Heights' (ibid.). It is the concomitant subjectivity of multiple voices that, also, can create a distance between the 'real world' and the diegesis. *Wuthering Heights* is an example of the 'fantastic' (described by Todorov) where the apparently supernatural can be explained rationally; for example Lockwood's description of Cathy's ghost which could be 'all a dream' (Brontë, 1978, p. 22).

> Fantastic narratives... assert that what they are telling is real – relying upon all the conventions of realistic fiction to do so – and then they proceed to break that assumption of realism by introducing what – within those terms – is manifestly unreal. They pull the reader from the apparent familiarity and security of the known and everyday world into something more strange, into a world whose improbabilities are closer to the realm normally associated with the marvellous. (Jackson, p. 34)

The use of the first-person narrative is a convenient device for 'fantastic' narratives because any bizarre events can be explained as being caused by subjectivity. Mark Nash (1976) has described how difficult it is for films, and it follows all audio-visual texts, to replicate this subjectivity; although Carl Theodor Dreyer does attempt to do so in *Vampyr* (1932) which uses such unsettling devices as having a point-of-view shot from a corpse in a coffin. This modernist technique was also deployed by William Faulkner in *As I Lay Dying* (1930/1963) where various members of a family recount their impressions, in the first-person, as they take their mother's corpse home. Their mother, Addie, is also one of the narrators.

Fantastic events can appear indisputably concrete when shown as images in audio-visual texts. However in *Twelve Monkeys*, directed by Terry Gilliam in 1995, we can never be sure whether James Cole (played by Bruce Willis) is a time traveller or a mental patient suffering from delusions and so the essence of the fantastic, the uncertainty of whether we are experiencing 'nature' or the 'supernatural', infuses the film.

Edgar Allan Poe, a mid-nineteenth-century North American writer, was a master of the fantastic, using his narrator's subjectivity to take the reader to the ultimate reaches of humanity. For example, the opening of *Ligeia*:

I cannot, for my soul, remember how, when, or even precisely where, I first became acquainted with the lady Ligeia. Long years have since elapsed, and my memory is feeble through much suffering. (Poe, 1967, p. 110)

With these elements of doubt surrounding the reliability of the narrator, his tale of Ligeia coming back from the dead can be explained as the phantoms of a deluded mind. This technique is little removed from that of the early novelists who sought, rhetorically, to convince the reader that their story was true (see Chapter 2).

Some writers use a 'stream of consciousness' technique to emphasise subjectivity and, at the same time, suggest a greater 'psychic realism'. This was based on the premise that thoughts are not structured grammatically like sentences and flow somewhat haphazardly; for example John Dos Passos' *The 49th Parallel* (published in 1930):

when you walk along the street you have to step carefully always on the cobbles so as not to step on the bright anxious grassblades easier if you hold Mother's hand and hang on it that way you can kick up your toes but walking fast you have to tread on too many grassblades the poor hurt green tongues shrink under your feet maybe that's why those people are so angry and follow us shaking their fists   they're throwing stones grownup people throwing stones. (Dos Passos, 1966, p. 21)

In the war film *The Thin Red Line* (1998) the audience is given access to the main characters' thoughts through voice-overs which offer a type of 'stream of consciousness'. This illustrates their interior lives and, although criticised by some for being trite (see MacCabe, 1999), offers a philosophical counterpoint to the extreme violence experienced by the characters.

Undramatised narrator

The undramatised narrator is where an 'outside' agent, who is often omnipotent, gives a description of events, so all the characters' thoughts and all occurrences can be known. Voice-overs in documentary are often characterised as a 'voice of god' because they appear to explain completely what is happening; this is a commonly used device in 'expository' documentary. In these texts, the camera is signed as simply showing real events without being involved in them. However, this ignores the fact that the presence of a camera often does affect what is being observed; very few people 'act natural' when on camera; not to mention the mediation of editing and framing. The undramatised narrator is most common in non-literary texts, such as film, where it appears that the narration is simply being shown by the camera-eye.

Observers

Some narrators, although dramatised, exist only as observers, as in Henry Fielding's *Tom Jones* for instance. These, however, are comparatively rare. More common are observer-narrators who slightly impinge upon the action they observe; for example, the characters of both Nick Adams in numerous Ernest Hemingway short stories (including 'The Killers' and 'The End of Something') and Nick Carraway in *The Great Gatsby* by F. Scott Fitzgerald. This enables the narrators to distance themselves from events and therefore appear to comment upon them in a more objective manner. These observers, potentially, can fulfil a narrative function; it is likely to be that of the donor or helper and not the hero or villain.

If the person doing the voice-over appears on camera (as in David Attenborough's wildlife programmes) then the narrator is an observer and a *dramatised* narrator. The character of this voice-over narrator is determined by a combination of the words spoken, which may be a script written by someone else, the voice (in terms of its non-verbal characteristics) and any attributes of the individual's persona the audience is familiar with. Conceiving the voice-over narrator like this helps make clear the point that this narrator is *not* a person, she or he is the addresser and can be, with the exception of extra-textual knowledge of the persona, wholly constructed by the text.

The fact that narrators can, and should, be treated like fictional characters, can be illustrated by looking at texts that use unfamiliar conventions, such as 1950s newsreels. Here the gung-ho, jolly attitude and Received Pronunciation of the voice-over usually jar on the modern ear. The narrator's unremittingly positive attitude toward events – often on events that are anything but happy – can make the narrator seem to be patronising to today's audiences. This is one reason why newsreels now sound more like propaganda (which, in effect, they were) than news. The narrator is the voice of the Establishment putting a positive spin on world events. However, before we congratulate ourselves upon our more sophisticated attitude, which does not allow such a patronising voice to explain the world to us, we should be aware that broadcast news fulfils the same function as newsreels. Title sequences, the studios and anchors all clearly state the institutional agenda that 'we will show you, in an unbiased fashion, what is going on in the world'. In reality, of course, it does no such thing (see Chapter 5 *Image and Representation*).

Exercise 3.2

Watch an extract from any documentary that employs a voice-over and analyse the 'character' of the narrator.

Narrative agents

These are agents who are integral to the narrative development and are most likely to fulfil Propp's hero or villain function. For example, Laurence Sterne's bizarre 18th-century novel *The Life and Opinions of Tristram Shandy* is such a self-absorbed 'autobiography' that its beginning concerns itself with his conception:

> I wish either my father or my mother, or indeed both of them, as they were in duty both equally bound to it, had minded what they were about when they begot me; had they duly considered how much depended upon what they were then doing. (Sterne, 1967, p. 35)

Without the character of Tristram Shandy there would be no text, his is a completely central role. Sterne's Shandy is also an example of a self-conscious narrator; one who is aware that she or he is relating the plot, albeit a plot that:

> Judged by ordinary story-telling standards *Tristram Shandy* is preposterous. The reader has to wait until the third book before the hero is born, and even then his future life remains undefined. The narrative consists of episodes, conversations, perpetual digressions, excursions in learning, with unfinished sentences, dashes, blank pages, fantastic syntax, caprices in humour, bawdy, and sentiment. (Evans, 1976, p. 228)

Narrative agents are not likely to fulfil the function of Propp's princess which would be too passive.

Telling versus showing

There is a fundamental tension in narratives between the *telling* explicitly or *showing* the events of the narrative. The former is probably easier because the latter requires the narrator to deal only in exteriors and imply knowledge (for example about a character's motivation) and hope that the audience infers correctly. In reality, of course, the only thing we know for sure about the world is what *we* are thinking and perceiving; we can only assess others' thoughts by what they show: their words and how they say them (non-verbal communication). For the nineteenth-century realist novelist 'showing' was the superior aesthetic; exemplified by Flaubert's *Madame Bovary* (1857). However, Flaubert did not simply show narrative events; Auerbach demonstrates how Flaubert operated by considering a description in part 1, of Chapter 9 of the novel:

> The paragraph itself presents a picture – man and wife together at mealtime. But the picture is not presented in and for itself; it is subordinated to the dominant subject, Emma's despair. Hence it is not put before the reader directly... The situation... is not presented simply as a picture... we are first given Emma and the situation through her. It is not, however, a matter... of a simple representation of the content of Emma's consciousness... Flaubert does nothing but bestow the power of mature expression upon the material she affords, in its complete subjectivity. (Auerbach, 1968, pp. 483–4)

Flaubert does not simply show surfaces; for example: 'she could bear it no longer... the smoking stove, the creaking door, the oozing walls, the damp floor-tiles; all the bitterness of life seemed to be served to her on her plate...' (ibid.). The choice of adjectives ('oozing') and selection of detail (the dampness) focus on the negative aspects of the setting; it could have been shown differently. So even in 'showing' it is possible to identify a narrative voice; the picture is partial.

'Showing' is the *raison d'être* of observational documentary, where the rhetoric of the form states that the camera is simply present as an observer and is not impinging upon events. This form was also known as 'fly-on-the-wall' documentary, a metaphor that is useful in characterising the narrator as it were a fly; that is, it can observe without being noticed. The term 'fly-on-the-wall' has been 'abused' in recent years as it has been increasingly used to describe 'docu-soaps' which feature such non-observational techniques as characters talking *to* an unseen 'reporter' and voice-overs which, anchoring the meaning of the images, 'tell' rather than 'show'.

'Showing' is the norm for audio-visual (including theatre) fiction texts; while novels are the obvious medium if an author wants to 'tell'. Writers are at liberty to relate the thoughts of any character they wish; for many readers the 'unreality' of this is not problematic. However, the realist aesthetic is immensely powerful in the western world and it may be that one way to distinguish formulaic novels, from those which are aspiring to be taken seriously by the critical establishment, is to examine their respective use of 'telling' or 'showing'. The former taking its aesthetic position 'seriously' while the latter is much more 'pragmatic' in its approach.

Media texts, of course, are nothing if not constructed and the *mise-en-scène* of audio-visual texts, or the setting in a novel, is often used to indicate what the narrator is stating about a character's situation. For instance, in Alfred Hitchcock's masterpiece of horror *Psycho* (1960), the colour of Marion Crane's underwear indicates the narrator's view of the morality of her actions: white for pre-marital sex (okay) but black when she is preparing to flee with stolen money (see also Appendix 1). Similarly, the use of high-angle shots can be used to diminish a character's power regardless of what they are doing or saying and low-angle shots can do the opposite.

Akira Kurosawa's classic film *Rashomon* (1950) details the accounts of four witnesses to a rape and murder; all the versions are different. However, the opening of the final account begins with an establishing shot that, unlike the others, is not a point-of-view shot. This suggests that this is the objective account and the subjectivity of the others suggests that they were lying.

This has not been an attempt to give an exhaustive account of the numerous types of narrative voice but has suggested ways in which texts' voices can be described and their use of various forms. Which voice is being used by the narrator determines the way the story is structured by the plot: the voice decides what to say and when to say it. The voice is not, however, the same as the plot for it can also gives us access to the story (that is, it can refer to material that precedes the plot). The narrative voice is the prime rhetorical device used by senders and analysing how it operates can give the reader insights into the way a text is constructed.

3.4 Ideological narrative analysis – *The Searchers*

Brian Henderson (1985) has shown how a narrative analysis can unlock an ideological reading of a text. His consideration of *The Searchers* (1956) attempts to explain why the film has been so influential; it is, for instance, referenced in many other films. *Auteur* critics explain the film's mythic power in terms of the authorship of director John Ford, who is certainly one of the great Hollywood directors. However, as Henderson points out:

> if myth is viewed as a social phenomenon then the power of a myth can only be explained by reference to the community that responds to it. (Henderson, 1985, p. 433)

So a film's power cannot solely reside within the talent of the director; directors, like everyone else, are influenced by society. This perspective considers *The Searchers* not as a film about 1868–73, when it is set, but about 1956, when it was produced. Henderson points out that during 1954 and 1955 a battle was raging over segregated schools in Virginia, USA when, after the 'Brown verdict', all-white schools were made illegal and busing introduced to ensure that schools consisted of both black and white pupils. The southern state of Virginia refused to be directed by the central government and this resulted in the biggest constitutional crisis since the Civil War. Henderson proceeds to show how this battle is articulated by *The Searchers'* narrative which is structured as follows:

1. a state of equilibrium at the outset – Ethan Edwards returns to visit his family
2. a disruption of the equilibrium by some action – the family is massacred by Comanche Indians
3. a recognition that there has been a disruption – Edwards realises his niece, Debbie, has been taken captive
4. an attempt to repair the disruption – Edwards and Martin Pawley search for Debbie
5. a reinstatement of the equilibrium – after many years Debbie is found and her Indian husband, Scar, killed.

In terms of Propp's spheres of action the film can be considered as follows: Edwards is the hero, he is played by the star (John Wayne) and is an experienced and dynamic character; Pawley is the helper;

Debbie the princess; the villain is the Indians led by Chief Scar. The Indians initiate the narrative disruption:

> beginning with horrible crimes by the Comanches, which follow no acts by whites but initiate the cycle of violence gratuitously, and proceeding through intermediate stages to their punishment by whites at the end. (ibid., p. 436)

By offering no justification for the massacre of the Edwards family the narrative suggests that the Indians' violence is simply a product of their 'savagery'. However, this ignores the history of the genocide perpetrated by the whites against the Native North American Indians: Indian violence was, in fact, a response to white violence.

So far, so conventional; however, part of the fascination of *The Searchers* is that it soon becomes clear that Edwards is not intending to rescue Debbie but *kill* her. Edwards is a racist and cannot bear the thought of his kin having sex with an Indian who has adopted her as one of his own race. This racial element is further heightened by the characterisation of Pawley as part-Cherokee; in the original novel he was completely 'white'. This alteration, by the film's scriptwriters, suggests a conscious attempt to deal with racial matters. Edwards's brother adopted Pawley, and it is Pawley who both kills Scar and protects Debbie from Edwards and thereby has, by the end, taken on the hero function. The scene where Edwards and Pawley meet Chief Scar is crucial to this: it is the first time that Pawley rejects Edwards's advice and makes his own decision to attend the meeting. Later, when it is clear that the Texas Rangers plan to charge into the Indian camp regardless of the fact that Debbie would be killed, Pawley takes it on himself to enter the camp furtively thereby saving his 'sister' and killing Scar (see Appendix 1). At the film's conclusion Martin Pawley is 'rewarded' for his heroic actions with marriage to a white girl, Laurie:

> The film's ending thus enacts Martin's position; the adopted one marries and enters the community as an adult male. He enjoys the full rights of kinship. (ibid., p. 447)

In the terms of 1956, the Indians represent black people who were not considered to be truly American by the racist, southern whites who were opposing the 'Brown verdict'. The verdict, however, constitutionally forced racist Americans to *adopt* blacks as Americans, just as Pawley – the part Cherokee – is given 'full rights of citizenship'. After the 'Brown verdict' the opposition to the possibility of kinship by adoption, rather than by blood only, was illegal hence Edwards, the racist, must depart. The film's opening and closing shots are among the most famous in all cinema: framed the same, a door opens to reveal Edwards approaching at the beginning and the end sees the door shut on his departing figure. Henderson notes:

> that the figure of the white Southerner often functions as a scapegoat on the race question. Our racial prejudice and *our* guilt for it are placed on his shoulders... mythically purging us of them. Thus, in *The Searchers*, Ethan is excluded for our sins; that is why we find it so moving. (ibid., emphasis added)

Figure 3.4   Ethan is excluded for our sins

While *The Searchers* articulates the adoption of black people into the 'race of whites' it cannot deal with the fact that Scar, and his people, are the *true* Americans. In addition, this adoption in itself can be nothing other than patronising:

> This may be read diachronically (a la Propp) that Martin cannot marry Laurie and enter society as an adult until he has proven himself as fully

white, indeed whiter than white, by the incredible number of performances that he accomplishes. (ibid., p. 448)

By killing Scar he unequivocally demonstrated his loyalty to the white race and so Pawley is *not* welcomed into the community as part-Cherokee. This may suggest that in 1956 desegregation was not about equality of the races but more to do with allowing blacks equal rights on white terms: 'you can come into our schools but you will be taught "white" history'.

This consideration of *The Searchers* has only drawn on a few of Henderson's ideas. His analysis shows how a narrative in a text can articulate ideological tensions using a conventional narrative structure. Many practitioners, however, choose to use alternative narrative structures to challenge the status quo.

3.5 Alternative narrative systems

As we have seen in Chapter 2, while there have been different modes of narrative throughout history, the basic structure has remained constant. Annette Kuhn has summarised the conventional, or 'classical', narrative mode of the twentieth century as:

1. Linearity of cause and effect within an overall trajectory of enigma-resolution.
2. A high degree of narrative closure.
3. A fictional world governed by spatial and temporal verisimilitude.
4. Centrality of the narrative agency of psychologically-rounded characters. (Kuhn, 1985, p. 216a)

Most, and probably by definition all, mainstream texts follow at least the first three of these conventions. Point 4 is exceptional because stereotypes are often deployed and while they not 'psychologically rounded characters', they are 'psychologically recognisable'. Texts that are intended to be alternative must in some way break these 'rules'; they therefore tend to exist outside the mainstream. A consequence of this is that they are 'non-commercial' in nature and, as most audiences prefer mainstream texts, most media institutions are not interested in producing them. The forms where alternative narrative texts have been produced, with some regularity, are literature, theatre and film; television is probably too commercial a medium to allow much experimentation and music's use of narrative is rather abstruse. Some consideration was given to theatre and novels in Chapter 2 and so this section will consider, briefly, *Pierrot le fou*, a film directed by Jean-Luc Godard.

The 'art' film – *Pierrot le fou* (1965)

Narrative synopsis

We see a young woman, Marianne (Anna Karina), playing tennis and then a man, Ferdinand (Jean-Paul Belmondo), in a bath reading out loud about the painter Velasquez. He asks his young daughter her opinion of what he's reading. Ferdinand's wife tells him to hurry to get ready for a party; he says he doesn't want to go. His wife says he will go and that he must gratefully accept the job he will be offered. Ferdinand gets ready and is introduced to the babysitter, Frank's niece (Marianne).

At the party men talk in monologues about cars, as do women who talk about deodorant. Ferdinand speaks to film director Sam Fuller (playing himself) about cinema and then leaves the party in disgust. He returns home and it materialises that he and Marianne were once lovers. They drive, hearing a report about the Vietnam War on the radio, to Marianne's flat and say they'll do anything for one another. At the flat a dead body lies on the bed but it is not mentioned. In the morning, Frank, Marianne's lover, turns up but Ferdinand – who Marianne insists on calling Pierrot throughout the film – and Marianne escape. Their departure is shown several times.

A voice-over says, 'Next chapter… despair, memory… quest for times past.' Ferdinand and Marianne steal petrol, in a slapstick fashion (*à la* Laurel and Hardy) and drive south. They stop at a café where the people introduce themselves; one says he is a film extra. Ferdinand and Marianne tell stories in a melodramatic fashion.

Continuing their journey they come across a car accident, with bodies strewn about the scene. They destroy their own car but also blow up their money. They walk through a river and fields and then steal another car. Ferdinand states that 'fun is all [Marianne] wants'; Marianne asks who he's talking to, he answers: 'the audience' and Marianne looks at the camera.

Ferdinand drives into water and they start a life on a 'Mysterious Island' (the title of a novel by Jules Verne). They make love. He decides to keep a journal. Marianne buys a record of pop music and tells Pierrot that it is as good as his literature. Marianne is getting bored and they decide to finish their Verne adventure and return to the thriller.

The pair entertain North American sailors with scenes from the Vietnam War. Marianne leaves Ferdinand to go dancing. She is then 'captured' by a dwarf who demands to know where the money is. Ferdinand realises that Marianne's 'brother', a gunrunner called Fred, is around and goes looking for her. Ferdinand finds the dwarf, with scissors stuck in his neck, and is then tortured by Fred's 'heavies' who want to know where Marianne is. Ferdinand tells them.

Having betrayed Marianne, Ferdinand, apparently suicidal, sits on a railway line but moves out of the way of an approaching train. We then see him in a cinema watching a newsreel about the Vietnam War. Next he appears to be working for a self-styled 'Libyan Queen'. Marianne then finds him; it is unclear how much time has passed. Marianne takes her Pierrot to Fred who appears to be leading a dance troupe on a beach. Fred gives Ferdinand a task to do and in the ensuing confusion, which appears to be out of a gangster movie, Marianne states that because she has breasts does not mean she cannot kill; she shoots two men.

Ferdinand feels set up but trusts Marianne to meet him so they can run away together. She then betrays him by leaving with Fred. Ferdinand follows them to an island where he shoots and kills both of them. He then wraps dynamite around his head, lights the fuse, decides he's being stupid and tries to put it out. But it's too late.

In writing this synopsis I am conscious of the large amount left out and how my summary actually seems to be more coherent than the film. There are a number of scenes that seem to take a long time because very little happens and much of the dialogue is elliptical, referring to other texts and genres, including *film noir*:

> Marianne is as mysterious to the spectator as to Ferdinand. She closely resembles the 'heroines' of Hollywood *film noir*: the hero leaves his home and family to follow her into a world of violence and *amour fou*. The film constantly refers to the *film noir* tradition: Marianne's frantic search for money seems to throw back to *Double Indemnity* (Wilder), her treachery to *The Lady From Shanghai* (Welles), her poses of destruction and self-destruction to *Out of the Past* (Tourneur). (MacCabe, 1980, p. 90)

In order to make sense of *Pierrot* we should consider these references; yet I have left many of them out of the summary for the sake of clarity. *Pierrot* also consciously plays with mainstream narrative conventions described above by Kuhn:

1. *Linearity of cause and effect within an overall trajectory of enigma-resolution* – the film opens with Marianne playing tennis, this scene is not used to introduce her character, nothing follows from it; why do we learn about the 'Libyan Queen'? And so on.
2. *A high degree of narrative closure* – while the narrative does close with the deaths of the protagonists, many details are left unresolved. It is not clear what racket Fred is involved in; who is the corpse in Marianne's flat?
3. *A fictional world governed by spatial and temporal verisimilitude* – although there are moments that are confusing, much of the film is shot conventionally. However, the film does break conventional diegesis: Mariannne's flat is departed from once in the story but this is shown several times by the plot; the use of voice-overs; the characters occasionally directly address the camera.
4. *Centrality of the narrative agency of psychologically rounded characters* – the characters' motivation remains throughout somewhat enigmatic and although my summary suggests that Ferdinand is the hero, this is debatable:

> *Pierrot...* is driven by the tension between the active principle of Marianne and the passive principle of Ferdinand. If Ferdinand can't even communicate sufficiently with this woman he loves to get her to call him by his right name then it is equally true that, as Marianne tells him, 'You speak to me with words and I look at you with feelings.' (Monaco, 1976, p. 164)

The protagonists' motivation seems to be governed more by a reversal of gender roles than any clearly defined psychological need. *Pierrot le fou* is an example of an 'art film' in which, in contrast with genre-based Hollywood production, a director's (Jean-Luc Godard in this case) individual expressiveness is deemed paramount. Because the 'art film' is considered to be a personal vision, the product of an *auteur*, and not as primarily a commercial product, it can therefore 'legitimately' dispense with a conventional narrative structure:

> The spontaneous nature of the film is vital to [Godard], for *Pierrot* grew out of a set of very personal emotions. He had reached a point in his career when he had begun to call the whole activity of cinema into question. (ibid., p. 161)

> From *Pierrot* until 1968 this crisis became more and more acute. Godard's attempt to articulate the cultural traditions of classical art and the

popular cinema was disintegrating under the more immediate pressures of the war in Vietnam. (MacCabe, 1980, p. 94)

One of the consequences of this crisis was the development of counter cinema considered, briefly, later in the chapter. The 'European Art Cinema' of the 1950s and 60s – exemplified by Bergman's *The Seventh Seal* (1957), Wajda's *Ashes and Diamonds* (1958) and Resnais's *Last Year in Marienbad* (1961) – could use conventional forms but did not rely upon genre in order to convey meaning (although, ironically, it can be argued that art cinema *is* a genre – see Chapter 5). The lack of genre was one of the reasons that these films were eulogised as art in contrast to the formulaic Hollywood product. It can also be distinguished institutionally:

> European art cinema... also has its own institutional structures for the consumption of films, notably a distribution and exhibition circuit which is separate from that of dominant cinema and is supported by certain kinds of film criticism. Audiences usually see the films in special places – art house cinemas and film societies. (ibid., p. 216ab)

There were, arguably, no British art movies in this period simply because British culture had difficulty in accepting cinema as an art form. Recently, the British director Peter Greenaway's films, such as *The Cook, The Thief, His Wife and Her Lover* (1989), have been considered as 'art film'. In the 1990s, the late Krzysztof Kieslowski has been the most celebrated 'art film' *auteur*, particularly for his *Three Colours* trilogy:

> On the final instalment in his trilogy, Kieslowski said:
> '*Red* is my most personal film, I think. It reflects not only my way of thinking about life, but about cinema: that film can come just that little bit closer to literature than one would imagine.' (Andrew, 1998, p. 52)

(Note how Kieslowski seems to be suggesting that literature is somehow superior to cinema as a form.) In order to make sense of 'art films' the audience often has to work hard at generating meaning. However, despite *Pierrot*'s unconventionality, it can still be related to Todorov's narrative structure:

1. a state of equilibrium at the outset – Ferdinand living a bourgeois existence

2. a disruption of the equilibrium by some action – Ferdinand loses his job and does not want one his wife has arranged
3. a recognition that there has been a disruption – decides to 'run away' with Marianne
4. an attempt to repair the disruption – tries to start a new life with Marianne
5. a reinstatement of the equilibrium – this fails and they both die.

Apart from the ending, this appears to be quite conventional. However, the cramming of the film's diverse detail into Todorov's 'pot' has meant that much has been left out. The Vietnam War, for example, is referred to many times but has no role in narrative development, it appears to be simply a backdrop to the action. Similarly, there are numerous voice-overs (mentioned only once in the synopsis) and their relationship with the image is not considered in a narrative analysis. In 'classical' film there is no, or little, narrative redundancy; the plethora of signifiers in *Pierrot* 'overflows' the constraints of narrative structure.

This is not the place to offer a detailed reading of *Pierrot le fou*, but Monaco (1976) suggests:

> If *Pierrot le fou* is frightening (as I think it often is) it is because it is full of emptiness. Space reigns supreme between these people. They are on the very margins of the film, in time and in space, and they never close the gap. (Monaco, 1976, p. 166)

Despite their professed love for one another, the characters have great difficulty communicating; the space between them (Ferdinand the intellectual, Marianne the hedonist) is too great. Marianne constantly calls Ferdinand 'Pierrot', a reference both to the clown of French pantomime and a 1930s French gangster. By the end of the film, Ferdinand has become that clown: his pathetic attempt at being a gangster having failed, he paints his face and, in a farcical finale, blows himself up. The characters embark on what is, essentially, a picaresque adventure: they do not know where they are going (other than south). This lack of direction works against conventional narrative which always knows where it is going: to the resolution when the disruption is overcome. Godard started his film career with *A bout de souffle* (1959), a homage to the Hollywood 'B' picture; by the time of *Pierrot* he had embraced the, often 'heavy', European art movie and made it modern, funny and cultish. However, post-May 1968 his cinema took another direction.

Peter Wollen, in his investigation of the post-May 1968, Brechtian, cinema of Godard, produced the following oppositions, which contrasted traditional (or old) cinema with the innovations of Godard's *Vent d'est* (1970) (also considered in section 4.11 of *Image and Representation*).

Table 3.1

Old cinema	Counter cinema
Narrative transitivity	Narrative intransitivity
Identification	Estrangement
Transparency	Foregrounding
Single diegesis	Multiple diegesis
Closure	Aperture
Pleasure	Un-pleasure
Fiction	Reality

From a narrative perspective we are interested in the first and fourth oppositions. One of the basic definitions of narrative offered at the beginning of Chapter 1 was 'it presents information as a connected sequence of events'. Narrative *intransitivity*, however, is characterised by 'gaps and interruptions, episodic construction, undigested digression' (Wollen 1985, p. 501).

One of the ways Godard disrupted narrative continuity was through the use of the 'picaresque', 'a pseudo-autobiographical form which substitutes a random and unconnected series of incidents for tight plot construction, supposed to represent the variety and ups-and-downs of real life' (ibid.). Although *Pierrot le fou* is more art movie than counter cinema, it utilises the picaresque in Ferdinand and Marianne's apparently aimless journey south. *Pierrot* can also be difficult to follow but does, overall, have a continuity that, at least, approximates traditional cinema. However by the time of *Vent d'est*:

> Digressions which, in earlier films, represented interruptions to the narrative have hypertrophied until they dominate the film entirely. The basic story... does not have any recognizable sequence, but is more like a series of intermittent flashes. (ibid., p. 502)

While conventional narratives take care to create a coherent narrative world which, necessarily, has a single diegesis ('a unitary homogenous world'), counter cinema offers multiple diegesis ('heterogeneous worlds. Rupture between different codes and different channels' [ibid., p. 504]). Caryl Churchill's play *Top Girls* (1982) begins with a dinner for a variety of characters including: Isabella Bird, a Victorian traveller; Lady Nijo, a thirteenth-century Japanese Emperor's mistress and Buddhist nun; and Dull Gret, a figure from a painting by Brueghel. This mix of history creates a multiple diegesis.

Pierrot occasionally seems to teeter on the edge of multiple diegesis, with its multitude of references to different genres; however, this is an example of the fifth point, aperture ('allusion, quotation and parody') which is endemic in the film.

Alternative narratives in film thrived, relatively, during the 1960s and 70s. In the non-generic novel there are, comparatively, numerous examples. Although novels are, like films and television, primarily produced by institutions for profit, the scale of investment required is obviously much less. Some alternative narratives, in novels, were considered in Chapter 2.

The growing influence of the Internet could have a profound influence on the development of narrative if only because it allows anybody, with access to the World Wide Web, to be their own publisher comparatively cheaply. However, in terms of narrative structure, the use of 'hypertext' could also be very important. Hypertext is basically a link within a WebPage document which will take readers, if they wish, immediately to another part of the document or to another page anywhere on the Web. The links are shown by being underlined and cursors 'turn' into a hand when placed upon them. The consequences for narrative are that the linear cause–effect, favoured by conventional structures, can be undermined by hypertext; it is the equivalent of instantaneously 'fast-forwarding' (or rewinding) a videocassette or switching tapes. Although readers have the choice of whether to click on the link, the existence of the link is dependent upon the WebPage's author.

This idea of information linked in one document, which informs the structure of the World Wide Web, was the vision of Ted Nelson in the 1960s; the early years of the twenty-first century will tell us how influential this will be on our conception of narrative.

Non-fiction texts also use alternative narratives although this is, arguably, more problematic than fiction texts because their 'referent' is reality.

3.6 Alternative narrative and documentary

Documentaries' narrative structures are often the same as fictional texts; this is particularly true of expository documentaries, by far the dominant variant. Take, for example, *When We Were Kings* (1996) which documents the 'Rumble in the Jungle' boxing match between Muhammad Ali and George Foreman in 1974: although this is a mixture of forms (it includes 'fly-on-wall' film, interviews and news footage), it is relatively simple to see the film in Todorov's terms:

1. a state of equilibrium at the outset – Muhammad Ali believes he is 'the greatest' and promotes Black Power
2. a disruption of the equilibrium by some action – George Foreman is the world heavyweight boxing champion
3. a recognition that there has been a disruption – Ali challenges Foreman
4. an attempt to repair the disruption – the bout in Kinshasa, Zaire
5. a reinstatement of the equilibrium – Ali triumphant.

The documentary, like fiction films, has agents who carry out functions: in Proppian terms Ali is the hero; Foreman the villain; Ali's promoter, Don King, the helper; the President of Zaire, the donor. It should be noted, however, that 'Ali's heroism… [is] as contrived as Foreman's villainy – after all neither was a hero *or* a villain' (Early, 1997, p. 12). However, there are alternative narrative forms in documentary.

Frederick Wiseman is renowned for his observational documentaries where the camera appears to be observing what is going on without being noticed by the participants. His films are often a collection of sequences filmed in one institution, for example *High School* ('one' and 'two') and *Hospital*. These sequences are not linked together chronologically, there is no beginning, middle and end; it appears that the events shown are ongoing and we are merely seeing a selection of them. Despite this, Bill Nichols has shown how the structure of Wiseman's films is analogous to narrative:

> In Wiseman's films the agents carry out functions determined by the institutional structure in which they are embedded rather than by a narrative structure. (Nichols, 1981, p. 213)

Nichols has even managed to isolate 11 'institutional' functions which take the place of Propp's 'spheres of action'. However,

Wiseman does *not* organise the text, as a whole, narratively, rather he creates, what Nichols calls, a 'mosaic'. That is, we are given a number of episodes shot within the institution but these episodes do not, necessarily, link together to give the audience an overall picture:

> The... sequences of a Wiseman film are already coherent and do not merge into one impression or one narrative tale so much as supplement each other (with each sequence conveying a recognizable aspect of the overall design). (ibid., p. 211)

It may be a fruitful exercise to compare Wiseman's mosaic with the oral mode of exposition described in Section 2.4. 'Mosaic' is present in this opposition and a case could be made for a number of others in this mode being similar to Wiseman's mode of address.

One of the effects of this non-narrative structure is for the text to sign itself as 'real'. So Wiseman's documentaries may appear to reflect reality primarily through their formal structure and not because of what they are showing. It could be argued that life is a mosaic, a collection of experiences that make up a day, a week, a year and, ultimately, a life.

Ironically, although most documentaries use a conventional narrative structure to represent their material, the most 'real' form may be one that acts in opposition to this structure (although it should be pointed out that Wiseman's documentaries do not command a mass audience). In fact it is possible to conceive narrative and 'everyday' life as a binary opposition.

Table 3.2

Everyday life	Narratives
real	mediated*
all middle	beginning, middle, end
diffuse	focused
conflict muted, random	conflict intense, continual
repeat performances	each story different
vague goals	curiosity about resolution
eventlessness basic	eventfulness basic
imitates art?	imitates life?

Source: adapted from Berger, 1997, p. 162
*Berger did not use 'mediated' here; he described narratives as 'fictional'. This misses the point, I feel, because it is useful to distinguish between fictional and non-fictional narratives. However, *all* narratives must be mediated whereas reality is... real.

I think Berger's last opposition is the most interesting. Post-modernists (see Chapter 2) suggest that *both* everyday life and art, defined in its widest sense as an artefact, are now imitating art. Given the choice, would you, as *Trainspotting*'s Renton said, 'choose a life' that was: 'focused, intense, varied and eventful' or one that was 'diffuse, muted, repetitious, eventless'? Well, we do not have a choice, except that human beings *do* turn life, with narrative, into an exciting experience: whether these are narratives about our own lives or fictional lives that use fictional narrative texts to facilitate escapism and the feeling of utopia. Maybe we are not *homo sapiens* ('man and woman as knower'); but are *homo narrans* ('tellers of tales').

4

THEORY OF GENRE 1

AIMS OF THE CHAPTER

➤ To consider genre as a theoretical construct; the basic schema is described with reference to crime and Western texts.

➤ To consider the relationship between genre and society and offer numerous case studies which use genre in particular ways:

- *film noir* and the 'hard-boiled' detective novel are related to the repertoire of elements

- TV cop texts illustrate generic oppositions

- a history of science fiction and its repertoire of elements

- melodrama as a genre and style.

➤ To compare genre to 'formats' with reference to lifestyle magazines.

4.1 Introduction

It is highly likely that, at some point in your education, you have studied genre and although the term itself may not have completely entered mainstream discourse, or language, almost everyone is familiar with the idea of grouping similar texts together. Indeed, one of the most successful series of books for teenagers is named after a genre: Point Horror. On the face of it, then, genre is a straightforward concept which refers to a type of text and:

> Genres can be defined as patterns/forms/styles/structures which transcend individual art products, and which supervise both their construction by artist and their reading by audiences. (Ryall, 1975, p. 28)

In this chapter we will focus on defining the 'patterns/forms/ styles/structures' of particular genres. We shall do this by considering the 'repertoire of elements' which mainly consists of characters, setting, iconography, narrative and style of a text; these elements offer the basic schema of a genre. However, before we consider various case studies we need to look at the relationship between generic texts, their audiences, the artists and the institutions that produce them.

The above definition suggests genre exists in the space between artists, audiences and the text itself. However, all media texts, with the possible exception of those distributed on the Internet, need a media institution to produce the text. In effect, an institution mediates between the artist and audience. Even novelists, who are among the most independent of artists, are likely to have an editor and will need a publishing house to print and distribute their work; similarly, painters need a gallery in which to display their art. Most other forms of texts are products of groups of people working together, although it has to be acknowledged that particular individuals often have a controlling voice in the production, for example the director of a film, or play, and a performer of popular music.

Characterising the text's producers as institutions, rather than artists as Ryall does above, also acknowledges that technological practices involved in media production affect the creation of a text. For example, the standard three camera set-up used for studio-based television work gives a distinct look to most sitcoms and soap operas. In addition, institutions are responsible for the marketing and distribution of a text.

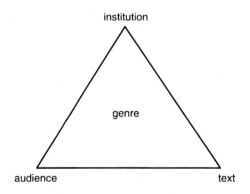

Figure 4.1

133

In *Image and Representation* (Chapter 4) we considered how authorial intent is, traditionally, the focus of artistic criticism; in other words, the objective is to try and work out what the author is saying. Genre criticism has a wider focus and does not privilege any one of its three components above the others. Genre criticism looks, broadly, at the three distinct areas:

1. it acknowledges that artists, working within an institutional context, produce a generic media text with the knowledge of the rules and conventions of that genre and with the awareness that audiences can be expected to be familiar with this knowledge
2. audiences use genre to categorise texts
3. institutions use genre in order to package texts which facilitates their sale to audiences.

Although genre is a 'stand-alone' key concept, points two and three mean it will also feature in *Media Institutions and Audiences*. The focus, in this book, is on genre as an 'organiser' of textual components. This organisation is a crucial part of the dynamic process of reading. While texts do exist, on their own, as artefacts, they can only 'come alive' with the act of reading. Without an audience, a text is useless as a text (although it may be still useful for swatting flies). A text is:

> a set of 'schemata', or general directions, which the reader must actualize. To do this, the reader will bring to the work certain 'pre-understandings', a dim context of beliefs and expectations within which the work's various features will be assessed. As the reading process proceeds, however, these expectations will themselves be modified by what we learn. (Eagelton, 1983, p. 77)

As we saw in Chapter 1, we engage in narrative prediction based on clues offered by the text and we base these predictions on expectations generated by the text; genre is one of the most influential of these expectations. Because the purpose of this chapter is to consider genre *in* texts, what follows, initially, discusses genre as if it were a fairly static phenomenon. However, it must be remembered that genres 'continually change, modulate, and redefine themselves' (Turner, 1993, p. 38); in Chapter 5 we will consider how genre develops through time and the existence of 'generic cycles'. In addition, genre texts do not offer *everything* that constitutes the genre to which they belong, it is a paradigm

134

against which we can assess the way a text is the *same* and *different* from the generic template.

It is worth noting the existence of sub-genres; for instance, Bram Stoker's *Dracula* (1897) is a horror novel that can also be categorised as a vampire novel. This sub-genre has many conventions that are common to the horror genre as a whole but also has conventions specific to itself, such as the vampire's aversion to garlic, sunlight and crucifixes.

4.2 Generic conventions

Danny stood with his back against the door, looking at the right angle where the hallways joined. The steady, irregular booming sound of the mallet against the walls grew louder. The thing that was after him screamed and howled and cursed. Dream and reality had joined together without a seam.

It came around the corner.

In a way, what Danny felt was relief. It was not his father. The mask of face and body had been ripped and shredded and made into a bad joke. It was not his daddy, not this Saturday Night Shock Show horror with its rolling eyes and hunched and hulking shoulders and blood-drenched shirt. It was not his daddy. (King, 1977, pp. 396–7)

The reference to 'King' gives a strong clue to the genre as a Stephen King novel is indelibly associated with horror. However, there is sufficient within this extract, from *The Shining*, for most people to identify the genre ('The thing that was after him screamed and howled and cursed. Dream and reality had joined together without a seam').

The use of the word 'thing' connotes that whatever is after Danny is not only *not* human but defies any pithy description that words can give; the 'ripped and shredded' face suggests extreme violence. The fact that dream and reality meld into one indicates a narrative world where a normal rules do not apply. And the screaming and howling offer aural signs of the horror genre.

What use do readers make of this information? Once a text has been identified as belonging to a particular genre then the reader has certain expectations about what will happen and what rules apply in this particular narrative world (diegesis).

Exercise 4.1

List everything you associate with the horror genre.

Of course individual horror texts do not have to follow all the expectations you have but if it fails to follow a sufficient number then it will no longer be a horror text. If a text breaks too many generic conventions, it runs the risk of alienating anyone in the audience who is reading the text because they expect it to be generic.

The first three chapters of this book showed how narrative is, basically, a schema which people use to make sense both of texts and the world. Genre is also a schema, however it is only used to make sense of texts; only in very unusual cases is it possible to characterise a life as being generic. Aristotle's original concept of genre was adapted as a tool to help with the analysis of popular texts; early, and classic pieces, of genre criticism include the work of Jim Kitses (1969), Robert Warshow (1970) and Colin McArthur (1972). This chapter leans towards a description of genre and will concern itself with identifying the conventions of various genres offering case studies on: *film noir* and the 'hard-boiled' detective novel; the television cop series (*NYPD Blue*); science fiction; melodrama. We shall also look at texts that may be considered as generic, such as game shows and tabloid newspapers, but might be better defined as formats.

However, one of the central problems about genre as a concept is the conundrum: which comes first, the genre or the text? On the one hand it could be said that genre is defined by the text; on the other, we understand the text's characters, setting, iconography, narrative and style because we classify them as belonging to a particular genre. This contraction will be dealt with in Chapter 5.

4.3 The basic schema of genre

When attempting to identify whether a text belongs to a genre, the best starting point is to list the following: types of characters, setting, iconography, narrative and style of the text and then consider whether it fits into any genre. It is useful to construct this as a matrix as in Table 4.1.

However, not all genre texts can be adequately categorised in this way; music, for instance, does not have a setting (ignoring performance for a moment) and not all genres have particular stars associated with them. In addition, some genre texts are a mix of more than one genre. This section will describe the constituents of the basic schema of genre with examples from the crime and Western genres.

Exercise 4.2

Using the matrix in Table 4.1, make notes on any of the genres you are familiar with.

Table 4.1

Genre	Setting	Character	Narrative	Iconography	Style	Stars
TV crime series film noir 'hard-boiled' detective novel science fiction melodrama						

Characters

As we saw in Chapter 1, characters can usefully be considered as 'spheres of action'. However, in terms of genre we are interested in the *type* of hero, heroine, villain and so on. Many genres have characters who can be classed as generic types; these can be stereotypical or specific to a genre. For example, a stereotypical prostitute can refer to characters in texts or people in reality; on the other hand, the character of the (usually male) captain, or lieutenant, in cop films and TV series is generic. This generic character is the boss (the 'organisation man' described in section 4.4) of the central protagonist and is usually attempting to 'rein in' the hero, who is after the criminals. This character is not a stereotype because we do not encounter this character either in 'real life' or, at least not often, in non-fiction texts. To summarise: stereotypes can both be generic types and exist in reality; generic types only reside in texts.

In contemporary crime genre texts, the protagonist (the Proppian hero) is usually a cop or private eye detective and in Westerns he is –

and it's usually a 'he' although exceptions include *Forty Guns* (1957) and *Johnny Guitar* (1954) – a good cowboy. In crime texts, the heroine is often threatened by the villain; in Westerns, which mostly marginalise females, the heroine is commonly reduced to staying at home cultivating civilisation. Villains, usually, are the criminals in crime texts and either the 'red Indians' (Native North Americans) or bad cowboys (for example, rustlers) in Westerns.

Setting

The setting refers to location in terms of place (space) and time. Crime texts are usually set in a contemporary urban environment or, classically in film, Chicago at the time of the Prohibition; Westerns are very particular in their space (the American frontier) and time (1865–90). The Western deals with the conflict between the wilderness and civilisation (a binary opposition), a conflict that occurred on the frontier between the end of the Civil War until both sides of North America were 'unified' by the trans-continental railway.

Iconography

Iconography refers to objects, or sounds, which are associated with a genre. Iconography, as a term, was derived in Erwin Panofsky's (1955) art criticism and referred only to the visual signs. However, as we also associate aural signs with particular genres then it is obvious that, for our purposes, iconography is both 'sight and sound'. We associate guns and decrepit city streets with the crime genre; iconography in the Western is very exact, possibly because of its very focused time period: the ten-gallon hat, the six-gun, horses, tumbleweed and so on.

Iconographic sounds refer both to diegetic and non-diegetic signs. In crime texts, the sound of a police car's siren (diegetic) is usually endemic just as a Western's theme music (non-diegetic) is likely to have lush strings, staccato brass and a fast rhythm emphasised by the bass drum. In the gangster movie, aural iconography:

> added immensely to the physical effect of the gangster film. The terrifying splutter of the machine-gun, the screaming of brakes and squealing of automobile tyres. (Griffith, 1976, p. 112)

It is arguable that iconography could also refer to more than objects and sounds: action movies, for example, are often notable for their 'tongue-in-cheek', 'over-the-top' style of acting. Be aware that iconography is *not* the same as Peirce's icon (see sections 2.3 and 5.8).

Narrative and theme

Assuming you've read the first three chapters, the term narrative is unlikely to create (much of) a problem for you. Although virtually all, indeed maybe *all*, genre texts follow the conventional narrative structure described by Todorov and Propp, they tell their *stories* in different ways. As we saw in Chapter 1, the typical crime story involves the hero solving the crime in order to catch the villain. Edgar Allan Poe, who invented the detective story with *The Purloined Letter* and *The Murders in the Rue Morgue*, defined the genre:

> The detective story formula centers upon the detective' investigation and solution of the crime. Both *Rue Morgue* and *The Purloined Letter* exemplify the six main phases of this pattern: (a) introduction of the detective; (b) crime and clues; (c) investigation; (d) announcement of the solution; (e) explanation of the solution; (f) denouement. (Cawelti, 1976, pp. 81–2)

Exercise 4.3

Relate Poe's formula to that of Todorov from Chapter 1.

We can see how closely the detective tale follows the classical narrative structure. Although Westerns, too, follow Todorov's pattern, typical Western stories are not so obviously reflective of narrative structure; Frank Gruber, a scriptwriter, described these stories as:

- Union Pacific/Pony Express fighting the elements to build a business
- homesteaders (cattlemen versus farmers)
- dedicated law-men
- empire (ranch) built and destroyed by second generation
- outlaw as good guy
- revenge
- cavalry versus Indians.

If we apply the above stories to the abstracts in Chapter 1, we can see how the Western articulates basic story structures:

- Union Pacific/Pony Express fighting the elements to build a business – 'the quest', an attempt to build a business in the wilderness (for example *The Iron Horse*, 1924)
- homesteaders (cattlemen versus farmers) – the 'biter-bit' where the farmers eventually throw off the cattlemen's yoke; can also be 'redemption' and 'the stranger saviour' depending on how the farmers defeat (which they usually do) the cattlemen (*The Westerner*, 1940)
- dedicated law-men – 'the quest', 'redemption' and 'the stranger saviour' (*High Noon*, 1952)
- empire (ranch) built and destroyed by second generation – 'rise and fall' (*Forty Guns*, 1957)
- outlaw as good guy – 'redemption' and 'the stranger saviour' (*Butch Cassidy and the Sundance Kid*, 1969)
- revenge – 'quest', 'the biter-bit' and 'the stranger saviour' (numerous Clint Eastwood Westerns)
- cavalry versus Indians – 'the quest' to destroy the Indians (*Fort Apache*, 1948).

In addition to Gruber's stories there is the tale of the 'white man' who goes native which can be characterised as a 'journey to another world' (*Run of the Arrow*, 1957).

One of the ways genres can be used is to consider which stories are dominant at a particular time. Will Wright (1975) created a typology of four, in contrast to Gruber's seven, Western narratives, in film, which help demonstrate the how the genre developed over time (the dates refer to the narratives 'predominant time'):

- Classical   1930–55   Lone gun fighter saves town or farmers (for example *Shane*, 1953)
- Transitional 1950–53   Hero and heroine defend justice but are rejected by society (for example *High Noon*, 1952)
- Vengeance   1950–60   Ill-used hero seeks revenge on villain (for example *Rancho Notorious*, 1952)
- Professional 1958–70   Professional fighters take jobs for money (for example *Rio Bravo*, 1959)

I would suggest a further category:

- Revisionist 1970–? The hero becomes disillusioned with the 'American way' because it involves genocide (for example *Little Big Man*, 1970).

Obviously not *all* Westerns made in any one of these periods necessarily reflected Wright's categories; however, the categories are useful in suggesting which variant of a genre is dominant at any one time. These narratives will, of course, also be structured by binary oppositions and will be in the 'guise' of one of Gruber's stories. In the crime genre, the tension is usually generated by the conflict between 'law and order' versus 'lawlessness and disorder'; this is an expression of the deep-seated, mythical opposition, of good versus evil. The notions of 'good' and 'evil' are evoked in many different types of genres but how they are *expressed* is dependent upon the genre.

Which oppositions are being mobilised, and which genres are popular, gives us a clue to the particular concerns society has at any one time (see Chapter 3 for an analysis *of The Searchers* and section 4.7 for how science fiction has developed through time).

Style

Genres often have a particular style associated with them: pop videos are characterised by frenetic editing, 'glossy' visuals, unusual camera movement and so on; cop series, particularly in North America, use the codes of the action movie with rapid editing and camera movement accompanied by fast music (a bit like pop video come to think of it); mass-market romance novels, such as those published by Mills and Boon, use 'purple prose' like:

> Slowly he rose, his hands trailing up her body, sending great waves of desire coursing though her, making her give small, animal-like sounds of tormented frustration. (Wentworth, 1994, p. 90)

Of course these particular styles are not necessarily specific to genres, but texts that do not use the 'generic styles' of their genre are likely to be breaking conventions. For example, while the prose style of Mills and Boon novels can appear in other genres, mass-market romance novels would not be recognisable without their particular brand of prose.

4.4 Genre and society

Because genres are characterised by 'the same but different', they are constantly evolving. Society, too, constantly changes, and the 'repertoire of elements' allows us to, tentatively, make links between what makes a particular form of the genre popular at any one time and the social situation that produced and consumed the variant. Genre texts, because of their commerciality, are very useful for this because if a particular generic variant does not find an audience, it is unlikely that many similar texts will be made. For instance, even though the Western was a staple Hollywood genre from the start of the North American film industry until the 1960s, very few have been made since; it is interesting to speculate why genres should fall out of fashion and this will be pursued in section 5.6.

Genres do not only change because society changes, they also evolve as distinct entities. As we saw in the section on Barthes's narrative codes, narratives make sense because they refer to other narratives; this is also true of genre. So producers of genre texts have to be knowledgeable about the appropriate genre and, if they successfully (that is, it is popular) offer a substantial variation on conventions, they are likely to be 'clued' – accidentally or otherwise – into the particular *Zeitgeist*. If they are not 'tuned in' then it is less likely that audiences will respond to the offered variation.

We can characterise this interaction between the producers and their audience (both groups, of course, are likely to be members of the same society) as follows.

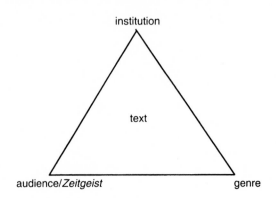

Figure 4.2

Individual genre texts are the product of the society – as expressed by the institution and audience expectation – and the history of the genre. This helps explain why particular narratives and themes are popular at any one time. In British TV crime series, for example, it may be possible to detect the public's general disillusionment with the police force by comparing *Dixon of Dock Green*, from the 1950s, when villains were apprehended by the genial Dixon fingering their collar and offering an admonishing word, with *Between the Lines*, of the 1990s, which concerned investigations into police corruption (see also section 5.6).

The period of the revisionist Westerns – including *Soldier Blue* (1970) and *Dances With Wolves* (1990) – may have been sparked off by the Vietnam War which had parallels with the 'frontier West': Vietnamese are, symbolically, Indians who, rather than being portrayed as the savages of the 'traditional' Western, are shown to be the victims of genocide. The massacre of Native American Indians was paralleled by the massacre of Vietnamese villagers, for example at My Lai in 1968, by North American forces.

The rest of this chapter will consider a number of case studies. The objective is to offer different ways of looking at genres. First there will be a consideration of 'hard-boiled' detective fiction and *film noir* using the repertoire of elements; this will be followed by the 'TV cop' genre and will demonstrate how oppositions can structure a genre text; science fiction will be considered, again using the repertoire of elements, and a brief history of the genre will attempt to show how genres can develop through time; a consideration of *Blade Runner – the Director's Cut* will offer a generic analysis of one text; there will be an examination of melodrama showing how it exists as a genre and a style.

4.5 *Film noir* and 'hard-boiled' crime novels – the repertoire of elements

Genre is a concept that appears in many different forms, such as television, literature and film. This makes it a useful concept in the analysis of the media themselves. For instance, if science fiction literature is different from science fiction film, it is likely that the difference is caused by the medium and/or its institutional context. Thus the essential character of a particular medium and its means of production can be isolated by considering differences in the way a genre is articulated. So although *film noir* and the 'hard-boiled' detective are not usually considered to be the same genre, the differences between them are a result of the media of film and literature for – as we shall see – they are, in essence, the same.

History

Film noir has its cinematic roots in German Expressionist cinema and literary seeds in the 'hard-boiled' pulp novels of 1930s North American writers such as James M. Cain, Dashiel Hammett, Jim Thompson, Chester Himes and Raymond Chandler. Contemporary writers who have also utilised the genre include Walter Mosley, Sara Paretsky, Elmore Leonard and James Ellroy. 'Hard-boiled' crime narratives originally came to prominence with the *Black Mask* pulp magazine; pulp literature was genre driven and also featured science fiction, war stories, Westerns and sports stories among others. Hammett, probably the most influential of 'hard-boiled' writers, had his first 'Continental Op' story published *in Black Mask* in 1923. 'Hammett was praised for the realism of his sparse, stripped-down style and for the way he did not "hold back" from sex, violence and the seamy side of life' (Krutnik, 1991, p. 35).

Krutnik compared the new 'hard-boiled' style to conventional crime fiction of the time; conventional texts relied upon the power of deductive reasoning which is replaced in 'hard-boiled' texts:

> by action, and the mystery element is displaced in favour of suspense. Gunplay, illicit or exotic sexuality, the corruption of the social forces of law, and personal danger to the hero are placed to the fore… the 'hard-boiled' hero - operates as a mediator between the criminal underworld and the world of respectable society. He can move freely between these two worlds, without really being part of either. (Krutnik, 1991, p. 39)

Hollywood was about two decades behind 'hard-boiled' literature because the self-regulatory system of censorship, administered by the Hays Office, did not look favourably upon such narratives. Despite the breakthrough of the John Huston-directed version *of The Maltese Falcon*, in 1941 (Huston's *Falcon* is often cited as the first *film noir* but Frank Krutnik states that the first of the 1940s was *The Stranger on the Third Floor*), it was not until two years later that the *film noir* cycle began. Krutnik suggests that this delay was because of the advent of the Second World War and the pressure upon Hollywood to deal with war-related issues.

The 1940s were also the time when the paperback mass market got established in the USA and many of the stories from the 'pulp' magazines were reprinted and then filmed:

> Their illustrated covers were an important sales feature, and… many of the covers were fairly lurid, suggesting sex and violence. A favourite subject was a woman with a gun, usually threatening a man. This image… can probably be claimed for *noir* iconography. (Walker, 1994, p. 31)

Manohla Dargis (1997) has pointed out that a number of influential *noir* film-makers all worked on an obscure German documentary, *Menshcen am Sonntag* (*People on Sunday*) in 1929. The director, Robert Siodmak, went on to make the classic *noir The Killers* (1946); screenwriters Billy Wilder and Curt Siodmak directed *Sunset Boulevard* (1950) and wrote *I Walked With a Zombie* (1943), respectively; assistant director Edgar G. Ulmer directed *Detour* (1945); cameraman Edgar Schufftan advised on *The Dark Mirror* (directed by Robert Siodmak, 1946) and assistant cameraman Fred Zinneman directed *Act of Violence* (1948). These artists were not the only ones who were responsible for the 'creation' of the *noir* genre but their German background is crucial. Fritz Lang was another German émigré who was instrumental in the development of *film noir*. They were all in the USA during the 1930s and 40s because they were fleeing the Nazis.

Although as a genre it is currently undergoing something of a revival with films such as *Se7en* and *Copycat* (both 1995), its classic period was between 1941 and 1958. There is some debate about whether *film noir* is a genre or a visual style and this will be considered later in the chapter.

Characters

Heroes

Although the central characters of 'hard-boiled' texts are usually male (recent exceptions are the film *The Last Seduction*, 1994, and novelist Sara Paretsky's private eye, V.I. Warshawski, who first appeared in *Indemnity Only*, 1982), they differ from the traditional 'clean cut' hero. Paul Schrader (1972) described three types of male protagonist in the classical *noir* period that are also applicable, dates apart, to 'hard-boiled' literature.

The private eye/lone wolf (1941–46)

In this period *film noir* offered the most faithful portrayal of the 'hard-boiled' hero featured in pulp detective fiction. The main protagonist is often a private dick (emphasising his masculinity) or, if not, a similarly 'lone wolf' character; neither has any family ties and often finds himself in between the criminal world and the law. The character also has access to all social classes: they inevitably deal with the lowlifes of the 'underworld' but often find themselves working for the rich (who may be being blackmailed) who live in grand mansions. *The Maltese Falcon* (1941) featured Dashiel Hammet's Sam Spade (played by Humphrey Bogart) who is a private eye hired to find the bird of the title.

Raymond Chandler, whose novels have been adapted many times including *The Big Sleep* (1946 and 1978), *Marlowe* (1969) and *The Long Goodbye* (1973), created private eye Philip Marlowe who exemplifies the 'lone wolf' hero, as the author described:

> Down these mean streets a man must go who is not himself mean, who is neither tarnished nor afraid. The detective in this kind of story must be such a man. He is the hero, he is everything. He must be a complete man and a common man and yet an unusual man. He must be, to use a rather weathered phrase, a man of honor. (Cawelti, 1976, pp. 150–1)

While the character is essentially, like most narrative heroes, good, he does not have a sanguine view of the world. He may have to resist threats and bribes, from both sides of the law, and political pressure to back-off in his investigation. His quest for the guilty party is often subordinated to his desire for justice which he will reach through making a personal choice (the law is often portrayed as too unwieldy or corrupt to attain justice). So even though they invariably succeed in their search for justice, the quest is often not what it initially appears to be:

> The classical detective's investigation typically passes over a variety of possible suspects until it lights at last on the least-likely person, [but] his hard-boiled counterpart becomes emotionally involved in a complex process of changing implications. Everything changes its meaning: the initial mission turns out to be a smoke screen for another, more devious plot; the supposed victim turns out to be a villain; the lover ends up as the murderess and the faithful friend as a rotten betrayer; the police and the district attorney and often even the client keep trying to halt the investigation; and all the seemingly respectable and successful people turn out to be members of the gang. (ibid., p. 146)

One of the great attractions of such 'hard-boiled' texts is the potential for subversion offered. In this genre we are moving away from the fairy-tale world of 'happy ever after'; certainly the villains usually get their punishment but the world remains, as the conclusion of *Se7en* stated, a sick place.

Less romantic heroes (1945–49)

Where the morality of the hero was more ambiguous and the narrative focused on crime in the streets and political corruption. In *The Postman Always Rings Twice*, by James M. Cain (1934), (filmed in Italian as *Ossessione* in 1942 and by Hollywood, eponymously, in 1946 and 1981) drifter Frank Chambers becomes a murderer and, in the film *Nora Prentiss* (1947), a respectable family man, Dr Richard Talbot (played by Kent Smith), ends his life being hideously scarred and then executed for the murder of *himself*.

Cain did not write detective stories but his characters are certainly 'hard boiled'; Chambers – the first-person narrator of *Postman* – and Cora fake an accident to cover up a murder:

> I hauled off and hit her in the eye as hard as I could. She went down. She was right down there at my feet, her eyes shining, her breasts trembling, drawn up in tight points, and pointing right up at me. She was down there, and the breath was roaring in the back of my throat like I was some kind of an animal, and my tongue was all swelled up in my mouth, and blood pounding in it... Hell could have opened up for me then, and it wouldn't have made any difference. I had to have her, if I hung for it. I had her. (Cain, 1985, pp. 34–5)

There is certainly no sense here of the narrator trying to put a positive spin on his actions; contemporary mores probably meant that Cain used a 'swollen tongue' as a substitute for 'swollen penis'.

Psychotic hero with a suicidal impulse (1949–53)

The main protagonist is often a killer and the narrative concerns despair and disintegration. This phase of *film noir* possibly reflects the moral confusion and disgust caused by the Holocaust and the nuclear bombing of Hiroshima and Nagasaki. *Kiss Me Deadly* (1955) features private eye Mike Hammer (Ralph Meeker) who enjoys slamming a drawer onto the hand of a weak individual in order to get information.

Hammer was a character created by Mickey Spillane who, as Cawelti shows, had essentially a right-wing view of the world, which contrasts with Chandler's liberalism:

> I've been almost anxious to get to some of the rats that make up the section of humanity that prey on people. People. How incredibly stupid they could be sometimes. A trial by law for a killer. A loophole in the phrasing that lets a killer crawl out. But in the end the people have their justice. They get it through guys like me once in a while. They crack down on society and I crack down on them. I shoot them like the mad dogs they are and society drags me to court to explain the whys and wherefores of the extermination. (from *I, the Jury* quoted in Cawelti, 1976, pp. 151–2)

Kitses makes the point that, like the gangster:

> the *noir* hero's need is… to rise above the two-bit level, and be 'somebody' [and this] resonates in the American psyche. Most Americans are unaware that their society's emphasis on the pursuit of happiness, on self-fulfilment and individualism, is a minority point of view, at odds with most of the world. (Kitses, 1996, p. 32)

The price North America, and the west in general, pays for its economic success is higher 'rates of crime, homicide, suicide, divorce, juvenile delinquency, alcoholism and child abuse' (ibid.) than the rest of the world; the west may be financially richer but it is at the cost of a poorer quality of life. The *noir* hero lives out this contradiction in the high price he usually has to pay for any 'success' he experiences in the narrative.

Many *noir* heroes are war veterans; men who had been taught to kill and had spent years in frightening and disturbing situations. These films often dealt with, what were in effect, post-traumatic stress disorders. It was unsurprising that the heroes often had a dubious morality and this, coupled with the unconventional sexual assertiveness of the female, often posed questions about conventional definitions of masculinity and femininity. The men were not the conventional 'shining armour' type and the women were not exactly princesses.

Heroines

In most generic texts the function of the central female character is to be the 'princess', who needs rescuing, and the reward (usually with sex) for the hero at the plot's conclusion. The sexual reward has become a generic joke in the James Bond series which often conclude with Bond, having dispatched the villain and eluded his boss, left alone with an implausibly named princess, such as Pussy Galore in *Goldfinger* (1964). Because heroines often fulfil the princess narrative function, it is unsurprising that the main female characters should be represented, primarily, by their passive sexuality. However *film noir* and the 'hard-boiled' novel often subvert this representation through the character of the *femme fatale*:

> The women are active, not static symbols, are intelligent and powerful, if destructively so, and derive power, not weakness, from their sexuality. (Place, 1980, p. 35)

Although the *femme fatale* remains a male fantasy at least she has the compensation of seducing, rather than being seduced by, the male protagonist and often leads him to a bad end. The problem for her is that she, too, usually meets her doom. The *femme fatale* was not created out of a vacuum by the 'hard-boiled' novel, she had her antecedents in the melodramatic character of the Vamp.

However, *femmes fatales* are not interesting merely for their sexual assertiveness, they often have desires that are conventionally male: money in *Gun Crazy* (1949); independence in *Laura* (1944); freedom in *The Big Combo* (1955); to own a nightclub in *Night and the City* (1950).

It is likely that the upheaval in gender roles caused by the Second World War precipitated the character of the *femme fatale*. Women were doing 'men's jobs' in factories and the men fighting abroad were nervously fantasising about what their wives/girlfriends were doing back home. The anxiety engendered by men's suspicions was personified in the character of the *femme fatale*, a character with a voracious sexual appetite, who was the opposite of the faithful, monogamous, virginal woman who populated many conventional genres. It has been argued (Rich, 1995) that the resurgence of the genre in the 1990s has its roots in a current crisis of masculine identity.

Classic *femmes fatales* include: Phyllis Dietrichson (*Double Indemnity*, 1944); Elsa Bannister (*The Lady from Shanghai*, 1948); Matty Walker (*Body Heat*, a 1981 remake of *Double Indemnity*); Bridget Gregory (*The Last Seduction*, 1994).

It is not only male Media Studies teachers who find *femmes fatales* seductive; feminist critics have used the character to make subversive readings of Hollywood texts (see Kaplan 1980). Although the *femme fatale*, like most women in conventional texts, is defined by her sexuality, her function as the princess is decidedly more ambiguous. In *Out of the Past* (British title, *Build My Gallows High*, 1947) Kathie Moffat ostensibly needs saving from the villain, Whit Sterling (Kirk Douglas), but it is soon clear that it is any man she wishes to use who is in need of rescuing. Kathie is contrasted with the good, virginal Ann:

> who is firmly rooted in the pastoral environment, static, undemanding and rather dull, while the other (Kathie) is exciting, criminal, very active and sexy. In the film the lack of excitement offered by the safe woman is so clearly contrasted with the sensual, passionate appeal of the other that the detective's destruction is inevitable. (Place, 1980, p. 50).

The *femme fatale* offers a sexual excitement that 'hard-boiled' men often desire sufficiently enough to accept at any price. The hero of *Double Indemnity*, also by James M. Cain, is an insurance salesman, a pretty safe occupation until he meets Mrs Nirdlinger who:

> was walking around the room, and I saw something I hadn't noticed before. Under those blue pyjamas was a shape to set a man nuts... all of a sudden she looked at me, and I felt a chill creep straight up my back and into the roots of my hair. 'Do you handle accident insurance?' (Cain, 1985, p. 234)

A sexy body is a passport to murder. Unsurprisingly, as the heroine is rarely the princess in this genre, the hero is often a 'victim hero'. This is certainly the case in the 1946 film version of *The Postman Always Rings Twice* where the casting of John Garfield, whose persona was of a straightforward, decent guy, meant his heroic 'transformation' would be a corruption of what was good in him. However, in the 1981 film version the opening scene, aided by the casting of Jack Nicholson, immediately shows that this Frank Chambers is already corrupt.

The *femme fatale*, however, does sometimes fulfil the function of princess. In *Laura* (1944), *Gilda* (1946) and *Nora Prentiss* (1947) she has no intention of seducing and destroying the male hero; it is the man's infatuation with her that creates the narrative disruption. This is brilliantly illustrated by the 'little known' *noir Nora Prentiss* where a respectable doctor 'falls for' Nora (see Appendix 1).

The faithful, monogamous, virginal woman, who populates many conventional genres, does appear in *film noir* and the 'hard-boiled' novel and is often contrasted with the *femme fatale*. In *Out of the Past* the virginal Ann, who hero Jeff Bailey (Robert Mitchum) did love, is told at the end that Bailey was betraying her by running off with the *femme fatale* (Kathie Moffett). The heterosexual union, the conventional 'happy ever after', sees Ann being chaperoned by the worthy, and slightly pathetic, cop Joe. The scene is one of desolation.

The decent 'hard-boiled' hero cannot save the 'evil' *femme fatale*; Sam Spade, *in The Maltese Falcon*, loves Brigid O'Shaughnessy and she pleads with Spade not to give her up:

> She put her face up to his face. Her mouth was slightly open with lips a little thrust out. She whispered: 'If you loved me you'd need nothing more on that side.'
>
> Spade set the edges of his teeth together and said through them: 'I won't play the sap for you.'
>
> She put her mouth to his, slowly, her arms around him, and came into his arms. She was in his arms when the doorbell rang. (Hammett, 1982 pp. 199–200)

Spade hands her over to the cops. Sara Paretsky offers a female private eye, V.I. Warshawski, who can use typically 'female' activities, such as preparing food, as part of a power play with the police:

> I methodically sliced cheese, green peppers and onions, put them on the pumpernickel, and put the open-faced sandwich under the broiler. I kept by my back to Bobby and the sergeant while I waited for the cheese to melt, then transferred the whole thing to a plate and poured myself a cup of coffee. From his breathing I could tell Bobby's temper was mounting. His face was red by the time I put my food on the table and straddled a chair opposite him. (Paretsky, 1993, p. 31)

No doubt it was the 'male' gesture of straddling the chair that really made Bobby's blood boil. The generic characterisation of the *femme fatale* is, however, certainly rooted in male fantasy, as Christine Gledhill points out:

> Rather than a coherent realisation of the unstable, treacherous woman, we tend to find in film noir a series of partial characterisations juxtaposed... so, for instance, in *The Postman Always Rings Twice* Cora exhibits a remarkable series of unmotivated character switches and roles something as follows: 1) sex-bomb; 2) hardworking, ambitious woman; 3) loving playmate in an adulterous relationship; 4) fearful girl in need of protection; 5) victim of male power; 6) hard, ruthless murderess; 7) mother-to-be; 8) sacrifice to law. Such a mode of characterisation,

needless to say, is in marked contrast to the consistent moral trajectory of the male. (Gledhill, 1980, p. 18)

Another way of characterising the *femme fatale* is as a 'spider woman' who captures her victims but also entraps herself:

> Norma Desmond in *Sunset Boulevard* is the most highly stylised 'spider woman' in all of film noir as she weaves a web to trap and finally destroy her young victim, but even as she visually dominates him, she is presented as caught... The huge house in which she controls camera movement and is constantly centre frame is also a hideous trap which requires from her the maintenance of the myth of her stardom: the contradiction between the reality and the myth pull her apart and finally drive her mad. (Place, 1980, p. 43)

Figure 4.3   Norma Desmond weaves a web to trap her young victim

It is worth noting now the argument that, in *film noir*, the mystery surrounding the crime is often overridden by the mystery surrounding the woman and the narrative can only display 'an inability... to cope fully with the woman-question' (Kuhn, 1982, p. 35). That is, the woman cannot be known; she cannot, in narrative terms, be resolved.

Villains

We have seen that the 'hard-boiled' hero can be psychotic and the heroine is often evil; so can villains be worse than these? Homophobic and xenophobic Hollywood was happy to type Joel Cairo and Kaspar Gutman, the villains of Huston's *The Maltese Falcon* (1941, a third film version of the novel), as homosexual and foreign. This is brilliantly shown by the *mise-en-scène* when Cairo is introduced: he is played by the wonderfully creepy German Peter Lorre who constantly rubs the top of his cane, a phallic symbol. Vince Stone, the 'heavy' in *The Big Heat*, showed no compunction about throwing boiling coffee into the *femme fatale's* face. *Noir* villains are both corrupt and vicious.

Setting

Although the city has always featured in crime fiction narratives, the city of the 'hard-boiled' novel, and *film noir* which followed, was very different. In nineteenth-century fiction the city was often a place of exotic adventure. However:

> When we step from the world of the classical detective formula into the milieu of the American hard-boiled story, the vision of the city is almost reversed. Instead of the new Arabian nights, we find empty modernity, corruption, and death. (Cawelti, 1976, p. 141)

The city in the 'hard-boiled' genre takes its cue from nineteenth-century melodrama (see below) where it was characterised as a dangerous place, particularly in comparison with the country. Like the gangster film, the settings are places where 'lowlifes' inhabit, such as seedy bars and nightclubs, cheap hotel rooms and precinct stations. Although the genre has associations with the gangster movies, it is distinct, as Ian Cameron states:

> the gangster movie dwells on [the city's] luxuries and spoils in a way which captures something of their allure; but in *film noir* the focus is on the seedy underside of the city: the casualties or crooks of capitalism. Where glamour and glitter are shown, there is typically a sense of alienation. (Walker, 1994, p. 30)

Not all *films noir* are set in the city: *The Postman Always Rings Twice* is set in the 'middle of nowhere' and Nicholas Ray's ambitious *On Dangerous Ground* (1952) starts, conventionally enough, in the city but when the protagonist, played by Robert Ryan, is sent into the countryside to assist in the investigation of a murder, he takes all of the neuroses of the city with him. Ray emphasised the division between the city and country by setting the latter part of the film in a snow-covered landscape: *film blanc*!

There is also a tendency for *noir* to eschew domestic settings in favour of the public so:

> For the hero a basic domestic ritual like eating is transferred from family to public eating place. Indeed, the lunch counter comes close to being one of the true icons of the form. (Dyer, 1993, p. 57)

This setting appears in the opening of *Detour* (referred to in Chapter 3) and emphasises the hero's desperate desire for the domestic bliss which he is already doomed never to have.

Contemporary 'hard-boiled' writers, such as Walter Mosely and James Ellroy (whose novels have been filmed as *Devil in a Blue Dress* (1995) and *L.A.Confidential* (1997) respectively), have set their narratives in the past. Mosely offered a 'black' take on the genre and Ellroy uses actual criminal cases to comment upon the ideological situation of the 1940s and 50s in USA.

Crime writing in the nineteenth century was characterised by what John Cawelti (1976) calls the 'classical detective story', as defined by Edgar Allan Poe – see earlier in the chapter. The genre celebrated the sleuth, the man (female in the case of Miss Marple, Agatha Christie's twentieth-century extension of the genre) who, through power of intellect, reconstructs the story to reveal it in the plot. It is possible that the 'hard-boiled' development of the crime genre, in the 1920s, was a response to the social upheavals of the time, which also spawned 'modernism' (see Chapter 2). David Glover has shown how this development had more in common with already existing masculine forms, such as the Western, than the traditional crime characters of Sherlock Holmes and his ilk:

> Manliness was equated here with action, speed, combat, confrontation and pursuit, and intelligence was conceived as essentially practical, mental alertness rather than intellectualism. (Glover, 1989, p. 73)

This suggests that 'hard-boiled' fiction is a particularly twentieth-century genre and, of course, *film noir* could not exist before the twentieth century. It is a modern genre dealing with alienation in contemporary society.

Iconography

While all media can use generic iconography, it is more influential in the creation of meaning in image-based texts. The 'hard-boiled' detective novel does have iconography in a conventional sense, including rainfall, guns and:

> Iconographically, the two most visually distinctive *noir* figures are the *femme fatale*, glamorously dressed in revealing gowns and coolly enigmatic, and the private eye, sloppily dressed in trench-coat and fedora, and suitably hard-boiled. (Cameron, 1994, p. 32)

However, the most obvious visual trademark of *film noir* is its expressionist style, characterised by chiaroscuro lighting (extremes of light and dark in the same frame) and unusual camera angles. The conventional lighting style of key, fill and back lighting was is often altered in *film noir* where the fill light is omitted creating deep pools of shadow; this is called low-key lighting.

> Strange highlights are introduced, often on the faces of the sinister or demented. The key light may be moved behind and to one side of the actor and is then called the 'kick light'. Or it can be moved below or high above the characters to create unnatural shadows and strange facial expressions. (Place, 1976, p. 328)

This style of lighting helps to define both characters and setting: the lighting of the female lead in traditional films uses a filter to diffuse the light and create a 'soft' beauty; *noir* lighting, in contrast, creates a hard, statuesque surface that seems more seductive but less attainable. The creation of dark pools of shadow obscures the setting creating a sense of threat and mystery.

Film noir is also characterised by an anti-traditional *mise-en-scène* that, rather than striving for balance, attempts to be disruptive and unnerving. Compositional framing devices such as the use of doors, windows, stairways, metal bed-frames and shadows create a claustrophobic and paranoid effect through which the nihilism and despair of the *noir* narrative world can be represented. Directors will often use an *extreme* high-angle shot to emphasise the oppression of characters within the frame. The conventional, horizontal eye-level shot is often eschewed in favour of bizarre angles and tilts and establishing shots are often withheld in order to increase audience disorientation. Mirrors are also used to create an unsettling composition (discussed below in 'Narrative and theme').

Wide-angle lenses also create a disturbing *mise-en-scène*:

> [they] have certain distorting characteristics... As face or objects come closer to the wide lens they tend to bulge outward... This effect is often used in *noir* films on close-ups of porcine gangsters or politicians, or to intensify the look of terror on the hero's face as the forces of fate close in upon him. (ibid., p. 331)

As was stated earlier, much of this expressionist influence came from German directors fleeing Nazism. They, and others, were able to break the rules of Hollywood convention because *films noir* were usually 'B' movies and thus under less producer control (Kerr, 1979). The necessity for rapid filming, another consequence of their 'B' status, meant directors had little opportunity of numerous 'set-ups' and the long-take was often a necessity. However, these limitations often led to experimentation, particularly with deep-focus photography where both the foreground and background can be clearly seen. In contrast, the use of real locations gave many *films noir* a documentary feel which was probably a consequence of the experience many directors had filming propaganda shorts during the war. The bank hold-up in *Gun Crazy* is a classic example of the use of a realist aesthetic (it was filmed 'live' in one take and improvised) in a highly stylised genre.

Modern *films noir*, inevitably, are in colour; but what is the colour of *noir*? Scorsese suggested red in *Taxi Driver* (1976), Kathryn Bigelow used blue in *Blue Steel* (1989) and David Fincher used brown in *Se7en*.

It is the predominance of the *noir* visual style that has led some commentators (for example Place, 1980) to suggest that *film noir* is not a genre but a visual style or film movement (like Soviet Social Realism and Italian neo-Realism). This argument suggests that because other genres use the *noir* visual style, *film noir* is not a genre as its key characteristic is not specific to it. Examples of films that use the style of *film noir* include Westerns such *as Rancho Notorious* (directed by Fritz Lang) and *Johnny Guitar* (Nick Ray, who also made the classic *noir In a Lonely Place*, 1950) and 'Women's pictures', or melodramas, such as *Mildred Pierce* (1945). Another of Place's arguments is that *noir* is not a genre but a 'Film movement [because it] occur[s] in specific historical periods... [and] Genres... exist through time' (Place, 1980, p. 37) refers to the classic *noir* period of

1941–58. However, this argument has been compromised in recent years by the spate of neo-*noirs* which appear to have extended the life of the movement into another era.

An interesting test case of whether *film noir* is a visual style or not is *The Big Sleep* (1946). It is routinely classified as a 'classic *noir*': it features a 'lone wolf' hero, Philip Marlowe (played by Humphrey Bogart); deals with corruption (blackmail, murder and pornography); has a convoluted plot (even the writer, Raymond Chandler, was reputed not to know who killed the chauffeur); has a character with *femme fatale* characteristics in the nymphomaniac (Carmen Sternwood). However, the hero never comes close to being seduced by the *femme* and the conclusion (probably) sees the normal heterosexual order restored (Marlowe gets the girl, Vivien Rutledge, played by Lauren Bacall) and the bad guys get their just desserts. Most tellingly, however, the film is shot in director Howard Hawk's typically anonymous style: '[a] cool, objective, classical style, [with] editing and camera-movement strictly functional' (Wood, 1981, p. 170). The lighting is used merely to illuminate the scene, the *mise-en-scène* and camera movement primarily mediate action; none are used particularly expressively. So is it a *film noir*?

For me, a film is not *noir* unless it uses the genre's lighting style; however, this is not to reduce *film noir* to being simply a style, or a movement. Films which use *noir's* expressionist style in another genre, like the Westerns cited above, become 'films shot in the style of *noir*' and remain – in this instance – Westerns. The visual style is integral to *film noir* but does not define it; the types of narrative, setting and characters are also important. *Noir*, then, is like melodrama (see below): it exists both as a style and a genre.

Narrative and theme

In the consideration of the 'hero' it has already been noted that among the themes of *film noir*, and its 'hard-boiled' source material, is the uncertain morality of the modern world: the protagonists may take Propp's 'hero' function but that does not mean that they are 'good'; as a fairy tale of the urban world, the genre only offers a nihilist view. This ambiguity of identity is often made concrete with the narrative device of mistaken identity and the use of mirrors in the *mise-en-scène*. Colin McArthur notes how the mirror is used iconographically in *The Big Heat* and the *femme fatale's* deception is visually signed:

Debby's allegiance to Vince Stone begins to shift to Bannion. The fact that she becomes 'two-faced' is graphically and terrifyingly rendered in the succeeding scene in which Stone, questioning her about her involvement with Bannion, throws the boiling coffee in her face. (McArthur, 1992, p. 69)

The mirror signifies the *femme fatale*'s duplicity and narcissism. The famous 'hall of mirrors' shoot-out in Orson Welles' *The Lady from Shanghai* makes concrete the shattering both of the bodies and the protagonist's illusion about the *femme fatale*, Elsa Bannister.

Two sources of audience disorientation are the uses of the narrative devices flashbacks and voice-overs. Flashbacks function to fragment, to a greater or lesser degree, the plot. In some films, like *The Killers* (1946), the large number of flashbacks told by different characters (one flashback is 'told' by a newspaper story) create a labyrinthine narrative structure. This is one way in which *noir* creates its trademark convoluted narratives. Voice-overs can be expected to anchor the meaning of the narrative. However, questions are often raised about the reliability of the narrator:

Voice-over(s) may seem to involve us with the experience of the protagonist, but it is experience recollected and the account inevitably removes us from the events themselves. Our access to events is filtered through the act of story-telling... Flashback further emphasises our distance from events. In these films we also tend to know from the outset, at least in part, what the outcome of the past events has been for the protagonist. (Pye, 1994, p. 99)

The audience's knowledge, at the start of the plot, of the protagonist's (often bad) end fuels the fatalism that frequently infuses the *noir* world. In an extreme case, *Sunset Boulevard* (1950), the movie opens with a voice-over stating that the body lying face-down in the swimming pool is *his*! The use of an unreliable voice-over is likely to have had Germanic origins:

it seems likely... the idea of Al's narration in *Detour* was arrived at by way of the concept of 'secondary revision'. Sigmund Freud argues that our recollection of the past is governed by a mechanism of unconscious censorship, such that memories of events which we find too distressing to acknowledge are either repressed completely or reworked by fantasy so as to eliminate their potentially traumatic elements. (Britton, 1992, p. 177)

Figure 4.4   The shattering of the protagonist's illusion about the femme fatale

Other typical narratives involve the pursuit of a missing object (*The Maltese Falcon* and *Kiss Me Deadly*); centre on the elusive *femme fatale* (*Laura*, *Gilda* and *Out of the Past*); or focus on gangsters (*The Big Heat* and *The Big Combo*, 1954). One other characteristic is the multitude of victims that litter the plot; Chandler commented upon this when he argued that Dashiel Hammett gave crime back to the working classes:

> Hammett gave murder back to the kind of people that commit it for reasons, not just to provide a corpse... He put these people down on paper as they are, and he made them talk and think in the language they customarily used for these purposes. (Chandler quoted in Cawelti, 1976, p. 163)

This working-class 'streetwise' aesthetic is evident in the style of the 'hard-boiled' novel.

As a postscript to this descriptive of typical generic narratives it is worth distinguishing the 'whodunit', which was described in narrative terms in Chapter 1, where the plot was concerned with 'exposing' the story, from the 'hard-boiled' detective narrative where:

> there is no story to be guessed; and there is no mystery, in the sense that it was present in the whodunit. But the reader's interest is not thereby diminished; we realize here that two entirely different forms of interest exist. The first can be called *curiosity*; it proceeds from effect to cause: starting from a certain effect (a corpse and certain clues) we must find this cause (the culprit and his motive. The second form is *suspense*, and here the movement is from cause to effect: we are first shown the causes, the initial *donneés* (gangsters preparing a heist), and our interest is sustained by the expectation of what will happen, that is certain effects (corpses, crimes, fights). (Todorov, 1988, p. 161)

Our original definition of narrative was as a 'cause–effect' chain and we saw how a whodunit made this chain explicit; Todorov demonstrates that the 'hard-boiled' novel moves both ways in the chain.

Style

The style of *film noir* has already been considered under iconography and while the prose style of the 'hard-boiled' novel is varied, it is unified by its 'streetwise' flavour which manifests itself in different ways. Hammett, for instance, uses a straightforward, 'objective' style:

Green dice rolled across the green table, struck the rim together, and bounced back. One stopped short holding six white spots in two equal rows uppermost. The other tumbled out to the centre of the table and came to rest with a single spot on top. (*The Glass Key*, Hammett, 1982, p. 11)

In Hammett the 'street' is evident in his subject matter. The close attention to detail with which the fall of crap dice is described elevates their movement to a plane of significance; it is not the mere tumble of dice, much depends upon where they fall. As Cawelti says:

Its impact derives not from figurative and emotional language but from the collision between flat, emotionally empty, but extremely lucid prose and the striking events and characters it describes. (Cawelti, 1976, p. 174)

Chandler, on the other hand, is much more 'poetic':

A man was looking up at the sign too. He was looking up at the dusty windows with a sort of ecstatic fixity of expression, like a hunky immigrant catching his first sight of the Statue of Liberty. He was a big man but not more than six feet five inches tall and not wider than a beer truck. He was about ten feet away from me. (*Farewell, My Lovely*, Chandler, 1975, p. 145)

Chandler wished to escape the pulp trappings of the genre and gain intellectual respectability, however the use of the 'beer truck' to indicate the size of the character, Moose Malloy, emphasises the 'street' perspective. His prose reflects the narrative voice of Marlowe, sardonic, cynical and bitter; the characteristic use of hyperbole make his books a delight to read.

Modern 'hard-boiled' writers continue this trend, for example in James Ellroy's *The Big Nowhere*:

Danny stood up, pissed at being patronized by a flunky harness bull. Not talking made the stiff sucker-punch him; his legs were rubber and his stomach was flip-flops. He flashed five-cell at the ground surrounding the dead man, saw that it had been thoroughly trampled by LAPD-issue brogans and that the prowl cars had obliterated any possibly tire tracks. (Ellroy, 1994, p. 2)

The use of the cops' vernacular ('flunky harness bull', 'sucker-punch', 'five-cell') is an expressive informing the reader that the narrator is street-wise; there is also, in the extract, Chandler's – as the addresser – sarcasm.

Figure 4.5 Comradeship is an essential ingredient of TV cop programmes

This has certainly not meant to have been an exhaustive survey of the genre; of course it is debateable whether it is valid to equate *film noir* and 'hard-boiled' detective fiction, although they are clearly similar. One final point concerns the use of French words in the critical discourse: the term *femme fatale* certainly sounds better than the 'fatal female' but the reason French terms are used is because French critics 'invented' the genre by noticing how a large number of apparently disparate 1940s 'B' movies had common elements. This perception arose when a large number of Hollywood films were screened in Paris at the end of the Second World War. One of the obvious similarities between the films was the expressionist visual style and the use of 'hard-boiled' source material which was published in France under the moniker *serie noir*.

4.6 The TV cop genre: *NYPD Blue* – oppositions in genre

The cop genre is one of the most popular genres on television. There are usually numerous programmes of the type broadcast at any one time and they often garner good ratings. Clearly part of the attraction will be opportunity to see action sequences and there is also the narrative pleasure, discussed above, offered by the solving of crimes. It is likely that, for many in the audience, the TV cop show gives much of our information about how the police actually operate, particularly as the realist aesthetic is often of prime importance in the representation of the narrative world. Part of this realism is signed by the seedy, naturalist, setting which many, particularly North American, contemporary TV cop programmes use; for example, *NYPD Blue*'s title sequence offers a montage of 'downtown' streets, a typical location where crime thrives and conditions are particularly difficult for the forces of 'law and order'.

This section will consider how genres are structured by oppositions: Geoffrey Hurd (1981) described seven oppositions that constitute the framework of television crime series. Although Hurd examined *The Sweeney*, a 1970s British cop series, Hurd's oppositions are applicable to contemporary television programmes such as *NYPD Blue*. The purpose of this section, then, is not to consider characters, setting, iconography and narrative but deal only with how the oppositions are articulated in *NYPD Blue*, focusing on the first ever episode, broadcast in North America in 1993. (The genre is also considered in Chapter 5.)

Narrative synopsis of episode one

Partners Kelly and Sipowicz are falling out over the latter's drinking problem and obsession with small-time gangster Alfonse Giardella. The episode opens with a judge throwing out Sipowicz's case, against Giardella, because it was clearly bogus. Kelly's wife is divorcing him and he is 'seduced' by Licalsi.

Sipowicz is suspended after assaulting Giardella. While taking solace from a prostitute, Sipowicz is shot by the gangster and left for dead; he is in a critical condition. Kelly, outraged, starts harassing Giardella's boss, Merino, in an attempt to get Giardella 'wiped out'. The episode concludes with the revelation that Licalsi is working for Merino and she is instructed to kill Kelly.

Hurd's oppositions

Police versus crime

Television programmes tend to concentrate on the police's role in apprehending criminals while neglecting the police force's repressive function in society (for example their role in monitoring pressure groups such as Greenpeace and Friends of the Earth).

NYPD Blue: The narrative disruptions in crime series are almost always caused by criminals (the 'villains); one exception was the early 1990s BBC serial *Between the Lines* which focused on police investigation of police misdemeanours – see Lacey 1998a). *NYPD Blue* conforms to this pattern with the generic characters of the gangsters (Merino is a Mafia type, complete with husky voice and emphasis on 'business'; which references *The Godfather*, 1971). However, *NYPD Blue* was unconventional in the beginning because it focused on the disruption caused by the main characters' disintegrating partnership; although it is not clear at this point that Sipowicz will be a main character in the series.

Law versus rule

The law is seen as an overriding moral embodiment of natural justice (that is, the bad 'guys' (villains) must pay, evil must be punished); the constraints, rules, which the police are under in their pursuit of justice, may be broken – it is the end result that is important. Switching medium for a moment, Clint Eastwood's *Dirty Harry* usually broke the rules in order to 'get his man'.

NYPD Blue: the episode opens with the failure of the law as Sipowicz's attempt to frame the obviously guilty Giardella (he is 'fat and leering' and his counsel is completely bald which are conventional ways of signing 'badness'). However, there is little doubt that this failure is temporary and Kelly spends much of the episode breaking the rules by interfering with Marino's operations.

Professionalism versus organisation

The hero is invariably characterised as a professional whose job is made harder by an 'organisation man'. The 'organisation man' is less interested in solving crime than maintaining his position within the hierarchy.

NYPD Blue: As is conventional, the lieutenant (a generic type) constantly tries to reign in both Sipowicz's and Kelly's attempts to get justice by circumventing the rules. However, there are two occasions where the lieutenant is seen to be in the right: (1) he takes Sipowicz 'off the street' and Kelly acknowledges this is the correct course of action by stating he will try and 'shape Sipowicz up'; (2) when Kelly barges in to see Merino he inadvertently knocks out the Organised Crime Squad's eavesdropping microphone.

Authority versus bureaucracy

The hero's authority is gained from her or his professionalism and not their position in the hierarchy. In many crime texts subordinates are shown to be better than their superiors.

NYPD Blue: most crime shows focus on the detective because their work is neither routine (at least in the world of television where the incessant form-filling of the modern cop is glossed over), unlike the uniformed cop nor desk-bound as it is for the managing hierarchy. Similarly, Internal Affairs, the police who investigate Sipowicz after he has 'roughed up' Giardella, are described as 'never been on the streets in their lives'.

Intuition versus technology

The 'hunch' is shown to be more affective than forensic science. Although 'forensics' can give vital clues, it is the intuitive way the hero uses the clues that leads to the apprehension of the villain.

NYPD Blue: when the lieutenant asks Kelly for a list of suspects Kelly simply writes one name: Giardella. He *knows* that Giardella is the guilty party and does not have need of procedure; forensics can be characterised as procedure.

Masses versus intellectuals

The policeman is shown to be a person with few intellectual airs but whose intuition is far superior to the expertise of, say, criminal psychologists. The Jimmy McGovern scripted serial *Cracker* (adapted as *Fitz* in North America) was notable for its hero being an intellectual, however this exception 'proves the rule'.

NYPD Blue: this opposition is not present in this episode.

Comradeship versus rank

Rank is unimportant to the hero, the most important relationships are defined by mutual respect, unlike the 'organisation man' who treasures his position in the hierarchy.

NYPD Blue: it transpires that Kelly had been 'carrying' Sipowicz for some time and Kelly's response to the shooting of his partner is typical: he will do anything to get even.

The application of these oppositions shows that *NYPD Blue* is a cop show; but we knew that already. Hurd's oppositions, however, are useful in defining and assessing how conventional a particular, generic, text is. While *NYPD Blue* is clearly a 'TV cop' programme it breaks the formula in two of the oppositions: the initial narrative disruption is Sipowicz's behaviour; his attempt to break the rules fails and both the central characters rail against bureaucracy, but are narratively shown to be in the wrong in this.

In addition, *NYPD Blue* offers variations in areas which Hurd's oppositions are not intended to cover, such as style. For example, the rapid editing within the same scene and use of handheld camera and telephoto lens gives an 'edgy' feeling to the *mise-en-scène*. The first episode also featured nudity and, for network North American television, graphic sex scenes. Producer Steve Bochco has a reputation for innovative television, he also produced *Hill Street Blues* and *Murder One*, and so we would expect him to put a spin on the generic conventions. Hurd's oppositions allow us to isolate what, if any, innovations the producer has introduced (although we should be careful not to draw too many conclusions from one episode).

Looking at the genre as a whole: what is the effect of privileging one of the oppositions above the other? As we saw in narrative, the assertion of one side of the opposition above the other is based upon ideological considerations; the same is true of genre. The 'TV cop show' hierarchy of oppositions celebrates the: police; law; professionalism; authority; intuition; masses; comradeship. However, the police are not just agents involved in solving or preventing crimes, they also have a repressive role in monitoring what governments define as 'subversive' groups. The lack of representations in the media of this activity helps contribute to society's lack of knowledge about this type of action. In addition, it is rare for the 'wrong villain' to be arrested and convicted in the world of TV cop series; although one episode of *Cracker* did feature the hero getting a confession to the murder of a child only to realise that the man was innocent and the killer was still at large. However, in Britain, numerous cases have recently come to light (and how many have not?) of the police breaking the rules to convict innocent people like the alleged IRA bombers, the Birmingham Six and the Guildford Four, who spent decades in jail before being released. Certainly the genre does emphasise the 'natural justice' involved in privileging the 'law' above 'rule' but the consequences of breaking rules are not often explored: how different would a series be if it showed the *negative* consequences of breaking the rules?

4.7 Science fiction – repertoire of elements and history

Science fiction (SF), in the late 1990s, has a peculiar status as a genre: it is at once very popular (witness numerous Hollywood blockbusters, *The X-Files* and its spin-offs) and ghettoised as a genre for 'anoraks'. SF is at the nexus of the 'high culture' versus 'low culture' debate; in North America it is recognised as Literature by many academics but is still treated contemptuously, in Britain at least, by the 'established' literary critics. Although written over 20 years ago, Terry Carr's description of the genre's reception still holds true:

> Seldom does a science fiction writer or reader meet with the once-familiar lift of a sophisticate's eyebrows, the tacit assumption that sf's themes are either crackpot or irrelevant. [But] We live in a world that has seen space travel, atomic power, television and myriad other science

fictional notions become everyday facts: the passage of time has brought vindication to those dreamy writers of thirty of forty years ago. (Carr, 1977, p. 9)

While the 'sophisticate' misses out on one of the most vibrant areas of literature, the mass audience (and this, of course, is the problem the 'sophisticate' has with all mass art, the fact that it is not elitist) has embraced books, computer games, television programmes and films. While SF literature has been popular for many years, television and Hollywood's attempts to exploit the genre have been more uncertain in their appeal. The cult TV series *Star Trek* had a rather precarious television existence in the 1960s, particularly when compared with the success of 'The Next Generation' spin-offs in the 1990s. *Star Trek 9* was released in 1998, however, the first was only made in 1979, ten years after the original series' demise, and only after the success of *Star Wars*. In 1997 four of the top 10, and eight of the top 20, 'worldwide' box office successes had at least some element of SF within them (*Screen International*, 19–25 December 1997. Box-office period: 29 November 1996 to 28 November 1997):

1. *The Lost World: Jurassic Park* $605m
2. *Men in Black* $533m
7. *Star Wars RE: 97* $255m
8. *The Fifth Element* $235m.

Among the top-rated television programmes was the aforementioned *The X-Files* (a movie version was released in 1998) with related 'cult' texts such as *Dark Skies* and *Millennium*; although these two failed to find a big enough audience to satisfy the North American networks. The fact a genre is *popular* is likely to suggest something about society at the time of this popularity just as, as we shall see in the following history of SF, certain themes predominate in different eras. When assessing the relationship between media texts and society it is easy to fall into the trap of drawing trite conclusions when, in fact, determining the actual affect society is having upon media production is exceptionally difficult, and may be impossible. That said, it is interesting to *speculate* what the effect might be: so why is SF popular outside its ghettoised position in the publishing world?

Since the end of the Cold War the stock 'commie' has no longer been a convincing villain (though the 1995 action movie *Crimson*

Tide resurrected the 'nuclear nightmare' scenario); one of the replacements for this 'sphere of action' was terrorists: Arabs in *True Lies* (1993) and disaffected military in *The Rock* (1995). SF, however, enables producers to jettison the need for a convincing scenario in which to situate the villain; in *Independence Day* (1996) an alien race bent on world domination is sufficient:

> 'It's politically incorrect to use any nationality for bad guys,' explained [director] Emmerich. Hence 'Aliens are the best movie villains since Nazis.' (Rogin, 1998, p. 15)

Although aliens are part of *The X-Files*, they are not constructed as the 'villain', this function was, initially, located in the 'smoking man'; as was discussed in Chapter 1, this type of programme, with its emphasis on conspiracy theories, may be tapping into a paranoia associated with an alienated populace who cannot find meaning in contemporary society. Jameson (1992) suggests this is a feature of postmodernism. This might be, as Chris Carter's production after *The X-Files, Millennium*, made explicit, an expression of *fin de siècle* at the end of the century.

In Hollywood, however, the reasons are probably also more prosaic. As Eco suggested (see Chapter 1) seriality is beloved of capitalism as it is one way of mass producing cultural products. In recent times 'SF in Hollywood' was sparked by the success of *Star Wars* in 1977 which spawned two sequels; the first of three prequels appeared in 1999. However Hollywood, and capitalist media industries in general, do not limit themselves to the seriality of the sequel; genres are often mobilised in the same way (genre as a marketing tool is examined in *Media Institutions and Audiences*) so the success of *Star Wars* was followed by *Close Encounters of the Third Kind* (1978), *Alien* (1979) and *E.T. – the Extraterrestrial* (1982). Although there were two high-profile SF movies produced in the early 1990s, *Total Recall* (1990) and *The Terminator: Judgment Day* (1991), the current boom in SF-related films began with the unexpected success of *Stargate* in 1994; the director Roland Emmerich and producer Dean Devlin followed up with *Independence Day*. For Hollywood, one success can create a cycle of generically related movies (see Chapter 5) and SF just happens to be the current favourite along with the ubiquitous 'action' movie (often the two are combined).

Although SF is popular in cinemas at the moment, this is probably less to do with the genre and more to do with Hollywood's current obsession with special effects/action movies. As we shall see in what follows, many of these movies can be described as 'non-genre SF'. The popularity of these films is merely due to audiences' desire to be amazed by the latest in computer-generated special effects and not because they deal with the central concerns of 'genre SF'; the use of these terms will be defined below.

Hollywood rarely markets SF films as SF: the marketing of *Judge Dredd*, for example, focused on the action elements, special effects and the presence of star Sylvester Stallone. While this, in part, reflects a contemporary trend in Hollywood of not marketing films generically but as events, it also is a recognition that SF literature is regarded as being outside the mainstream. If a big-budget Hollywood picture is perceived to be targeting a niche 'anorak' audience, it would mean commercial disaster.

The reasons why SF is ghettoised as a genre have been chronicled in Brian Aldiss's history, *Billion Year Spree*. Any history of a genre, even one as compressed and partial as the one below, should offer some insights into how the form relates to society. The repertoire of elements focuses upon contemporary generic conventions but these are likely to have been different in the past, so a knowledge of how the genre has developed is necessary to understand where it is now.

A history of SF

Genres, of course, are subject to history; that is to say that they are a product of particular societies at particular times. Some have argued that SF goes back to Greek myths, such as that of Icarus, or Shakespeare's *The Tempest*; even *The Epic of Gilgamesh* includes a 'fantastic' journey. However, to determine when SF began it is necessary to define the genre. In essence SF is about *now*, this can be a 'what if...' scenario or a narrative that deals with what it means to be human. Brian Aldiss offers a more academic definition:

> Science fiction is the search for a definition of man and his status in the universe which will stand in our advanced but confused state of knowledge (science). (Aldiss, 1973, p. 8)

From this definition Aldiss concludes that the first SF novel was *Frankenstein* (written by Mary Shelley) which was published in 1818. Aldiss suggests that the scientific developments of the Industrial

Revolution made the period germane to the gestation of SF. Unlike earlier texts that could lay claim to be SF, Shelley emphasised science rather than fantasy. Although Baron Frankenstein's attempt to create life was, and is, impossible, Shelley suggested it was a result of scientific experimentation rather than the magic wand.

In terms of dealing with humanity, *Frankenstein* articulates the life versus death binary opposition; as the film *Zardoz* (1973) suggested, without death we have no life. At first the monster is compared to Adam:

> The creature's career roughly parallels Adam's, with the vital exception of the missing Eve: he is first created, and then brought to full intellectual awareness of the world in which he lives – at which state, 'benevolence and generosity were ever present before me' (Chapter 15) – and then undergoes his version of the Fall, 'the spirit of revenge enkindled in my heart' (Chapter 16). (ibid., p. 27)

Frankenstein's monster is truly a pathetic creature who, in his own self-awareness, realises that he can never enjoy the happiness of humanity:

> Remember that I am thy creature; I ought to be thy Adam, but I am rather the fallen angel, whom thou drivest from joy for no misdeed. Everywhere I see bliss, from which I alone am irrevocably excluded. I was benevolent and good; misery made me a fiend. Make me happy, and I shall again be virtuous. (Shelley, 1968, p. 364)

Dr Frankenstein is playing god by creating life and the novel deals with 'the disintegration of society which follows man's arrogation of power. We see one perversion of the natural order leading to another' (Aldiss, 1973, p. 27). Berger has shown how the monster represents both life and death, because he is not the product of sexual intercourse but of dead bodies.

Because, unlike God, Frankenstein refuses to make a female companion for his creation the monster cannot become the new Adam, and thereby celebrate life, but is another Fallen Angel who revels in death. He kills his creator in a scene that was replayed a century and a half later in *Blade Runner*, a film dealt with later in the chapter.

Frankenstein is a Gothic novel, a genre that has elements in common with SF; in Chapter 3 we considered how narrative voice can be used to create the 'fantastic', a text where the amazing can happen but the laws of the 'natural world' are not broken because the narrative voice is distanced from us. Edgar Allan Poe also used the Gothic to explore the limits of what it is to be human. As Harold Beaver notes:

> All [Poe's] imaginary trips – by ship, balloon, laudanum, hypnosis – were aimed at setting the soul free from the demands of the body and so from restraints of normal perception; simultaneously releasing the mind from its own tomb, the prison of its endlessly inturned and ramifying nervous complexes. (Poe, 1976, p. xx)

Table 4.2

Life	Death
Creation (sex)	Destruction
Naturally born	Naturally die
Growth	Decay
Change	Permanence
Controlled by man (social animal)	Controlled by God (the soul)
Outside: light, air, sun	Inside: dark, putrid
Unitary: from an embryo	Decomposition
Feeling	Insensate

Source: Berger, 1992, p. 151

The questions raised by the mind:body duality, another binary opposition, is clearly important to Poe, who often deals in the 'inner space' of the mind. At the turn of the nineteenth century, Sigmund Freud's investigations into the human psyche suggested that many of the motivations for our behaviour are repressed and have their origins in the libido (sex drive). Gothic literature often deals with this repression and it found an audience for its particular view of the world in Victorian society. At a time when sex could not be discussed in 'polite company' the 'necking' antics of a certain Count Dracula (author, Bram Stoker) could be openly read because the sex was not explicit. The 'Gothic mould' is probably where SF and horror meet and some critics even suggest that SF is a branch of horror (Heyward, 1996). This is certainly true of texts like *Alien* (1979) but ignores the fact that, although both genres can deal with what it is to be human, SF bases its diegesis upon the scientific and not the metaphysical.

The mind:body duality of humanity was, and is, matched by a duality in society: the rich and the poor. Nineteenth-century literature was graced by a number of utopian visions which, when compared with the then current 'state of things', suggested the world was, in fact, a dystopia. Samuel Butler, in *Erewhon* (spell it backwards) (1872), described a future where machines controlled humans, a feeling probably not dissimilar to that experienced by the workers in the 'satanic mills' of Victorian England or the Chicago stockyards in the USA.

H.G. Wells, along with Frenchman Jules Verne, is often cited as the 'father of modern science fiction'. His first book, *The Time Machine*, was published in 1895. It is a first-person narration, once removed: the diegetic narrator tells us the Time Traveller's 'fantastic' tale with a hint, at the end, that it may be true. The protagonist journeys, in his machine, to a future where the cultured Eloi are eaten by the craven Morlocks. Wells' future is a perverse Darwinian view of what might happen if the rich continued to 'feed' off the poor. The middle classes evolve into effete and useless individuals; the workers mutate into sub-human monsters who cannot bear the light of day.

> The attitude of the book is complex: by virtue of their vestigial aptitudes for solving at least mechanical problems, the Morlocks possess in greater measure that self-reliance on which mankind had prided itself. Clearly neither alternative is acceptable, and the book becomes a potent plea for the whole of man, warning against the fragmentation of function and the isolation of class which the progressively mechanizing society of England was supporting. (Scholes and Rabkin, 1977, p. 202)

Although Wells was not the first to use the conceit of having the narrator travel into the future, his use of science (a *machine* is required) stamps him as an SF writer; in an earlier version of the device, Washington Irving's Rip van Winkle sleeps into the future.

Wells was a socialist and hence critical of the rampant capitalism that thrived in Victorian England. Brian Aldiss eulogises both Wells and Verne as they used the genre to analyse the human condition; however Aldiss vilifies Edgar Rice Burroughs, a contemporary of Wells, for trashing the genre as a respectable and literate vehicle. Wells' *Men Like Gods* is compared to Burroughs' *Pellucidar*, both published in 1923. Both are fantasies, both use people as symbols, both have their excitements. Yet their differences are many.

173

The fourth dimension is perhaps as unlikely as a hollow earth and Barn-staple's adventures no more probable than Innes'. However, Wells' fantasy device, the fourth dimension, serves merely to lead us to his utopia; the utopia is so much the thing, that the feasibility of the device which gets us there does not much matter, provided it is dealt with briefly and interest-ingly. On the other hand, Burroughs' Inner World is the whole story, and the narrative is largely taken up with the stones and arrows loosed there, and the fangs and claws bred there. (Aldiss, 1973, p. 157)

Here is an excellent example of the distinction between what is called 'genre SF' and 'non-genre SF' (Clute and Nicholls, 1993): the former deals with questions of humanity while the latter merely uses the trappings of the genre for an action-adventure narrative. It is potentially confusing to describe non-genre SF as belonging to the genre of SF. Alternatively we can call 'genre SF' 'hard SF', and non-genre, 'soft SF'. It was such 'pulp fiction' as Burroughs' which gave SF such a bad name in 'literate circles'; even as recently as the 1970s pulp magazines could be defined as:

Cheaply produced publications... the contents [of which] are almost exclu-sively by hack writers, working to a predetermined editorial formula tailored to appeal to readers of undeveloped intellect. (Ward, 1975, p. 432)

As we saw in the section on 'hard-boiled' fiction, in pulp there reside many masterpieces; however Burroughs was certainly guilty of helping to ghettoise SF. Despite Burroughs' influence, 'serious' writers continued to produce 'genre SF' in the early years of the century; Karel Capek (*R.U.R.*, 1920), Aldous Huxley (*Brave New World*, 1932) and Olaf Stapledon (*Star Maker*, 1937) among them. Of greater influence than these writers, however, was Hugo Gernsback who coined the phrase 'scientifiction' to define the particular brand of pulp he published in *Amazing Stories* from 1926. Gernsback accepted the Burroughs' inheritance which saw space as the new frontier and merely a setting for, what are essentially, Westerns or 'good guys versus bad guys' narratives. The yarns of E.E. 'Doc' Smith (his Lensman series for example) epitomise what came to be known as space opera:

The term 'space opera' is modeled on 'horse opera', a critical term for Western fiction. Space opera denotes those works which have the typical structures and plots of Westerns but use the settings and trappings of science fiction. (Scholes and Rabkin, 1977, p. 170)

174

Probably the biggest space opera of them all, in terms of audience, is *Star Wars* (1977, RE 1997) which director George Lucas acknowledged as being a 'Western in space' with the reference, when Luke returns home to find his parents murdered, to the 1956 film *The Searchers*.

While Aldiss concedes the yarn-spinning capabilities of the pulp writers he believes their brand of 'non-genre SF' tarnished the literary credentials of the genre so now the only SF literary texts that are treated with any critical respect are those by established writers; that is, writers who have proven they can also write mainstream novels (such as J.G. Ballard and Iain Banks). Aldiss provides an excellent description of the pulp writer's task and how genre was germane to it:

> It must have been a painful experience to write for the pulps in the thirties. One had to conform to formula or get out. There was not sort of cultural tradition or precedent to appeal to. Low rates of pay engendered much hack-work. (Aldiss, 1973, p. 220)

For Aldiss, J.W. Campbell and his *Astounding* magazine rode to the rescue in 1938. Campbell's writers, such as A.E. van Vogt, Robert Heinlein, Isaac Asimov and Theodore Sturgeon, offered an antidote to trashy fantasy. If Campbell had a dominant ethos as an editor, other than a dislike of 'shoot 'em up' and 'splatter' narratives, it was that he liked his writers' speculations about the future to be based on technological development.

Take Asimov's 'Robotic' stories, for instance: he posits a future where robots become an integral part of society. The series of short stories do not simply speculate about what life would be like in such a society but use the robot, in a quintessentially SF manner, to pose questions about what it is to be human. The stories are prefaced by an extract from a 'Handbook of Robotics, 56th Edition, 2058 AD':

The Three Laws of Robotics

1. A robot may not injure a human being, or, through inaction, allow a human being to come to harm.
2. A robot must obey the orders given it by human beings except where such orders would conflict with the First Law.
3. A robot must protect its own existence as long as such protection does not conflict with the First or Second Law. (Asimov, 1968, p. 8)

Heinlein constructed his 'future history' collection of short stories that dealt with different issues within one world; such as, in *Lifeline* (1939), what would happen if a machine could predict when we would die. Although Campbell's writers usually dealt with the potential benefits of technology, the post-Second World War era saw many SF writers become disillusioned with scientific and political developments. It was not just that technological development resulted in the nuclear bombing of Hiroshima and Nagasaki, there was also the schism between 'east' and 'west' which led to the Cold War.

Although the post-Holocaust narrative has always been important in SF (Mary Shelley wrote *The Last Man* in 1826), it was only after the use of the atom bomb that the destruction of humanity by humanity became possible. The aftermath of such a conflagration is usually portrayed as hellish where the few survivors cling on to the remnants of humanity: this can lead to a better society when the mistakes of the past have been learned as shown, albeit ambiguously, in George R. Stewart's *Earth Abides* (1949); or show humanity blindly lurching towards another apocalypse as in Walter Miller Jnr's *A Canticle for Leibowitz* (1959). George Orwell's dystopia *Nineteen Eighty-Four*, considered briefly at the beginning of Chapter 1, was also published at this time.

The Iron Curtain 'descended', presaging the start of the Cold War where two opposing political systems, communism and capitalism, accused each other of attempting to subvert their nation states. Eastern Europe was split from the west by a line through Germany (which was itself divided between East and West) and the Austrian–Czechoslovakian (as it was then) border. The east was considered to be part of the Soviet (Russian) bloc. This 'border' was called an 'iron curtain' by Winston Churchill (the British Prime Minister during the Second World War) as it represented the split between so-called communist states and the capitalist states of the west. The threat of nuclear war was very real and this manifested itself, in North America, with the 'red scare' and the McCarthyite hearings (HUAC). Numerous people went to jail in the USA, the 'land of the free', because they were accused of being communists. This paranoia manifested itself in SF with 'body snatcher' narratives like Robert Heinlein's *The Puppet Masters* (1951).

In straight 'alien invasion' narratives the identity of the villain is obvious. In the 'body snatcher' variant humans are 'taken over' from 'within'. This reflected the right-wing obsession with communism which was represented as being an insidious credo surreptitiously taking over society. The possibility that 'the people' would embrace communism was not considered credible. The difficulty that conservatives had was that, unlike say black people, white communists looked like 'everybody else'. The 'body snatcher' neatly expressed this fear of 'the enemy within'; homosexuality was regarded as similar to communism for the same reasons.

Invasion of the Body Snatchers is probably the best known 'body snatcher' movie; the first version, made in 1956, was based on Jack Finney's story from 1954. Communism was represented, at the time, as a disease which turned all its adherents into emotionless automatons at the service of the state; in *Invasion of the Body Snatchers*:

> Drifting down from the sky, seed pods from outer space replicate human beings and replace them (as they sleep) with perfect, emotionless, vegetable doubles – thus successfully colonising the earth with the asexual outer-directed drones of a harmoniously single-minded society. (Hoberman, 1994, p. 29)

The script ended with hero, Dr Miles Bennell, ineffectually trying to convince everyone of the menace: 'There's no escape... not time to waste. Unless you do, you'll be next!' In typical Hollywood fashion, this 'unhappy' ending was changed and the FBI rode to the rescue.

Body Snatchers, however, is a particularly polysemic text: arguably it is satirising the paranoia associated with the 'red scare'; it could be mocking the stifling conformity of 'small town America'; the director, Don Siegel, even suggested that the aliens were Hollywood producers trying to 'take over' an individual's artistic expression! However, the large number of texts featuring 'aliens who look like humans' movies in evidence at the time, does suggest that they touched a chord with contemporary audiences.

Meanwhile, across the 'great pond', Britain was coming to terms, or *not* as the case probably was, with no longer being the 'world power' it had been before the Second World War. The British Empire was being dissolved and the USA was clearly the dominant western nation. It *could* be that the British penchant for disaster-based SF reflected the disillusionment engendered in the post-war period. Writers such as John Wyndham and, slightly less so, John Christopher produced, what Brian Aldiss has dubbed, the 'cosy catastrophe':

> The essence of cosy catastrophe is that the hero should have a pretty good time (a girl, free suites at the Savoy, automobiles for the taking) while everyone else is dying off. (Aldiss, 1973, p. 294)

Wyndham's alien invaders were not 'body snatchers' but plants in *The Day of the Triffids* (1951) and sea-monster creatures from Jupiter (or Saturn) in *The Kraken Wakes* (1953); however post-nuclear apocalypse did feature in *The Chrysalids* (1955), and *The Midwich Cuckoos* (1957) had the women in a village impregnated by aliens. J.G. Ballard's disasters were obvious from the titles: *The Wind from Nowhere* (1962), *The Drowned World* (1962), *The Drought* (1965) and *The Crystal World* (1966).

From 1957 onwards SF had a different relationship with reality; that was the year of Sputnik, the Soviet spaceship, which was the first human-made artefact to orbit the earth. In 1961, Yuri Gargarin, also Soviet, became the first person in space.

Apologies are due, in this potted history, for the apparent convenience of how trends seem to fit into decades; obviously they do not. However, the details must fit in the 'pot' so the 1960s saw the development of New Wave SF; the term was derived from film, the French *nouvelle vague*. This signified a break with traditional 'genre SF' and was associated with the inner space and the near future. Neither of these themes were new, Edgar Allan Poe had explored inner space in the first part of the nineteenth century (see *The Tell-Tale Heart*), but New Wave SF also reflected the liberalism (or libertarianism in the case of Robert Heinlein) of the 1960s in its treatment of sexuality and drugs. J.G. Ballard was one of the best writers to emerge from this period, his short story 'Track 12' has a man's identity drowning in the magnified sound of his adulterous kiss. The New Wave also:

> introduced a tone of knowingness and literary sophistication, with an almost obligatory commitment to formal experiment. The much-publicized cultural innovations of the 1960s, from the wave of psychedelic drugs and alternative life-styles to the Tolkien cult of the fantastic, 'postmodernist' fictional mode of novelists such as John Barth, Richard Brautigan, and Thomas Pynchon, all contributed to the sense that experience as a whole was becoming 'science-fictional' (Parrinder, 1980, p. 17)

The population explosion of the time was dealt with in such novels as John Brunner's *Stand on Zanzibar* (1968) and Harry Harrison's *Make Room! Make Room!* (1966). Philip K. Dick, one of the most significant writers of the twentieth century, also emerged in the 1960s; although he had been publishing since the mid-1950s. *The Man in the High Castle* (1962) is an alternative-world narrative where the axis powers (Germany and Japan) won the Second World War. *Do Androids Dream of Electric Sheep?* (1968), later filmed as *Blade Runner*, was a dystopian nightmare where, typical of Dick, the characters, and readers, are not sure what is meant to be reality within the novel. In *The Three Stigmata of Palmer Eldritch* (1965) Martian colonists use a drug to make life bearable but this is superseded by Palmer Eldritch's drug which dispenses with reality all together.

In the 1970s, SF began to gain some academic respectability in Britain; Ian Watson taught one of the first SF courses at Birmingham Polytechnic. During this decade he also produced a series of intellectually challenging novels such as *The Jonah Kit* (1975) and *The Martian Inca* (1977). *The Embedding* (1973), for instance:

> Through a complex tripartite plot… engages in a searching analysis of the nature of communication through language; the Whorfian hypothesis that languages shape our perception of reality… is bracingly embodied in at least two of the subplots: one describing a cruel experiment in which children are taught only an artificial language, and the other showing the aliens' attempt to understand *Homo sapiens* through an analysis of our modes of communication. (Clute and Nicholls, 1993, p. 1302)

Probably the most far-reaching innovation in the genre in recent times has been the emergence of the sub-genre of cyberpunk:

> Cyberpunk literature has a very pessimistic view of the future, predicting the rise of multinational capitalistic corporations, and showing the negative effects the forthcoming new technologies may have on everyday human life. In the cyberpunk world technology and punk collide, bringing the technology down to the street level. (Patron-Saints/Gibson website, 1998)

It is, given the sub-genre's emphasis on information technology, appropriate that the above definition should have been 'downloaded' from the Internet. Cyberpunk will be investigated later in the chapter with *Blade Runner*.

Having looked at the history of SF, what follows is a consideration of the current repertoire of elements. Although what is offered below is intended to be useful as a guide to what helps define SF as a genre (what is Aldiss' 'characteristically cast in the Gothic or post-Gothic mould') it should not be regarded as prescriptive. Like Propp's morphology, it is meant only to be used as a framework and not a legal document. Some critics suggest such attempts at definition are bound to fail:

Abstract conceptualisations of science fiction rooted in the search for common textual conventions or iconographic typologies are doomed either to vacuousness or bizarre proscriptiveness. (Longhurst, 1989a, p. 193)

However, as SF does exist as a genre there must be some common elements that exist outside Longhurst's vacuum.

Characters

Human generic types, in science fiction, are few: possibly only the 'mad scientist' and the 'practical engineer'. The scientist's madness does not have to be clinical, it may express her or his visionary status.

Exercise 4.4

Describe or draw your idea of the 'mad scientist'.

These scientists can be good (*Back to the Future's* Dr Emmett Brown, 1985), misguided (Mary Shelly's Baron Frankenstein) or bad (Felix Hoenikker in Kurt Vonnegut's *Cat's Cradle*, 1963). The character is important to 'genre SF' because she or he is the narrative agent (helper, hero or villain) who provides the innovative science which can overcome, or cause, the narrative disruption.

Related to the scientist was the 'practical engineer':

As pulp sf matured there was a significant shift in the characterization of the scientist hero. Especially in *Astounding Science Fiction*, the role of the theoretical genius was de-emphasized relative to that of the practical-minded engineer; archetypal example of this species were the personnel of George O. Smith's *Venus Equilateral* (1947), forever scribbling equations and designs on the tablecloths in Joe's Bar. (Clute and Nicholls, 1993, p. 1077)

Like many genres, SF has the 'man of action' (to resolve narrative conflict); and while women often fulfil the function of the princess they may at least be granted intellectual credibility by being cast as a scientist. Occasionally she is the daughter of the 'mad scientist'.

Aliens can be described as characters because if one is present in a narrative, the text is certain, at least, to have SF elements (1970s sitcom *Mork and Mindy* is a possible exception). However, aliens cannot be characters, in the traditional sense, because they are not human. They do, however, often represent repressed human desires; a repression that is described in psychoanalytical discourse as the Other. It is possible that human beings can never truly comprehend an alien mind as its way of seeing is likely to be profoundly different to our own. Clearly any human creation of an alien can only reflect the human psyche and so what often emerges is something that is conceived as being 'other' to what we are, something which is normally repressed from normal discourse.

Exercise 4.5

Create, in any form you wish, your own idea of an alien being.

You may have found that your starting point in creating an alien was to have thought of something that is 'non-human'. One way of doing this is to consider what is the opposite of 'humanity', however this opposite can only be expressed and comprehended in human terms. Hence a description of an alien is likely to reflect the repressed thoughts and desires in our minds: they appear to be 'non-human' because we have disavowed them. Another possibility is that 'your' alien is similar to ones created in other texts. Like all genres, intertextuality is one of the prime ways in which meanings are created in SF.

Annette Kuhn described Margaret Tarratt's Freudian theory on aliens:

> Aliens and extraterrestrial forces... are actually externalizations of civilization's conflict with the primitive unconscious, the Id; and many of these science fiction monsters are disguised representation of repressed sexual desires. (Kuhn, 1990, p. 92)

Another way in which the Other manifests itself is as the 'feminine': female sexuality is represented as monstrous and therefore in need of male control:

> The archaic mother – constructed as a negative force – is represented in her phantasmagoric aspects in many horror texts, particularly the science fiction horror film. We see her as the gaping, cannibalistic bird's mouth in *The Giant Claw*; the terrifying spider of *The Incredible Shrinking Man*; the toothed vagina/womb of *Jaws*; and the fleshy, pulsating, womb of *The Thing* and the *Poltergeist*. (Creed, 1990, pp. 135–6)

While Creed's idea fits with the definition of SF as a genre that deals with 'what it means to be human', it also makes clear that, inevitably, the definitions of what it means to be human, in this case femininity, are ideological. Female sexuality is thus represented as

'monstrous' in order to justify the repression of women in patriarchal society. See Chapter 5 for a consideration of how horror films
express the same ideological conflicts.

Stanislaw Lem, in *Solaris* (1961/1973), created an alien sea that
covered the eponymous planet; humans, in orbit, studied the creature. However, they find themselves to be the object of study as, in
an apparent attempt to communicate with, and understand,
humanity, the planet makes flesh the scientists' deepest desires and
fantasies. In the case of the protagonist, Kelvin, this manifests itself
in the resurrection of his recently deceased, young, wife. The consequences of the materialisation of their deepest desires are such that,
Lem suggests, we are better off without them. *Solaris* was filmed in
1972 and directed by Andrei Tarkovsky.

One of the most significant SF writers, Ursula Le Guin, has also
created convincing aliens: in *The Word for World is Forest* (1972),
when one of the alien characters is about to die it expresses curiosity
about what is going to happen next; in *The Left Hand of Darkness*
(1969), probably her most famous novel, the aliens are androgynes
(can be either male or female). More recently, Mary Doria Russell
received plaudits for her alien creations in *The Sparrow* (1997).

It is possible that texts in which aliens are not articulating the
Other but are used *simply* as a narrative villain, as in *Independence
Day* (1996), are 'non-genre SF'.

Other non-human characters in SF are robots, androids and
cyborgs: robots are machines that can do the work of humans;
androids are robots that look like humans (they may be indistin-
guishable); cyborgs are part-machine, part-human. Clearly, these
artificial beings are ideal objects with which to investigate notions
of humanity (see *Blade Runner* later in the chapter).

Prometheus, in Aeschylus' *Prometheus Bound* (approximately
463BC), steals fire from the gods and teaches humanity rudimentary
mental and manual skills and thus prevents Zeus, the top god,
fulfilling his plan to destroy human beings. A consequence of the
failure of Zeus' plan to create a more perfect race was that we are
left with our imperfections. SF narratives concerning the creation of
robots, androids or cyborgs can be seen as versions of the
Promethean myth with humans in the Promethean role; by creating
creatures we are 'playing with fire' (see the 'uncontrolled machine'
narrative below).

Many of these Promethean creatures are 'more than human' in
that they are superior to the flesh and blood version. This reflected

the need for beings that can withstand the heightened physical pressures of the modern city:

> The merely human body wasn't designed for the stresses and shocks of a mechanical world. The body had to be armoured against modernity. Superheroes appeared on the American industrial landscape in the 30s – the Man of Steel had the right stuff to exist in the Machine Age. As embodied by the new bodies of superheroes, robots or replicants, the 'utter helplessness of the human being' could be overcome – technological trauma produced its own antidote; or, as the poster for *Blade Runner* put it, 'Man had made his match...'. (Bukatman, 1997, p. 72)

In *Blade Runner*, the replicants (cyborgs) are physically better than humans but are treated as slaves.

Settings

Although numerous genres rely upon time, as well as space, to define their setting, SF is unique in the flexibility offered to both dimensions. SF settings can, literally, be anywhere anytime.

Time

- *Past* – time travel narratives (such as *Back to the Future*)
- *Present* – 'what if...?' scenarios such as, 'what if an alien was accidentally left on Earth when studying humanity?' (*ET – the Extraterrestrial*)
- *Future* – *Do Androids Dream of Electric Sheep?* by Philip K. Dick.

Time is also used to investigate paradoxes created by time travel: what if you travelled into the past and killed your father or mother, would you disappear in a puff of something? In *The Terminator* (1984) the time-loop paradox concerns John Connor sending Kyle Reece back in time to be his father; if he had not done so he would not have existed, so the future events cause the past events. Constance Penley (1990) suggests that there is a Freudian reason for the attraction of such time-loop paradoxes: the 'primal scene fantasy'. The 'primal scene' is the first time we see, or fantasise about, our parents having sexual intercourse; we are revisiting, in a way, the scene of our conception. This, Freud argued, is important in coming to terms with who we are. In *The Terminator*, the primal scene concerns John Connor who *chooses* his own father Kyle Reece. Reece is a contradictory figure:

> Kyle is the virile, hardened fighter barking orders to the terrified Sarah, but alternately he is presented as boyish, vulnerable, and considerably younger in appearance than her. His childishness is underscored by Sarah's increasingly maternal affection for him (bandaging his wounds, touching his scars), and in the love scene, he is the young man being initiated by the more experienced, older woman. Kyle is thus both the father of John Conner and, in his youth and inexperience, Sarah's son, John Conner. (Penley, 1990, p. 122)

The Terminator is certainly one of the most fascinating SF films; as Sean French (1996) suggests, John Conner's initials could represent Jesus Christ, they are both saviours of humankind, or that of the director, James Cameron, who also directed the *Terminator* sequel and SF movies *Aliens* (1986) and *The Abyss* (1989); he also scripted *Strange Days* (1995).

The primal scene was also visited, bizarrely, in Robert Heinlein's short story 'All You Zombies' where, with the aid of sex change operations, the central character contrives to be both his father and mother!

Space

While most people would associate 'outer space' with SF, the genre also investigates inner space. As was noted in the above history, Edgar Allan Poe explored the limits of humanity by investigating the minds of often deranged individuals. Philip K. Dick's *We Can Do Memories Wholesale* (1966), adapted in 1990 for cinema as *Total Recall*, plays upon the idea that if it were possible to implant memories then it would be impossible to tell the difference between what was real and false. The film *Fantastic Voyage* (1969) concerned a journey, by a crew in a submersible vehicle, through a scientist's bloodstream in order to destroy life-threatening brain damage.

Although outer space is a familiar SF setting, from 1957 onwards, when the Russians launched the first human-made satellite, the location was not exclusive to SF. The Oscar-winning *Apollo 13* (1995) is not SF at all; however, if a film using a similar scenario had been made in the 1950s, it would have been. This is a case of history catching up with the genre.

Outer space, of course, can consist of virtually anything a writer can imagine but usually consists of other planets and/or galaxies and 'deep space'. As technology has developed, a new space has opened up: cyberspace. This is virtual reality or the space created by information technology:

> whether presented as an actual physical space (*Tron*) or a metaphorical sense of space, like an extended, immersive computer interface (*Neuromancer*). (Bukatman, 1997, p. 45)

Unsurprisingly, given SF's genesis at the time of the Industrial Revolution, the city is a distinctive setting. The city, as a binary opposition, is contrasted with the countryside and while SF's utopias have often been agrarian, dystopias are invariably city-bound. We will examine *Blade Runner's* dystopia below; in 1927, Fritz Lang's *Metropolis* – to which *Blade Runner* owes conceptual debt – offered a visually stunning cityscape but the workers suffered working below the surface. Isaac Asimov's *The Caves of Steel*, one of his robot stories and featuring detective Lije Baley, created a future earth that is, virtually, totally city-bound:

> City culture meant optimum distribution of food, increasing utilization of yeasts and hydroponics. New York City spread over two thousand square miles and at the last census its population was well over twenty million…
>
> Each City became a semiautonomous unit economically all but self-sufficient. It could roof itself in, gird itself about, burrow itself under. It became a steel cave, a tremendous, self-contained cave of steel and concrete. (Asimov, 1958, p. 23)

By the 1980s, the emergence of cyberpunk offered a very different setting:

> The shift from the expansionist and visible machineries of the industrial age to the invisible technologies of the information age created a representational crisis for the genre. The purpose of much science fiction in the 80s, especially cyberpunk, was to construct a new position from which humans could interface with the global, yet hidden, realm of data circulation; a new identity to occupy the emerging electronic realm. (Bukatman, 1997, p. 46)

It is arguable that cyberspace allows a direct interaction between inner and outer space (defined as being outside the mind). Virtual reality represents the 'inner space' of technology, the chips as neurones, in three dimensions.

Iconography

Exercise 4.6

What objects do you associate with SF?

It should matter little whether or not you are a fan of the genre, it is likely that you have been able to create a list. This list below is not meant to be definitive:

- *ray-guns*: see the 1956 classic *Forbidden Planet* and *Star Wars* (1977)

- *synthesiser music*: exemplified by the use of the Theremin in *Forbidden Planet*; *Star Wars* emphasised its action-adventure credentials with a 'symphonic score'. Synthesisers connote the modern and, if the sounds are particularly bizarre, the weird

- *futuristic clothing*: a difficult one this as future fashions are, obviously, unknown. Luc Besson neatly side-stepped the problem by employing Jean-Luc Gaultier as designer in *The Fifth Element* (1997); clearly Gaultier's designs, like high-fashion in general, are 'out of this world' anyway. Of course what counts is whether the clothing connotes the future: for example, *Rollerball's* (1974) idea of the 'futuristic', while convincing at the time, already looks hopelessly dated. *Blade Runner* avoided the problem by having many of the characters dress up as if they belonged in a 1940s *film noir*

- *spaceships*: that is spaceships which do not look like those which actually exist. The appearance of the space shuttle in the James Bond movie *Moonraker* (1979) was clearly not an example of SF iconography

- *aliens*: at the time of writing these are clearly of fictional creation (unless you buy the Area 57 conspiracy stories). Conventions of what aliens should look like are totally influenced by fictional texts: for example, the large brain cavity of super-intelligent races (*Close Encounters of the Third Kind*, 1978 and many texts before) and the insect-like killing machine of the *Alien* franchise, reprised in *Independence Day*. In action-adventure, 'non-genre SF', insect aliens are characterised as 'bugs' and are merely fodder for splattering as in *Starship Troopers* (1997)

- *high-tech gloss*: computers with flashing lights and bleeping noises and technical environments which are very clean. This utopian view of the future is exemplified by *2001: A Space Odyssey* (1968).

One of the pleasures of *Alien* was the juxtaposition of high-tech gloss with the grotty and dirty parts of the spaceship

- *computer-generated special effects*: look at the credits of virtually any film and somebody is credited with special effects; however, one of the reasons that SF is a popular starting point for the current spate of action-adventure films is the genre offers a great opportunity to wow an audience with the latest computer-generated visions. Part of the success of *Star Wars* was due to the use of computer-*controlled* cameras for the multi-track filming; *The Abyss* (1989) was the first film to use the technique of morphing.

Narratives

- *first contact*: what might happen when the human race meets an alien race? While there have been occasional bouts of excitement about 'life on Mars' in recent years, 'first contact' narratives are not concerned with what happens when we meet a microbe. Usually the speculation centres on meeting an intellectually and technologically superior race which may want to destroy us or simply co-exist (for example *Last and First Men* by Olaf Stapledon (1930) and *The Star Beast* (1954) by Robert Heinlein, respectively).

- *exploration of space*: classically the *raison d'être* of the *Star Trek* (the sixties and 'next generation' series) which 'boldly went where no man (in the sixties) or person (in the nineties) had gone before'. These narratives, essentially, use space as a location of the new frontier: Westerns in space. *Star Trek* was originally conceived as a '*Wagon Train* (a popular Western series) in space'. Once the original space of the pioneers had disappeared, in 1890, Americans needed other ways to sustain the myth of the frontier. This myth conceived America: 'as a wide-open land of unlimited opportunity for the strong, ambitious, self-reliant individual to thrust his way to the top' (Slotkin, 1973, p. 5).

  The ideological basis of *Star Trek* is recognisably North American: a multiracial and multinational United Nations of the world promulgating the 'American way of life'; although Chekov did not appear until – apparently – the Russians complained about the absence of one of their number in the crew. Although *Star Trek* is 'genre SF', this narrative is also the staple of space opera: see above in the history dealing with Edgar Rice Burroughs.

Rushing and Frentz (1995), in a fascinating study, relate the myth of frontier to 'the cyborg hero in American film'. Showing how the staple myth of the hunter has become travestied to a point where the human hunter becomes the hunted, which manifests itself, in SF, as the 'uncontrolled machine' narrative.

- *the uncontrolled machine*: where a machine, usually a computer, created by humanity becomes more powerful than those who made it and decides to take over. Frederic Brown wrote many witty short stories including 'Answer' where all the computers of 96 billion planets were linked and the first question asked was 'Is there a God?' The answer: 'Yes, *now* there is a god' (Brown, 1977, p. 121). The uncontrolled machine also formed part of *The Terminator*'s scenario which, of course, is also an 'after a nuclear holocaust narrative'; a point which illustrates that these narratives are not mutually exclusive.

- *after a nuclear holocaust*: as suggested in the above history, the post-Second World War era spawned numerous texts which dealt with the aftermath of a nuclear war. John Wyndham's *The Chrysalids* (1955) dealt not only with splintered human society of the aftermath but religious fundamentalism and Darwinian evolution. It is in narratives such as these where the subversive aspect of the genre becomes apparent. The official line on nuclear war was quite sanguine (the British government issued a booklet, in the 1980s, called *Protect and Survive* which suggested hiding under a bed would protect the population from nuclear fallout); fans of SF knew that a nuclear war would mean the end of civilisation as we knew it.

- *time travel*: this narrative has already discussed in relation to Wells' *The Time Machine* and *The Terminator*. Stanislaw Lem's *The Star Diaries*, in a hilarious parody of the narrative, had hero Ijon Tichy stuck in a time loop. Ijon Tichys from different eras keep popping out of the loop resulting in the over-population of the spaceship and causing numerous arguments as none of the Tichys will cooperate with each other:

I really can't recall whether I was still the Sunday me, or had already turned into the Monday me. Not that it made any difference. The children sobbed that they were being squashed in the crowd, and called for their mommy; the chairman – the Tichy from next year – let out a string of curses, because the Wednesday me, who had crawled under the bed in a futile search for chocolate, bit him in the leg when he accidentally stepped on the latter's finger. I saw that all this would end badly, particularly now as here and there gray beards were turning up. Between the 142nd and 143rd vortices I passed around an attendance sheet, but afterwards it came to light that a large number of those present were cheating. (Lem, 1976, p. 17)

If you met yourself from another time would you co-operate? Would you want to give orders or take them?

- *alternative worlds*: narratives based on the premise that history developed differently from what has happened; for example, what if the Reformation never occurred? (see *Pavane* by Keith Roberts (1968) and Kingsley Amis's *The Alteration*, 1976). These narratives offer parallel universes, worlds that are very similar to our own and the differences between them make us consider our own reality. For instance, the above novels suggest what effect the Reformation *did* have on our society.

  The alternative world might also be based upon a particular cultural environment, such as Frank Herbert's *Dune* novels which create a civilisation based upon the premise that water is the most valuable commodity. Another type of alternative world might be utopia or, its opposite, a dystopia. Joanna Russ's *The Female Man* (1975) offers the former and Margaret Attwood the latter in *The Handmaid's Tale* (1985) (see Lacey, 1996).

- *doppelganger*: a narrative that centres on an alien being's, or a machine's, ability to mimic humanity exactly. The question that usually arises in such narratives is 'how can you tell the difference?' which therefore focuses on what it is to be human. In *Invasion of the Body Snatchers* (original version directed by Don Siegel in 1956; other versions were produced in 1978 and 1993), the film reached a climax when the 'hero' kissed his 'princess' to find her unresponsive and cold; she had been taken over. Emotion was what defined humanity in this text. In *The Thing*, the John Carpenter directed 1982 remake *of The Thing from Another World* (1951), the alien 'thing' managed to overcome this distinction to such an extent that the unemotional Nauls, who appears to have been 'taken over', turns out to have been human.

Loss of identity – and, more particularly, the individual's fear of being swallowed up by a faceless mass and becoming a drone – was a prime concern in 50s sci-fi movies, in which it was usually an allegory of the totalitarian political system. In subsequent decades such losses became more of an abstract concern, representing the fear of suiting up and 'selling out' as part of the rat race, the sacrifice of the soul in pursuit of riches or pleasure. (Billson, 1997, p. 64)

Humanity can be 'taken over' by materialist concerns or desires formed by contemporary, bourgeois, culture. For instance, in *The Stepford Wives* (1975) the men of a small North American town replaced their wives with androids because they were much more efficient and obedient.

The final part of this section considers a generic analysis of a single text. One of the most influential SF films of recent years is *Blade Runner* which has become a touchstone for the 'look' of futuristic SF films. For some, its adaptation of Philip K. Dick's original novel was a travesty; although Dick died before it was released he is reported to have liked it. *Blade Runner* articulates many of the themes of SF and spawned a new subgenre.

Blade Runner – the Director's Cut – single texts and genre

Blade Runner was originally released to general critical and audience incomprehension in 1982 and re-released in 1991 as a so-called director's cut. I will not recycle the tale of *Blade Runner*'s transformation from a big-budget box-office flop to one of the most written about cult movies but will consider how the film deals with various SF themes. It is also interesting, in terms of the history of SF, because the film was influential in the creation of cyberpunk:

> The purpose of much science fiction in the 80s, especially cyberpunk, was to construct a new position from which humans could interface with the global, yet hidden, realm of data circulation; a new identity to occupy the emerging electronic realm. (Bukatman, 1997, p. 45)

William Gibson, reputed inventor of cyberpunk with his novel *Neuromancer* (1984), has acknowledged *Blade Runner*'s influence upon his work. While the film is, undoubtedly, primarily SF it also has many elements of *film noir*: the 'hard-boiled' lone wolf character; a convoluted plot; a blurred distinction between the good and the bad; the suggestion of lives being controlled by conspiracy; an expressionist visual style and so on:

The link between noir and cyberpunk was neither superficial nor coincidental, but was connected to those 'intolerable spaces', once *urban* and now *cyber*. The task of narrating urban alienation and separation now fell to the hybrid of crime fiction and science fiction that was cyberpunk. (ibid. p. 51)

The only scene in which information technology is emphasised is when Deckard (a name similar to Descartes who defined humanity with the phrase, 'I think therefore I am') analyses photographs found in one of the replicant's (a cyborg) room. He slips the images into a scanner which then is voice-activated. Deckard intones instructions, 'enhance three to thirty-six, and back. Stop'; the scanner clatters like a camera taking photographs rapidly (a postmodern mix of old and new technology that characterises the film) as it zooms in on the requested area. The enhancement is massive as tiny parts of the image are blown-up beyond contemporary possibilities.

Deckard obviously spots something, signed by his intent expression, his leaning forward body posture and introduction of music, but what he has seen is not clear to the audience. He then instructs the enhancement of an area that is within a mirror (an iconographic object in *film noir*), peculiar light-bulb like objects appear and then, as Deckard asks for a 'track left', a sleeping body appears. At this moment, also we appear to be looking *behind* an object which, of course, is impossible in a two-dimensional image. Bukatman suggests this, and the representation of the city, reflects the 'new' mathematics of chaos theory:

The limitless complexity of the film suggests some precepts of chaos theory, which holds that chaotic systems are not random but complex, non-linear systems produced through massively repeated, simple operations. New dimensions lie between the dimensions of traditional mathematics: *fractal* dimensions. (ibid., p. 58)

This scene, however, is not simply an exploration of fractal space, it is a detective searching for clues. That the answer is found in technology, and not on the city streets, emphasises the proto-cyberpunk credentials of the film. The sleeping body appears (it does not quite look like her) to be Zhora, the snake woman whom Deckard then tracks down and kills. Although Deckard does not like killing replicants, he is blackmailed into doing the job, like *noir* heroes his moral position is slightly suspect. When Rachel visits him to show him photographs, evidence she thinks of her humanity, he brutally refuses to let her leave and, with the music connoting the 'sinister' and the lighting casting venetian blind lines across the scene, it looks as if he is going to rape her. He appears to be treating her like this because she is not human. He instructs her to say, 'kiss me' and 'I want you'; he is the personification of brutal masculine desire. However, the tension is dissipated when Rachel relents her opposition to Deckard because she desires him.

The play with 'a two-dimensional image which appears to be in three dimensions' also occurs later in the film when Deckard examines Rachel's photographs. These photos are given to replicants to help them use memory to cope with the emotions they develop through experience. One photograph suddenly *appears* to come alive, although as the 'live' image lasts for less than a second it is difficult to be certain that it moves. This scene emphasises that most people use photographs to capture their past and, as they grow older, they become more precious as memories pile up and fade. Indeed, it could be argued that our past existence is nothing more than what we can remember, and other people's memory of us.

Strange Days, the 1995 cyberpunk movie, takes this conceit a step further using the device of the S.Q.U.I.D. This is a recording device that enables the recording of experiences which can be played back. The central character, Lenny Nero, deals in black market 'squid' tapes which can give the recipient the *complete* experience of their own memories or someone else's. The film opens with an extreme close-up of an eye, similar to that at the beginning of *Blade Runner*; there are also ambient sounds that refer to the earlier film. *Strange Days* is an immensely ambitious movie, it attempts to articulate aiteral *fin de siècle* where an LAPD death squad kills a black leader and troops are constantly on the streets to maintain law and order. However, instead of the apocalypse that the narrative appears to be inevitably drawing us towards, we are left with a compromised ending (see Appendix 1).

Eyes are a central symbol in *Blade Runner*, they are, metaphorically, the 'window to the soul' and, for most people, the most important organs of perception. When Roy Batty is trying to discover how to lengthen his life he teases Chew (the manufacturer of cyborg eyes) with the line 'if only you had seen with your eyes what I have seen with your eyes'. This implied voyeurism also refers to cinema where audiences see with the camera's eye. When Deckard searches Zhora's dressing room he claims he is looking for eye-holes used by peeping Toms (the scene is an intertextual reference to *The Big Sleep* an, allegedly, classic *film noir*). During the opening sequence to the film we see the astonishing dystopic land-

Figure 4.6   *Blade Runner:* SF + *film noir* = cyberpunk

scape of Los Angeles for the first time; this is intercut with an extreme close-up – it fills the whole of the widescreen – of an eye. The flares that illuminate the dark panorama are reflected in the eye. This eye is disembodied: we can only assume it is Holden's waiting to interrogate Leon (see Appendix 1 of *Image and Representation*). This disembodiment suggests the eye represents an abstract image of cinema spectatorship; it is a way of putting the audience into the picture, as if it were part of the *mise-en-scène*. The film deals with what it is to be human and the audience is reminded that it is watching a text.

The eyes also offer a hint about whether Deckard is human or not. Throughout the film, the eyes of the cyborg characters reflect back light, like a cat's; Deckard's do not, except on one occasion. In keeping with the rest of the film the hint both illuminates and obscures the question about the status of the central character's humanity. Another 'eye reference' is the Voigt-Kampff text that measures the dilation of the pupil (offering another extreme close-up of an eye) caused by an emotional response; it appears to be a sophisticated lie detector.

> *Blade Runner* performs an ingenious variation on the definitions of humanity that dominated science fiction film in the 50s: *I Married a Monster from Outer Space*, *The Thing from Another World*, *Invaders from Mars* or *Invasion of the Body Snatchers*, humans simply have feelings while non-humans simply do not. *Blade Runner* denaturalises that division and subtly inverts it: *what has feelings is human*. (ibid., p. 69)

Deckard, as a killer of replicants, cannot afford to feel for them; this is inverted at the climax when Batty who, having sought immortality from his maker Tyrell (there are echoes of *Frankenstein* here), accepts his death and saves, because he *feels* for, the blade runner. The replicants, like Sebastian, suffer from 'accelerated decrepitude'; they only have four years to live, a fail-safe built in to prevent them becoming too human which suggests maybe we become more human as we grow older. They are, however, *better* than human; they are constructed to work 'off-world' in hostile environments. In the climactic scene there is no real contest between Deckard and Batty, it is completely one-sided, there would have been only one winner.

The city in *Blade Runner* is postmodern: it is full of waste and is a city in ruins. Postmodernism is characterised by borrowing material or recycling. This is most obviously present in the architecture:

recollections and quotations from the past are subcodes of a new synthesis. Roman and Greek columns provide a retro *mise-en-scène* for the city. Signs of classical Oriental mythology recur. Chinese dragons are revisited in neon lighting. A strong Egyptian element pervades the decor. The Tyrell corporation overlooks what resembles the Egyptian pyramids in a full sunset... Pastiches, as an aesthetic of quotation, incorporates dead styles; it attempts a recollection of the past, of memory, and of history. (Bruno, 1990, p. 187)

The Tyrell building itself was designed to 'be sort of Mayan pyramid with Art Deco detail' (Trumbell, 1995, p. 16); the 'Mayan temple' look is appropriate because it is associated with human sacrifice which gives an ironic spin to Tyrell's motto of 'more human than human'. Los Angeles is a melange of past and (prospective) future and if it is the end of history – which postmodernism suggests – then humanity has failed, we are to be left in a dystopia. There are no real animals left, only replications; the environment is an eco-nightmare. The battle between Batty and Deckard suggests humanity will go the way of the animals as it is outstripped by its superior creation. *Blade Runner* is a fascinating spin on the 'uncontrollable machine' narrative: the 'monsters' that Tyrell has produced deserve to live and they certainly are not likely to create a more inhospitable environment than that which humans produced.

With global warming a certainty, can we be sure that the ecological nightmare of *Blade Runner* is not our future? In 1999 the genre was still alive in Hollywood with the box office hit *The Matrix*.

SF film versus SF novels

While one of the strengths of genre as a tool for analysis is its ability to cut across media, there are also likely to be differences between how media use generic conventions. SF is, primarily, a literature genre, not only because that is where it originated, but the symbolic (in Peirce's terms) nature of language allows much greater flexibility of representation. This flexibility is required by SF because it is not primarily concerned with mimesis, the reproduction of reality. On the contrary, SF is anti-mimetic; it often deals with different realities whether they be set on different worlds or in different times. This is probably one reason (the 'non-genre SF' of Hugo Gernsback is the other) why SF was, and is in unenlightened circles, often treated as trivial. Because the central bourgeois aesthetic is realism, and SF appears to outsiders to be mainly fantasy, it is regarded as having no relevance to contemporary society. However, as we have seen, 'genre SF' is defined by its engagement with issues of what it means to be human; a project that could not be further from fantasy.

In recent years, however, the development of computer-generated special effects has narrowed the gap between what SF novelists can create on the page and the Hollywood technicians can magic into film. While the novel as a form is likely to remain best at representing the interior world of characters, it will become increasingly easy, if not as cheap, to adapt SF books for cinema as it is literature set in the contemporary world. Despite this, most contemporary SF movies are little different from those described by Susan Sontag over 30 years ago:

> Science fiction films are not about science. They are about disaster, which is one of the oldest subjects of art. In science films disaster is rarely viewed intensively; it is always extensive. It is a matter of quantity and ingenuity. (Sontag, 1979, p. 491)

Another institutional difference between film and literature is the degree to which texts are censored. Films tend, in the west, to be much more heavily censored than literature; while the former uses (Peirce's) icons (see section 2.3), the latter uses symbols. One effect of this is that graphic detail can be shown much more powerfully using images. Despite the fact that director David Cronenburg's version of *Crash* (1996) caused apoplexy in British Conservative politicians and the *Daily Mail*, the following details from the novel were not shown:

> I moved my mouth down his abdomen to his damp groin, marked with blood and semen, a faint odour of a woman's excrement clinging to the shaft of his penis. A zodiac of unforgotten collisions illuminated Vaughan's groin, and one by one I explore these scars with my lips. (Ballard, 1973, p. 201)

Although Ballard's reputation as a writer is in the field of SF, *Crash* is not a generic novel. However, this extract illustrates the point: can you imagine this scene being filmed outside the realms of pornography? The censor's hypersensitivity is not simply a consequence of the graphic nature of images: cinema tends to be more of a mass medium than literature and class prejudice suggests that texts which address a mass audience, one which will obviously include the working class, need to be more sanitised than those solely addressing the middle class.

One final reason for the 'uneasy' relationship between 'genre SF' and cinema is that science fiction thrives in the short-story form and these tend not to lend themselves for feature-length adaptation. Although Arthur C. Clarke's short story 'The Sentinel' did provide the inspiration for *2001: A Space Odyssey*, the latter was much more fully developed. Sadly, in Britain at least, SF remains critically ghettoised; but that is only sad for those who sneer at this 'pulp fiction'. What other genre offers such potentially entertaining texts and fascinating insights into who we, as humans, are?

4.8 Melodrama – a genre and a style

Unlike any other genre, except pornography, 'melodrama' is often used as a term of abuse. Melodrama refers to texts, like soap opera, that focus, in an exaggerated way, upon relationships in a domestic setting. However it is also a *style*, like *film noir* described above, that helps shape texts of other genres; this is particularly true of film and the theatre.

The Lumière brothers organised the first public film screening in Paris on December 28, 1895. Although these were essentially 'home movie' type presentations it was not long before melodrama and action, arguably the two generic roots of cinema, made their presence felt. The most popular type of theatre in the nineteenth century was melodrama, a form originally developed in the eighteenth century in opposition to the official, Patent, theatres:

> In 18th century England and France, royal patents granted, to two or three theatres, monopoly over the 'official' repertoire and the rights of censorship over all other forms of 'illegitimate' or 'Minor House' entertainment. (Gledhill, 1987a, p. 14)

In unofficial theatre, dialogue was banned and so a great emphasis was placed on actors' non-verbal communication and on the use of signs such as meteors, lightning, spectres, crosses in flames and rising tombs. Similarly, film was silent until the late 1920s (although screenings often included sound effects and usually had a musical accompaniment) and so the image had to carry the bulk of narrative development and characterisation. The melodramatic style of acting developed in the theatre, based on histrionic gesture, was an ideal form of expression for early film, as was the use of emblems.

In melodrama, theatrical *mise-en-scène* was created as if it was a painting, the proscenium arch became the frame that, in turn, became the model for the cinematic frame. Music, too, was integral; melodrama means 'music with drama'. Theatrical devices were developed that were also forerunners of cinema; for example the use of dissolves and fades, eliminating the curtain drop, to sign that shifts in time and/or space had taken place.

Melodrama often featured conflict between the bourgeois, or middle-class, family and the aristocracy. For example, narratives dealt with the battle to preserve a daughter's honour against the attentions of a corrupt aristocrat, exemplified by the eighteenth-century sentimental novel *Clarissa* by Richardson. This battle symbolised the desire for private conscience and individual rights against aristocratic dominance; these desires are still valued in modern society. Melodrama was, in its early years, a political weapon that asserted the rights of the burgeoning middle classes against the ruling aristocracy.

After the demise of the aristocracy as a powerful social force, melodrama moved from dealing with confrontation to assimilation. During the nineteenth century the family came increasingly under pressure as industrialisation forced the separation of work and home. Melodrama at this time dealt not with how things were but how they ought to have been, often evoking an 'Edenic' past of a home and family that centred on the mother.

It is unsurprising that many of the early fiction films should take their inspiration from theatre, the art form closest to cinema. Audiences were familiar with sitting in the theatre and so early films often consisted of a camera placed in the position of the stalls and the actors performed as if they were on a stage. There was, at first, no camera movement and no editing; however, cinema soon developed as a form:

> Technically the cinema solved the problems of the stage, and the verbal limitations of the novel, in their common search to realise the melodramatic imagination. (ibid., p. 27)

D.W. Griffith is credited as the director who created a mature film language for western cinema, a language that is still in use today. Griffith certainly didn't 'invent' many of the technical devices with which he has sometimes been credited; Edwin S. Porter, for example, used dissolves, cross-cutting, close-ups and camera movement in the early years of the century. However, Griffith's use of the devices was more sophisticated; they were not self-evident technical tricks but integral to the storytelling. A number of Griffith's greatest films, *Birth of a Nation* (1914), *Way Down East* (1920) and *Orphans of the Storm* (1921) were adapted from stage melodramas. Another melodrama, *Broken Blossoms* (1919), dealt with miscegenation but was atypical in that all the main characters die in the end. Griffith had to buy back the film from the studio in order to get it distributed and he marketed it as the first 'art' film.

The success of *The Jazz Singer* (1927) meant the end of 'silent' pictures and, it was argued, this would be the end of melodramatic cinema. As we shall see, this was not the case.

Early genre criticism focused on the, supposedly, masculine genres of action, particularly the epic of the Western and tragic heroes of gangster movies.

> The 'classic' genres were constructed by recourse to 'adult' realism – while 'melodrama' was acknowledged only in those denigrated reaches of the juvenile and the popular, the feminised spheres of the woman's weepie, the romance or family melodrama. (ibid., p. 34)

These 'classic' genres were eulogised by film theorists, however they seemed to forget that many of these films were infused with melodrama. It wasn't until the 1970s that melodrama became critically respectable, particularly through the work of Thomas Elsaesser and Laura Mulvey (both included in Gledhill, 1987).

Much of the early critical work focused on the subversive characteristics of 1950s Hollywood melodrama where the idea of the traditional middle-class family was called into question after many women had experienced financial independence during the Second World War. Many 1950s melodramas, particularly those directed by Douglas Sirk and produced by Ross Hunter, were critical of the traditional family. In addition, Elsaesser (1985) has described how technological developments in 1950s Hollywood helped to switch the emphasis from dialogue to the *mise-en-scène*. The developments of colour, deep-focus, crane and dolly-shots made a more complex *mise-en-scène* possible. The growing influence of Freud's theories added to the essentially inward-looking focus of the genre. It should be noted that this criticism of North American family life only become, academically, apparent in the 1970s through the work of Paul Willemen among others. Their argument was that great *auteurs* (the film director as author) could use the excess of melodramatic *mise-en-scène* to create a 'secondary text' and subvert the conventional narrative structure of their films which were, after all, Hollywood productions. However:

> If it is true that only an *auteur* such as Sirk is capable of bringing stylistic pressure to bear upon the purely ideological melodramatic material and thus causing it to 'rupture' and reveal its own textual gaps in terms of the dominant ideology, then only an elite audience, indeed one already committed to subversive ideas, would be able to read the secondary text. Such a position does not explicate the spectator position melodrama allows for its intended audience. (Feuer, 1984, p. 6)

In writing about the 'woman's picture' Jeanine Basinger suggested that contemporary audiences *did* see the ideological contradictions inherent in the melodrama; they did not have to be skilled in *mise-en-scène* analysis, or the intricacies of psychoanalytical theory in order to do this, understanding the narrative was sufficient. The stock narrative of the 'woman's picture' of the 1930s and 40s shows the central character thrown out of, or leaving, a secure family situation which leads her to forge a successful career for herself. A woman, as the narrative's hero, was shown being able act decisively and through her actions able to motivate narrative development. However, the patriarchal ideology, which informs much of Hollywood, could not allow this success to be the narrative resolution, the woman needed to be recouped for the family where she 'belonged'. So the successful woman's life is represented as essentially empty and she usually returned to her family and her 'appropriate' role as mother and wife.

We have seen how narrative often reinforces the values of the dominant ideology with the victory of the hero, who embodies the values of society, and the defeat of the villain who has transgressed those values. Basinger suggests that, like the gangster movie before it, where crime pays spectacularly until the final frames, the women's picture offered a narrative of subversion:

> It's obvious that seeds of unrest, even rebellion, were planted in some female minds by the evidence they saw on-screen, despite the conventional endings that turn a story into a cautionary tale. When morality has to dramatize its own opposite to make its point, the opposite takes on a life of its own. The film becomes accidentally ambivalent, contradictory. It sends two messages, though they're allegedly resolved by a hokey finale. (Basinger, 1994, pp. 11–12)

This 'hokey finale' often manifests itself as a *deus ex machina* ending that is inherently implausible. Many melodramas offer only an ambiguous conclusion: for example *All That Heaven Allows* (Douglas Sirk, 1955) and its 'remake' *Fear Eats the Soul* (*Angst Essen Seelen Auf*, Rainer Werner Fassbinder, 1973) see our protagonists reunited at the end but the man is seriously ill; in *My Son the Fanatic* (Udayan Prasad, 1997) it is difficult to see what future the protagonists have (see also Stafford, 1998).

So, possibly, melodrama is subversive not only in the excess it offers but also, more straightforwardly, in its narrative.

In the 1950s, the development of widescreen cinema created another tool for the melodramatist's armoury. Nicholas Ray, director of *Rebel Without a Cause* (1955), was one of the first directors who used widescreen cinema to melodramatic effect. For example, the scenes in *Rebel* where Jim's family argues on the stairs: the camera's tilt, signifying domestic disruption, is made almost vertiginous by the width of the screen. Ray's *Bigger Than Life* (1956) was also filmed in a widescreen format and probed the economic and gender tensions lying just beneath the surface of a respectable teacher's family.

In cinematic melodrama, attention to the *mise-en-scène* is crucial; it is often more important than dialogue and narrative. In *Meet in Me in St Louis* (1944), Vincente Minnelli expresses a young girl's hysteria at the prospect of being forced to move home in an expressionist *mise-en-scène* that features the destruction of her snowpeople (standing in for her family). The musical, including opera, is the melodramatic form *par excellence*.

One of the ways of decoding the excess in melodramatic *mise-en-scène* is through the deployment of a psychoanalytic discourse that emphasises the sexual.

Exercise 4.7

Consider Figure 4.7, noting how Schwarzenegger is signified as masculine.

The excess in this image is intended to emphasise Arnold Schwarzenegger's masculinity. From a psychoanalytical perspective, power is represented by the phallic symbol whether it is wielded by men or women. However, the phallic symbol has a great advantage over the penis, which it represents: it can never go limp:

Figure 4.7   Schwarzenegger who 'never goes limp'

This leads to the greatest instability of all for the male image. For the fact that the penis isn't a patch on the phallus. The penis can never live up to the mystique implied by the phallus. Hence the excessive, even hysterical quality of so much male imagery. The clenched fists, the bulging muscles, the hardened jaws, the proliferation of phallic symbols – they are all straining after what can hardly ever be achieved, the embodiment of the phallic mystique. (Dyer, 1982, p. 71)

Such excessive imagery is ideally viewed on the cinema screen, where size, and quality of image, really counts.

Excess in prime-time serials cannot easily centre upon mise-en-scène, for television's limited visual scale places its representational emphasis elsewhere. Acting, editing, musical underscoring and the use of the zoom lens frequently conspire to create scenes of high (melo)drama, even more so when these televisual conventions are overdetermined by heavily psychoanalytical representations. (Feuer, 1984, pp. 9–10)

As Feuer points out, North American soaps like *Dallas* and *Dynasty*, which were very popular in the 1980s, overcome the 'poverty' of the TV image by the use of expensive, opulent sets which meant that *Dallas*, for example, cost in the region of $1 million an hour. Despite its small size (at the time of writing widescreen televisions are just becoming consumer items), television can use some 'cinematic' techniques to melodramatic effect, for example cross-cutting between different narrative strands is a staple technique of soap opera.

Melodrama is not concerned with creating three-dimensional characters ('round' in E.M. Forster's terms) but with using recognisable types: 'the patient, suffering heroines; the upright, but often somewhat ineffectual heroes; the unscrupulous, scheming villains, usually with sexual designs on the virginal heroines; the saintly mother-figures; the stern 'Victorian' father-figures' (Walker, 1982, pp. 3–4). These are examples of generic types, they are characters that we associate explicitly with Victorian melodrama or, more likely as these texts are still occasionally screened, 'silent' films.

Melodrama is characterised by the following:

- identification of moral polarities of good and evil within the narrative
- is comparable to tragedy except character is generally of lower social status and confronts clearly identified antagonists
- the use of music for dramatic emphasis

- clear-cut solutions to conflict
- excess and exaggeration
- use of character types
- coincidence as a narrative device
- celebration of overt emotionalism
- use of emblems as visual signs.

More than anything, melodrama is characterised by excess; if it isn't 'over-the-top' then it probably isn't melodrama. Melodrama, in the form of romance, soap opera and the 'woman's picture' in particular, is often thought of as genres that are aimed at females and the excess is characterised as an expression of hysteria (see Chapter 5).

We know that many genres can be defined by their use of setting, character, narrative and iconography. Melodrama, however, can appear in many different genres – for example the Westerns *Run for Cover* (1955) *Johnny Guitar* (1954), both directed by Nicholas Ray, or the *film noir* 'woman's picture' *Mildred Pierce* (Michael Curtiz, 1945).

While there are many texts that can be easily defined as melodrama, many others use melodrama as a general aesthetic mode of representation, or style. For instance, in *Se7en* the schematised domesticity of the Millses is melodramatically elucidated:

- their apartment is routinely disturbed by trains: emphasising Tracy's alienation from city life and the corruption therein – the estate agent had showed them the flat for only a few minutes at a time thus avoiding train noise
- Mills plays, embarrassingly, with his dogs whom he refers to as the 'kids': stresses his need for a family which is sublimated into the masculine (dogs)
- Mills drinks beer to Somerset's wine: the connotations of the drink are, respectively, proletarian and sophisticated.

The use of coincidence as a narrative device is one of the techniques that help create narrative economy; for example in *Se7en*:

- the DA is making a statement about the second murder just as Mills arrives to investigate
- when Tracy is asking Somerset's advice about whether to have an abortion, the conversation comes to an empasse and Somerset's embarrassment is saved by his pager

- Somerset had been in a similar position to Mills when he was younger
- when the detectives eventually find John Doe's apartment the killer arrives just after they do.

Another parallel between genre and melodrama is iconography, which acts in the same way as emblems did in the theatre, as a short cut to meaning. Melodramatic character types are also utilised in many different genres. In fact there is little point in trying to separate the 'melodramatic' from the specific generic conventions in texts, it a pervasive style; it is difficult, for instance, to imagine a non-melodramatic horror text.

We have considered melodrama in the theatre and cinema; but nineteenth-century literature also used the style of melodrama. It is ironic, given the low status with which traditional aesthetics classifies many melodramatic texts, that some of the great British novelists, Charles Dickens and Thomas Hardy among them, should use the melodramatic style in their novels. Take Dickens's characterisation of the utilitarian Thomas Gradgrind in *Hard Times* (1854):

> Thomas Gradgrind, sir. A man of realities. A man of fact and calculations. A man who proceeds upon the principle that two and two are four, and nothing over, and who is not to be talked into allowing for anything over. Thomas Gradgrind, sir – peremptorily Thomas – Thomas Gradgrind. With a rule and a pair of scales, and the multiplication table always in his pocket, sir, ready to weigh and measure any parcel of human nature, and tell you exactly what it comes to. It is a mere question of figures, a case of simple arithmetic. (Dickens, 1969, p. 48)

This is certainly an 'over-the-top' characterisation even using an, almost, archetypal name in case the audience misses the point. The use of narrative coincidence, characterised as Fate, was a favourite device of Thomas Hardy: for example, Tess's letter going, not only under the door, but under the carpet to be left unread in *Tess of the D'Urbervilles* (1892). Melodrama is clearly one of the dominant modes of discourse in western society.

4.9 Genre and format

We have considered a variety of genres in this chapter and this final section will look at the differences between 'genre' and 'format'.

Format is, primarily, a television industry term that describes a particular variant on a generic form; it is also used to describe the type of technology used in a media product, for example, VHS videotape and 35mm film.

The game show genre can be defined in terms of the repertoire of elements:

- setting – television studio
- characters – studio audience, 'ordinary' people for contestants and an avuncular host
- narrative – the questions or tasks must be overcome to win the prizes
- iconography – a high tech, glitzy set
- style – basic 'live' television including: focus on host; audience and contestant reaction shots; segmented structure.

However, game shows are also formats; *Catchphrase*'s (Yorkshire television) particular format consists of contestants guessing a phrase based upon fragments of a picture. This format can be sold elsewhere in the world allowing other programme producers to use local contestants and, in this case, catchphrases from their own culture. While most game shows will conform to the generic conventions they are likely to have different formats.

Not all formats can be considered to be part of a genre. For instance, newspapers are obviously formatted either tabloid or broadsheet. Audiences have expectations about these formats: the purchaser of a broadsheet newspaper expects to find 'hard' news within its pages and they are sometimes referred to as the 'heavies'; the tabloid purchaser is more likely to be seeking enter-tainment. In Britain we also need to distinguish between two types of tabloid, the 'red tops' (*Sun*, *Star* and *Mirror*) and the middle-market (*Daily Mail* and *Express*); the former offer very little hard news, the latter fall somewhere between the broadsheets and 'red tops'. Newspapers are obviously formats in the way they look: the broadsheet, twice the size of the tabloid, is ideal for a more serious newspaper as it has much more room to develop stories on a page and can include a number of 'leads' on the front. There has been a tendency, since the 1960s, for newspapers to go from broadsheet to the tabloid format, a change usually accompa-nied with more lightweight news values. However, there are serious tabloid newspapers; for example, *Liberation* in France and the *Los Angeles Times*.

Although we have certain expectations about a newspaper based on its format, these are not, I suggest, detailed enough to qualify the forms as generic. Try to apply the repertoire of elements to newspapers.

Exercise 4.8

What are the generic setting, characters, narrative, iconography and style of tabloid newspapers?

The answers to these questions are almost certainly too general; for example, home-based stories; celebrities; shock-horror narratives; tabloidese language. All these may be true of some of the stories in a publication but what of others and the feature articles? So any expectations generated by newspapers, for those unfamiliar with the publication at least, are to do with the format which tells us only how 'serious' the text is; newspapers are not generic.

A more ambiguous case could be magazines: are they genres and/or formats? Certainly the physical format of magazines tells us very little; most magazines are the same size regardless of content. Special interest magazines are, arguably, generic; for example, think about the content of mainstream film magazines like *Empire* and *Premiere*: no setting but they have characters in the form of film stars/makers; narratives that deal with making or made movies; glamour photography and film stills are possibly iconographic; predominance of images over writing and friendly/slightly sarcastic style. General interest magazines, however, are more problematic.

Exercise 4.9

Can you apply the repertoire of elements to lifestyle magazines such as those in Figures 4.8 and 4.9.

The notion of setting is redundant but 'characters' are present in the focus on celebrities, whether from sport, show business or simply individuals considered as elite (for example, the British royal family); the narratives expressed are relatively limited, with a focus on 'publicity puffs' (stars selling their latest 'product'), relationships and 'how to' guides; iconography can be considered to be the glossy look which complements the glamour photography and the layout. Although lifestyle magazines do have elements that approximate

Figure 4.8

Figure 4.9

the repertoire of elements there seems little point in stretching these categories to make the texts fit. Like genres, lifestyle magazines do offer the 'same but different'; it is quite astonishing to think how many sex surveys must have been compiled over the years. The typical contents of these magazines are:

Female and male

- 'true life stories'
- health
- relationships
- pin-ups
- sex
- fashion
- star profiles
- beauty (called 'grooming' in lads' mags)

Male only

- the extreme,
- sport,
- technology
- the arts.

These are the ingredients of successful lifestyle magazines and they can arguably be considered to be formats, like the game show mentioned above. In Britain, *Loaded* started the current in male lifestyle magazines and its format has been followed by *FHM*, *Maxim* and *Front*.

In conclusion, there is little point in defining whether a text is generic or the product of a format; what matters is the isolation of conventional elements which then allows us to identify how closely individual texts follow the norm or in what way they diverge.

The next chapter considers genre from a broader perspective and problematises, to an extent, the concept and looks at its relationship to society as a whole.

5

THEORY OF GENRE 2

AIMS OF THE CHAPTER

➤ To consider the 'chicken or egg' conundrum in relation to genre.

➤ To outline twelve generic approaches.

➤ To explore (Jungian) mythical characteristics of genre.

➤ To investigate the adventure genre using 'action' films such as *Independence Day*.

➤ To deal with gender-specific genres with reference to soap opera.

➤ To consider two types of generic cycle: cycles of popularity and the genre's life cycle.

➤ To investigate the relationship between genres and reality, illustrated with the British TV cop genre and the horror film.

➤ To apply semiotics is to genre and cover the ideology of genre criticism.

➤ To show how scheduling relates to genre.

5.1 Introduction

This chapter offers a more advanced perspective on genre, looks at the concept's theoretical problems and considers its relationship with society.

5.2 Genre – the chicken or the egg?

What do you think comes first: the genre or the texts that make up the genre? It may appear obvious that the texts must come first because it is difficult to conceive of, say, the soap opera genre without actually having texts that are soap operas. However, if you accept this you must then answer the question:

> Unless you had a predetermined idea of what soap opera was, how did you know the actual texts were soap operas?

Clearly we do have a predetermined idea, the repertoire of elements, but this must have originated in the generic texts (so it is not really 'predetermined'). It therefore follows that we could not know that the 'texts themselves' were soap opera until we had actually watched soap operas. It is the same conundrum as, 'which came first, the chicken or the egg? There can be no chickens without eggs; but without a chicken, what can lay the egg? As Tudor states in relation to the Western:

> almost all writers using the term *genre*, are caught in a dilemma. They are *defining* a 'Western' on the basis of analysing a body of films which cannot possibly be said to be 'Westerns' until after the analysis. (Tudor, 1976, p. 120)

Put another way, this problem highlights the 'conflict' between the philosophical positions of idealism and empiricism. The former offers an ideal type, a genre's repertoire of elements, while the latter examines the actual texts in order to define a genre.

The use of a repertoire of elements is also problematic: if we define texts based upon their conventions of narrative, setting, iconography and so on, all we are doing is stating that a text belonging to, say, genre 1 is different from another text which belongs to genre 2. This difference, of course, is self-evident because this was how the genre was defined in the first place. It could be that genre leads us into a critical cul-de-sac so, in order to make genre useful as a concept, Tudor concludes that:

> *Genre* notions… are not critic's classifications made for special purposes; they are sets of cultural conventions. *Genre* is what we collectively believe it to be. (ibid., p. 122)

So, genre is of little use critically but of great use in 'common sense' terms; which is how the mass audience uses the concept. Genre's version of the 'chicken/egg' problem does not exist in 'common sense' discourse. However, within the 'collective audience' we cannot assume equal knowledge of a genre's conventions:

it is quite possible that, before reading Chapter 4, you were not familiar with the genre of *film noir*; now, assuming you have read the chapter, you can read texts that belong to that genre as *genre* texts. Previously you will have used other frameworks in order to make sense of them. This framework may well have been generic: you may have read them as 'detective films' or 'thrillers'. Similarly, you may have dismissed SF as fantasy; now you know 'genre-SF' deals with the issue of what it means to be human.

While Tudor's conclusion that genre is a concept that belongs to audiences is attractive, from an academic point of view we should attempt to make the concept useful in the analysis of texts; after all, analyses like those undertaken in Chapter 4 can be revealing. As was concluded in the discussion of Propp, the 'use value' of a theory is the true test of its success. We are, as media students, at liberty to ignore the philosophical *dilemmas* inherent in genre criticism, if we find the notion of genres useful (although we should not forget the philosophy). It is likely that anyone who attempts to understand a genre from an academic perspective has already experienced that genre as a cultural convention so the academic already has a predetermined idea of what to expect. We cannot academically consider genre without 'collectively believing in it'.

5.3 Twelve generic approaches to media texts

Chapter 4 consisted, primarily, of a number of case study *descriptions* of genres. However, it is valid to ask 'so what?' If all genre criticism can do is identify a type of text, something that most audiences can do in a few seconds, then it is not likely to produce any insights into those media texts or the society that produces and consumes them. While identifying genres is important, this must be the first step in analysis; Berger (1992) suggests 12 approaches to media texts:

1. *'A historical study of the evolution of genre'*: in Chapter 4 we considered the history of science fiction.
2. *'Relation of a text to a genre'*: as genre is a mix of 'the same but different', the difference can be isolated by comparing the text to the genre's repertoire of elements. Much of Chapter 4 was an attempt to isolate defining the elements of a number of genres. We also considered how Steve Bochco's 'innovative aesthetic' influenced the TV crime serial in *NYPD Blue*.

3. *'A study of how genres relate to one another'*: why do some genres combine as 'hybrids'. This can be considered in two ways: how genres combine to create another genre, or sub-genre, like cyberpunk (see Chapter 4); how two genres, which deal with similar discourses, can readily combine like SF and horror.

4. *'How do the popular genres of a particular period compare with one another?'* For instance, is the visual style of North American television programmes related to the current popularity of action moves and why is SF popular in both television and film?

5. *'Comparison of American texts and genres with texts and genres from other countries?'* How do British hospital dramas compare with North American productions (see later in chapter ?) Berger is guilty of ethnocentrism here; of course generic texts of any nation can be compared with those of any other nation; for example it is fruitful to compare Brazilian *telenovelas* with soap opera (see Trinta, 1998). Tony Rayns suggested, of the 'cop movie' *Violent Cop* (*Usono otoko, kyobo ni tsuki*, Takeshi Kitano, 1989):

> The fact that it is Japanese explains some of its departures from Hollywood norms: the climax and the coda are both blacker than anything American audiences are taught to expect, and the moments of violence are more intense, more detailed and above all more personalised than in any Hollywood equivalent. (Rayns, 1994, p. 53)

6. *'Distinctive aspects of heroes and heroines (and villains and villainesses) in the various genres'*: as we saw in Chapter 4, the heroes of 'hard-boiled' narratives are very different from those of 'classical detective fiction'. Similarly, in Chapter 1, Barthes's 'semic' narrative code determines the characteristics associated with 'heroes' and 'villains'.

7. *'Analysis of what different genres reflect about society and culture'*: what is the appeal of 'hip hop' music to black (and, increasingly, white) audiences and why does dance music primarily address a young audience? The relationship between genres and sub-cultures will be considered in *Media Institutions and Audiences*.

8. *'Impact of mythic and folkloristic content on texts and genres'*: some genres may be more likely to use myths and folklore as their structural basis than others; it is possible that science fiction, with its elements of fantasy, is more readily able to use mythic structures than, say, situation comedy. The next section

considers how 'adventure' and 'romance' underpin most
generic texts.
9. *'Rise in popularity and decline in popularity of genres'*: why is the
Hollywood musical, at the time of writing at least, a 'dead'
genre? (Generic cycles are covered in section 5.6.)
10. *'Differences in genres in different media'*: we have seen how Hollywood takes science fiction out of the 'literary ghetto', where
much of it is placed by book publishers, and turns into something that appeals to a mass audience.
11. *'What uses and gratifications do different genres provide for audiences?'*
12. *'How do technical matters involving production and aesthetics impact
on different genres?'* These will both be dealt with in *Media Institutions and Audiences*; the 'uses and gratifications' audience
theory will be described with reference to genre; Kerr (1979) has
shown how the 'B' movie status of classic *film noir* allowed it to
be a subversive genre.

Berger's list does make a convincing case for genre criticism regardless of the shaky philosophical foundations upon which the concept
is built.

5.4 Genre as Jungian myth

the unconscious mind of modern man preserves the symbol-making
capacity that once found expression in the beliefs and rituals of the prim-
itive. And that capacity still plays a role of vital psychic importance. In
more ways than we realize, we are dependent on the messages that are
carried by such symbols, and they profoundly influence both our atti-
tudes and our behavior. (Henderson, 1964, p. 107)

Disciples of psychiatrist Carl Jung believe that humanity has a
'collective unconsciousness' that manifests itself in archetypal
symbols. Cawelti takes up the idea in relation to genre and isolates
what he calls 'formulaic archetypes', or moral fantasies: 'Adventure;
Romance; Mystery; Melodrama; Alien Beings or States' (Cawelti,
1976, p. 39).
We shall focus on 'adventure' and 'romance' which are the most
influential and, in a sense, *ur*-genres; that is, they are the basic paradigms that inform *all* generic creations.

215

Adventure

> The central fantasy of the adventure story is that of the hero – individual or group – overcoming obstacles and dangers and accomplishing some important and moral mission. (ibid.)

This fantasy manifested itself, in early literature, in epics and myths that narratively dealt with a triumph over death. How this fantasy is articulated in more modern times depends upon which genre is currently popular:

> The cultural treatment of a myth responds to historical and political contingencies, and may appropriate archetypal imagery… for rhetorical means. (Rushing and Frentz, 1995, p. 48)

For instance, in nineteenth-century literature the adventure archetype was popularly fulfilled by the 'knightly adventure' which often consisted of the quest for the Holy Grail. Cawelti points out that, in the twentieth century, the 'victory over death' manifested itself as: a 'triumph over injustice' in the Western; the saving of a nation in spy fiction; overcoming fear and defeat of the enemy in war stories. At the end of the late twentieth century, action-adventure narratives predominated, in cinema at least; these may be 'super-genre' films that are often marketed as 'event' pictures.

A super-genre film refuses to be categorised simply as one genre, it is eclectic. *Star Wars* (created by George Lucas, 1977) is often cited as a turning point for the use of genre in Hollywood. It was more than just a mix of science fiction, Western and fairy-tale fantasy, the film also harked back to the Saturday matinée adventure serials, such as *Flash Gordon*, of the 1930s and 40s. Steven Spielberg's Indiana Jones films referenced these texts even more explicitly. However, as Larry Gross points out, this tendency within cinema, which he calls the 'big loud action movie', started in the 1960s:

> James Bond after *From Russia with Love* gives up spying for what? For an entirely new super-kinetic cartoon-type action movie… from *Goldfinger* on, espionage and plot mechanics disappear almost entirely. Pure-action set pieces, large in scale, take over. (Gross, 1995, p. 8)

The key word is 'kinetic', this cinema is about motion; indeed one of the early forms of film projectors was called the 'kinematograph'. Previously, Hollywood had marketed and categorised films generically, such as:

- musical
- gangster
- screwball comedy
- thriller
- swashbuckler

- Western
- war
- horror
- woman's picture
- biopic

and so on.

Modern Hollywood, however, favours the 'super-genre' text that eschews narrow generic categorisation. As we have seen, *Blade Runner* is a mix of *film noir* and science fiction; it also contains chase and fight (kinetic) sequences that characterise the action movie. Gross outlines the new format of commercial cinema, post-*Star Wars*, as follows:

1. Spielberg's Lucas' elaborate and expensively produced elevation of B movie genre plots.
2. A reduction of narrative complexity.
3. The Cinematic, the Image and Technology dominate the narrative experience.
4. Of crucial importance is these films' self-deprecating humour. (ibid., p. 9)

According to Gross, a consequence of this is:

Since 1981, the institutionalisation of the Big Loud Action Movie has proceeded apace. It has realigned the creative atmosphere in Hollywood shaping the release slates of all the major studios and virtually crushing European art cinema. (ibid., p. 10)

Much of what Gross describes can be described as being high concept film-making; a term which will be considered in *Media Institutions and Audiences*.

The top ten films of 1997 (10 January 1997–11 January 1998), measured by North American box-office receipts and reported in *Screen International*, 30 Janurary–5 February 1998, were:

1. *Men in Black*
2. *The Lost World: Jurassic Park*
3. *Titanic* (it had only been on release for four weeks)
4. *Liar Liar*
5. *Air Force One*
6. *Star Wars* (RE: 1997)

7. *My Best Friend's Wedding*
8. *Face/Off*
9. *Batman and Robin*
10. *George of the Jungle*

Seven of these are categorisable as Gross's big loud action movie. The studios also eschew the use of traditional genres in describing their films. For example, Columbia Tristar's slate of 18 films advertised in early 1998 included:

- thriller × 3
- comedy drama × 2
- futuristic thriller
- action thriller
- romantic adventure
- comedy satire
- romantic comedy-drama

- drama × 3
- romantic comedy
- action drama
- dramatic thriller
- action adventure
- comedy thriller

There is clearly a preponderance of action and adventure here, especially if we include 'thriller' in the equation. With the exception of 'thriller', none of the descriptions are traditional generic categories. The fact that one of the films, the 'futuristic thriller' *Gattaca*, could easily be called science fiction shows how the studios are wary of science fiction's ghetto image. One exception to this wariness about generic categorisation is the horror movie, a genre traditionally addressed to a young audience: 1997's *I Know What You Did Last Summer*, *Scream 2* and 1998's *Halloween H20* and the *I Know* sequel continued the 'comeback' of the 'teen horror' initiated by *Scream* in 1996. Ten of Columbia-Tristar's categories are hybrids; the last one seems desperately trying to cater for every cinema-goer.

Titanic is a good example of the 'super-genre' movie in that it has an almost schizophrenic split between its halves: romance (melodrama) followed by action. Associated with the rise of the 'super-genre' movie is the event picture. The would-be event picture of 1998, *Godzilla*, was widely lauded for its marketing campaign ('Size does matter') which began a full 18 months before the movie's release. However, even though it exceeded $100 million, its return at the North American box office was disappointing: it reputedly cost $120 million dollars to make and an extra $60 million in 'p and a' (prints and advertising). Although *Godzilla* did generate a lot of box-office revenue, and network TV rights were sold for a basic $25 million, the film failed to live up to the expectations generated by the marketing, in contrast to the same producers' *Independence Day*.

Exercise 5.1

Make a list of the hero's gender in any action-adventure texts you can think of.

Who takes on the role of hero is culture-specific: how many texts make a teacher the hero (or student for that matter)? Similarly, what groups are deemed to be appropriate villains? In 'adventure' narratives, as you probably discovered in the above exercise, most of the heroes are male and this may be one reason why action-adventure texts appeal predominantly to males. The villains in 'super-genre' movies are usually either megalomaniacs, aliens, monsters or natural disasters. As in the archetypal adventure narrative, the hero does 'triumph over death' by defeating the villain, however the emphasis is on action, immediate response and instant effect.

Any action by the villains is, usually, counteracted by the actions of the hero. This is conventional Proppian narrative; in action films, however, the *actions* are the point rather than narrative progress. In *Batman and Robin* (1997), the reason Mr Freeze wishes to destroy Gotham City is immaterial, what matters is the special effects of him freezing the city. Similarly, Batman, and his cohorts, 'utilise' other special effects to negate Mr Freeze. The consequences do not matter, only the event is important. In such postmodern texts we are not expected to get beyond the surface of the medium. It could be argued that *Batman and Robin* is simply, like cinema, about action, or movement (the film also draws on the conventions of comic strips). Modern Hollywood is in the business of producing rollercoaster rides which are all form and no substance.

Despite appearances, not all action movies are immune to interesting investigation as Michael Rogin's intriguing analysis of *Independence Day* shows. At the climax of the film, 'white trash' Russell Casse is the only one left with a missile and 'he aims it at the alien's primary weapon, visually imaged as a bodily orifice with leg-like protrusions on either side' (Rogin, 1998, p. 68) but finds that the release mechanism has jammed. However he refuses to abort his mission:

Russell shouts, 'All right you alien assholes. In the words of my generation, up yours.' Speaking his last words, 'Hello Boys, I'm back!' Russell
Casse pays back the alien sex abusers by flying up the alien asshole.
(ibid., p. 69)

The resulting conflagration, Rogin entertainingly argues, leads to a
conclusion that:

> Bifurcating to two maternal orifices at its climax, *Independence Day* allies
> anal penetration with death, escapes maternal power and rescues hetero-
> sexuality. The return of the Jewish-black [Jeff Goldblum and Will Smith]
> alliance also saves Clinton's [Bill Pullman] Democratic Party, menaced by
> the defection of southern whites, for the anal explosion wipes out not
> only the aliens but also the Reagan Democrat. (ibid., pp. 71–2)

While such a conclusion is, at first reading, bizarre, Rogin does
justify his perspective with detailed reference to the text.

Adventure texts are characterised by a strong narrative thrust
which, as we shall see later in the chapter, may appeal specifically to
males. One of the reasons this genre predominates, in cinema at
least, may be because men make the majority of decisions. There
are, arguably, similar tendencies in British television: when considering a large number of drama programmes that featured female
nudity in the summer of 1998, John Dugdale opined:

> What's interesting about these projects... is that they are not only written
> by women, but form part of a plethora of programming scheduled to
> attract female viewers fleeing the World Cup. It's strange, then, that they
> are so concerned to lay on enough nudity to lure the lads, a policy which
> may have something to do with fact that the screenplays were written for
> male head of serials and channel controllers. (Dugdale, 1998)

Traditionally women have found romance as the most appealing
archetypal genre.

Romance

It should be noted that Cawelti's 'romance' is not the same as the
'literary romance' which refers to narratives in which adventure,
love and chivalry occur. Cawleti calls this the 'feminine equivalent
of the adventure story' (Cawelti, 1976, p. 41). They are characterised
by having central female characters and 'its organizing action is the

development of a love relationship' (ibid.). Although adventure narratives also usually have a 'love' relationship, it is peripheral to the hero's struggles against the villain. In romance any danger 'function[s] as a means of challenging and then cementing the love relationship... The moral fantasy of the romance is that of love triumphant and permanent, overcoming all obstacles and difficulties' (ibid., pp. 41–2).

This form probably thrives most in the novel, particularly the 'airport novel' (novels with several hundred pages) in their 'bonkbuster' form. As the latter term suggests, sex is a potent feature of modern romance. Referring back to the 1997 box-office chart, only *My Best Friend's Wedding* and the first half of *Titanic* can possibly be classified as romances. We have already considered romance, as melodrama, in some detail in Chapter 4. Is this male preference for action, and female for romance, a consequence of genetics or gender?

5.5 Genre and gender – soap opera

Soap opera has long been considered a genre that primarily appeals to females. This was implicit in their original scheduling, in North America, as 'daytime' programmes for housewives. They were sponsored by detergent companies, hence their name, and dealt with domestic issues that were seen to be the prime concern of the woman in the family. This emphasis on the domestic, or private, space contrasts with the 'adventure' genres which occur in public spaces.

Table 5.1

Public	Private
street	home
the general public	family
work	leisure (This opposition ignores 'work' in the home, which is exactly what happens: in patriarchal society a housewife's work is not given any status.)
action	rest
outward	inward
reason	emotion
business relationships	personal relationships
male	female

In (patriarchal) western society the world of work, the public sphere, has been valued over the private arena. Soaps turn this opposition around:

> The essence of soaps is the reflection on personal problems and the emphasis is on talk not on action, on slow development rather than the immediate response, on delayed retribution rather than instant effect. (Geraghty, 1991, p. 41)

In doing the opposite, soap operas challenge the male version of what is important in life; when the 'private' is privileged over the 'public' this, implicitly, denigrates men's favoured sphere. In addition, soap opera, like its precursor the 'woman's' film (see Chapter 4), places:

> the emphasis... on the central woman protagonist whom the reader is invited to support and whose reasons for action are understood by the audience although not necessarily by the male characters... the woman's pre-eminence in the narrative is based on her understanding and control of the emotional arena. (ibid., pp. 116–17)

Soap opera, and its source *ur*-genre romance, is often characterised as escapist; a text where women can escape to and experience the feeling of 'utopia'. However, Ien Ang has shown that, in an investigation of the North American soap *Dallas*, which portrayed the lives of the rich and powerful, women related to it as a 'realist' text. This is not to say that women believed in the verisimilitude of the programme but believed in the realism of the emotions portrayed in the programme:

> In this sense the realism of *Dallas* can be called an 'emotional realism'... what is recognized as real is not knowledge of the world, but a subjective experience of the world. (Ang, 1985, p. 45)

The repetitive, and continual, nature of the genre's overall narrative structure could be said to mirror the work of a housewife which is boring and never-ending:

> For the household drudge, the soap operas, with their slow pace, repetition, dislocated and overlapping story lines and their emphasis on the ordinary rather than the glamorous, provide a narrative which can be understood without the concentration required by prime time television. (Geraghty, 1991, p. 43)

Of course, women do not have to be housewives in order to enjoy soap opera. Another appeal of soaps to the female audience is the fact that 'women express perfectly efficient and rational behaviour, a feature quite rare in other televised women' (Zoonen, 1994, p. 121). There have even been suggestions that the appeal of soaps to women is more elemental:

> the open-ended, slow paced, multi-climaxed structure of soap-opera is in tune with patterns of female sexuality. (Modleski, 1982, p. 98)

In contrast, men are apparently more interested in the instant gratification provided by the adventure genre. Fiske has compared the narrative structure of soaps to a popular 'action' programme of the 1970s and 80s, *The A Team*.

Table 5.2

Soap opera	The A Team
1. lack narrative closure	narrative closed each episode
2. emphasises problem solving, intimate conversation, and feelings	emphasises action, minimal dialogue
3. multiple characters and plots	structuring around main protagonist with whom the audience is expected to identify
4. close correspondence between story time and real time (characters' lives continue between episodes)	live only in their performance
5. segmentation: abrupt switching from strand to strand	singular plotted narrative
6. male characters can be sensitive	sensitive male characters often a threat and/or characterised as gay
7. female professional characters	power resides only in men
8. the primacy of the domestic setting	the dominance of the public domain

Source: adapted from Fiske, 1987

As a consequence of this, soaps in general have:

> personal relationships (as their backbone). They provide dramatic moments – marriage, birth, divorce, death – and the more day-to-day exchanges of quarrels, alliances and dilemmas which make up the fabric of the narrative. (Geraghty, 1991, p. 41)

In terms of the 'uses and gratifications' theory (see *Media Institutions and Audiences*) soaps help audiences articulate their personal identity: by watching how 'ordinary' people deal with 'ordinary' problems, audiences can compare characters' experiences with their own. Soaps are also very useful for social interaction, and this has even 'spilled over' into newspapers and magazines (there are dedicated soap publications). 'Realist' soaps, like *Brookside* and *EastEnders*, also take care to offer information within their narratives; for instance, a narrative strand dealing with a Down's syndrome child in Brookside was carefully researched to present a 'factual' context for the experience of coping with such a child. Research, by Dorothy Hobson (1989, 1990), has shown women have two ways of talking about soaps:

> The women [Hobson] interviewed tended to speculate about narrative development, and the future feelings of characters based on their own opinions about realistic plots and stories... Secondly... they use soaps to think and talk about their own lives. (Zoonen, 1994, p. 118)

This is not to say that all men find the attractions of soap opera difficult to comprehend. Indeed, the central thesis of Geraghty's book is that soap operas have evolved to incorporate the concerns of men and minority groups, such as gays and lesbians. Similarly, it is possible that traditional gender roles are changing in society and men may be becoming more 'feminised' and women gaining more power. As the old definitions of gender blur, it is unsurprising that what used to be seen as a female genre should start appealing more to men.

Geraghty points out that the first episode of *EastEnders* (BBC1), broadcast in 1985, featured an opening shot of a boot kicking down a door. When *Brookside*, which was first shown at the inception of Channel 4 in 1982, attempted:

> to incorporate issues of work and trade unionism [this] led to an emphasis on the male characters who operated in the public sphere. The presentation of Bobby Grant, in this period, was extremely powerful... [his] relationships with his family were also explored in a moving way which allowed the audience access to a depth of masculine feeling which in *Coronation Street* tended to be expressed with a shrug and a sigh. (Geraghty, 1991, p. 171)

The new 1980s soaps also focused on children, although it was a number of years before *Coronation Street* responded to these developments. However, *'Corrie'* has never fully up-dated itself; the lack of ethnic minority characters in the late 1990s, in particular, gives a sense that the *Street* is living in a 'time warp' where the Salford of the 1950s still exists. More recently *Emmerdale Farm* (Yorkshire television) became *Emmerdale* and featured an aircraft crash and a hostage drama in order to boost its audience figures.

Why should soaps have evolved, at this time, to incorporate more masculine appeal? There is evidence that conventionally male spheres are becoming more appealing to females. In the 1998 World Cup, a traditionally male soccer event, audience figures for the first week's televised matches in Britain showed a substantial proportion of women watching the games:

> Women have been tuning in to the football coverage in higher numbers than expected, accounting for about a third [actually the figure was 37 per cent] of the audience so far, with British women more likely to view that their Continental counterparts. (*Campaign*, 19 June 1998)

In Britain, at least, football has been traditionally considered as a male bastion; possibly even this tradition is about to founder on women's increasing interest (see also Lacey 1998b). It is tempting to suggest that the change in gender roles has precipitated this development but, in practise, it is impossible to be sure of casual links between media texts and society. However, one way of assessing changes in society is to consider genres as cycles.

5.6 Generic cycles

Genres are cyclical in two senses: there are cycles that conform to a genre's rise and decline in popularity; genres also possess a 'life' cycle.

Cycles of popularity

When considering 'cycles of popularity' we are looking at how media industries respond to audience choices. When any text becomes exceptionally popular you can be certain that 'follow-ups' will not be far behind. These are in the form of sequels and other producers' attempts to get on the 'band wagon' with their own versions of these texts. These 'versions', inevitably, take their cue from the genre. In British television, after the success of the 'docu-soap' (or, possibly, 'docu-sitcom') *Driving School*, numerous other examples of the genre followed, including programmes on a hotel, a holiday rep, an airport, an airline, and even on traffic wardens. Similarly, the pop chart success of Take That heralded numerous 'boy band' clones in the 1990s.

In music it is possible that generic cycles, like punk and grunge, are more than simply a case of industry exploitation of a popular form. For example, although EMI signed the Sex Pistols in an attempt to cash in on the group's success, the band remained as obnoxious as punk demanded; this led to a much-publicised split. Musical popularity is often 'bound up' in youth sub-cultural groups and therefore is, at least for a time, driven more by audience, and the 'street', than industry production. Of course, whether it is 'street' driven or industry driven is, to an extent, irrelevant to the existence of a cycle, the salient fact is that certain genres are popular at particular times.

This type of cycle is, probably, most discernible in cinema; we have already seen how SF/special effects films have dominated in recent years. Back in 1988, for instance, the only non-comedy in the North American top ten box-office hits was *Die Hard*. However, it is clear that these cycles must start somewhere replacing previous generic cycles:

> by the late 80s, there were odd cracks in the smooth surface... Genres drowned out by the boom (in comedy) – and others which had died long before – began reappearing: the thriller itself had been so neglected as a form that *Jagged Edge* (1985) was the first non-period whodunnit in the US Top 20 since Hitchcock's *Rear Window* (1954)... By the time of *The Silence of the Lambs* (1991), the thriller was everywhere. (Pirie, 1996, p. 27)

Pirie suggests that major genre breakthroughs, and the late 1990s 'SF fest' heralded by *Stargate* (1994), 'resemble major financial breakthroughs in that they are contra-cyclical – that is, they occur *against* the prevailing market wisdom or trend' (ibid., p. 26).

So although, in the late 1990s, the major Hollywood studios pursue success through the manufacture of special effects/SF movies, the cycle will end when another generic text is successful *against all expectation*. Critics who berate Hollywood as being simply a manufacturer of product, and films' successes as primarily due to following trends and marketing, tend to forget that if audiences are bored the film will bomb. Although many producers undoubtedly wish that cultural texts were products in the manner of, say, baked beans (which are all the same), the essential ingredient of even formulaic texts is 'difference'. While genres are certainly characterised as the same, without the 'but different' audiences are likely to feel they are simply watching the same movie as the last one and their 'good faith' purchase of a ticket will be compromised. This leads us to consider the second type of cycle, the 'life cycle' of generic development: while beans are required to be the same, the *difference* in genre texts inevitably leads to evolution.

Generic life cycle

If a generic variation is successful, the following texts are likely to use this variation which then becomes a staple part of the genre. For example, the 'spaghetti Westerns' (mostly filmed in Spain) of the 1960s took the Western genre, threw in expressionist camera angles and threw out much of the dialogue:

> They are filled with stylized violence and cruelty; they are as serpentine with intrigue as they are loyal to the idea of destiny as the far, flat horizon. They know no other human impulses than greed, treachery, silent honour and the unswerving imperative of revenge. (Thomson, 1981, p. 1417)

They parodied the Western genre so successfully, Thomson suggested, that:

> its influence is total. There are so few Westerns made today because the genre has been revealed as not a true fable of rock, lead and dust, but a fabrication of pasta. (ibid., p. 1419)

As we saw in Chapter 3, although Westerns are usually set in the late nineteenth century, they reflect ideological concerns of the time they are produced. As society changes, so do genres.

The trick for the media producer is to offer a variation on a generic formula that will appeal to an audience. Producers who are adept at introducing appealing variations can expect a financially spectacular career; possibly only artists like Steven Spielberg and Stephen King have come close in reaching this 'Holy Grail' of popular culture production. This begs the question as to why audiences, as a mass, suddenly respond to a new genre cycle or 'take' to a new generic variation? To try and answer this question we need to consider the relationships between texts, producers and society. It is safe to assume there is a relationship between texts and the society that produces and consumes these texts; what this relationship consists of is, however, problematic. Texts are often thought as being mimetic, that is, they reflect reality; however, this reflection is not neutral, it is – inevitably – shaped by ideological forces.

Texts 'reflecting' reality

As we have seen, genres change as society changes: in our consideration of soap opera and gender, the change in gender roles, particularly during the 1980s, was also apparent in modern soaps. Any new soap is likely to base itself on the successes of *EastEnders* and *Brookside*, which attempt to deal with the social issues of their time. This is despite the fact that *Coronation Street* is even more highly rated, in terms of audience; it, however, in the 1990s, has offered very little in terms of generic innovation. Presumably its appeal is more to do with the nostalgia it offers than its observations on contemporary society. In generic terms *Coronation Street*, which was originally considered to be a drama-documentary, is obviously the antecedent of other British TV soaps, but as the genre evolves it is unlikely to do so with reference to the old-fashioned *Street*.

At the end of the twentieth century a sub-genre of soap, the hospital drama, is experiencing a great deal of success. The central characters of programmes such as the North American *ER* and British *Casualty* are the doctors and nurses who usually, against the odds, manage to take great care of their patients. The appeal of these programmes is primarily as entertainment; however, we can ask why the cycle has reappeared at this time? It may too trite to suggest this genre articulates the *fin de siècle*, or a millennial angst, with its emphasis on the vulnerable bodies (particularly gruesome in *ER*) which the heroes repair. It is trite because it is guilty of a 'vulgar Marxist' perspective which sees a direct cause–effect chain between, in this case, texts and the time in which they are produced. The link may be there but a more sophisticated argument is needed to legitimate the possible connection.

Traditionally, British soaps sign themselves as being realist texts and so, to remain credible (*Coronation Street* excepted), they must respond to changes in society. So if the National Health Service were dismantled in Britain, it would no longer be credible for hospital genres to operate in an NHS framework; indeed, the disruption of the organisational change involved is likely to feature as an important narrative strand. We use realist texts, particularly news and documentaries but also fictional texts, to inform us about how our world is changing.

Exercise 5.2

Write down a description of a typical Australian (if you are Australian, try Brit ('pom') or North American).

How much of your perception of Australians, and Australia, comes from the media in general and the soap *Neighbours* in particular? What view do Australians get about northern British people if their only information is *Coronation Street*? Which texts inform most North Americans about the British or Australians? and so on. We are likely to have much more familiarity of foreigners through media representations than in actuality. The degree to which the media affect our perceptions is very contentious and is probably inseparable from society as a whole (media representations are, of course, part of society). A policeman suggested, in the BBC documentary *Cops on the Box*, that in the 1970s some members of the 'flying squad' (an elite police division stationed at Scotland Yard in London) modelled their behaviour on Regan and Carter, characters in Thames Television's *The Sweeney* (cockney rhyming slang: 'Sweeney Todd–flying squad') – see below. Maybe postmodernists are right and there is *no* difference between reality and media texts: media texts frame reality and reality *is* media texts.

Assuming a relatively simplistic relationship between texts and society, the next section considers the British TV cop genre.

The British TV cop genre

The TV cop programme is one of the most interesting genres broadcast on television. It is a genre that is continually being 'reinvented' as new variations are tried in an attempt to replace tiring cornerstones of the schedules. Charlotte Brunsdon has suggested that this genre:

has proved so resonant with the both producers and audiences because it repeatedly, even obsessively, stages the drama of the responsible citizen caught in the embrace of what increasingly seems an irresponsible State. (Brunsdon, 1998, p. 225)

Dixon of Dock Green was a staple of the British early evening Saturday schedule from the 1950s to the 1970s. It featured the patriarchal Dixon, an unarmed British bobby who could restore order by his very presence. *Dixon* belonged to the post-war era of consensus, when the police were shown as being 'whiter than white'. One episode which did feature a thieving policeman showed up the problems the programme had in dealing with police who were anything other than a 'pillar of society'. When Dixon apprehended the 'bent' copper, the thief was characterised as a 'rotten apple' and told to 'take your tunic (uniform) off and then I'll arrest you'. Clearly *Dixon*, as programme, could not deal with the image of a uniformed policeman being arrested.

Such coyness may seem strange to modern audiences who are used to the idea of 'bent' coppers, however at this stage of the genre's development it was impossible to deal with 'the policeman as villain'; this was not, however, because the genre 'disallowed' such a representation. The model used at the beginning of Chapter 4 emphasised that institutions are important in the creation of genre texts and the inability of the British TV cop show to articulate police corruption, at this time, was, primarily, a result of institutions 'refusing' to deal in such a controversial area. There are, no doubt, other areas now that certain institutions will not cover; such as the police's role in monitoring pressure groups mentioned in Chapter 4.

In the more liberal 1960s it became institutionally possible to offer representations of the police as other than paragons of law and order. *Z Cars* introduced a new realist aesthetic to the genre, and television in general, by – among other things – showing that the police had weaknesses. This evolution did incur the wrath of some:

The police constable of Lancashire withdrew support from the original *Z Cars* on the grounds that the presentation of policemen as 'human beings', not immune from the pressures and problems of everyday life, might undermine public confidence, though the decision was later reversed when the success of the series became apparent. (Hurd, 1981, p. 54)

However, the representation of the police in *Z Cars* did not stray away from the central tenet that the police were the heroes. It was not until the 1970s that alternative representations of the police appeared on British TV screens, most powerfully in *Law and Order*. The fact that *Law and Order* has not been given repeated viewing (on UK Gold for example) suggests that the Establishment did not welcome its portrayal of endemic police corruption. However, another serial from the 1970s, *The Sweeney*, is regularly repeated. Although still couched in terms of the 'police as heroes', *The Sweeney* did offer a different take on the 'reality' of police law enforcement. By the 1970s the corrupt nature of the Metropolitan police had attained notoriety and Robert Mark was appointed Commissioner of Police with a brief to clean up the 'Yard'. This high profile 'crusade' was inevitably covered by the news media which probably 'opened up' the ground for the *The Sweeney*:

> *The Sweeney* relates to a public's *already discursive* knowledge of the police: knowledge conveyed in other police series, in news reports and in the much publicized views of senior policemen like Sir Robert Mark. A cop series takes some of that public knowledge (carefully selected to deny the outrageous – with little of nothing about racism in the police force, or deaths in police custody) and refracts this through generic conventions, which are themselves subject to change. (Tulloch, 1990, p. 71)

Like *Z Cars* before it, *The Sweeney* was lauded for its realist style; its hero, Regan, and his helper Carter, where aeons away from *Dixon of Dock Green* which bizarrely, given its 'distance' from that decade's 'reality', was still running in the 1970s. But as Tulloch says, the 'realism' of *The Sweeney* is carefully selected and Regan's rule breaking is narratively legitimised:

> Regan has a *mandate* for his 'entrepreneurial' violence and rule-breaking. His (tragic and partial) corruption is the price the 'good' society pays for its protection from chaos. (ibid., p. 69)

The programme was the model for Hurd's oppositions in the TV police serial covered in Chapter 4. Regan and Carter epitomised: law versus rule; professionalism versus organisation; authority versus bureaucracy; intuition versus technology; masses versus intellectuals; comradeship versus rank. Summarising the work of Alan Clarke (1986) and Andrew Ross (1987), John Tulloch states:

The Sweeney is certainly a child of its time, marking a shift from earlier crime series which still consensualized crime as part of the 'unusual' disruption of post-war reconstruction, to the more confrontationist politics and increasing para-military function of the police from the late 1960s on. (ibid., p. 70)

It has been suggested that the pre-eminence of the TV cop genre has been superseded in British television of the 1990s; however, despite this, it is still evolving:

Arguably, the dynamic genre of the mid 1990s is the medical drama. There is at the same time a move towards the medicalization of crime within the crime series, with focus moving away from the police as the solvers of riddles to pathologists and criminal psychologists (*Cracker, Dangerfield* [1995-], *Silent Witness* [1996-], *McAllum* [1997-], *Bliss* [1997-]. (Brunsdon, 1998, p. 242)

One of the 'straight' TV cop programmes that developed the genre in the early 1990s was *Between the Lines* produced, like *Law and Order*, by Tony Garnett. *Between the Lines* focused on the branch of the police who investigate crimes by the police (for a consideration of how it articulated Hurd's oppositions see Lacey, 1998a). Brunsdon has concluded that it:

offers a very politicized image of the police, with explicit recognition of high-level political pressure, [there are] mention[s] of the Home Secretary and other less clearly identified sources of power. (Brunsdon, 1998, p. 240)

It remains to be seen how recent high-profile British cases, such as the release of the Guildford Four and Birmingham Six and the travesty of an investigation that sought the murderers of Stephen Lawrence, will inflect on the genre. If the relationship between society and such 'realist' genres was direct, we would have already seen police racism, and deaths in custody, being dealt with by the genre. The fact that such contentious issues have not, to date, appeared – to my knowledge – in the TV cop genre suggests there is an 'inbuilt' selection mechanism that screens out radical representations that directly challenge the status quo. Although, by reputation, *Law and Order* did offer a subversive take, it is very much a product of its time in an institutional sense: the programme almost certainly owes its existence to the organisational structure, and public service ethos, of the BBC. Even though the BBC remains a public service institution, reorganisation within the Corporation in the 1980s has probably made it impossible to get a highly controversial programme about the police made.

In order to address this 'inbuilt' mechanism of censorship we need to use the concept of ideology:

> In Bennett and Woollacott's view 'periods of generic change and innovation in popular fiction often coincide with those in which the ideological articulations through which hegemony was previously secured are no longer working to produce popular consent.' (ibid., p. 74)

Much of our information about the police derives from the TV cop genre. As soon as, say, both *Dixon of Dock Green* and *Z Cars* failed to create a convincing, modern representation of the police a new variant could be introduced. Hegemony is the way the dominant ideology secures popular consent to its worldview and if there is a mismatch between the dominant representations of, in this case, the police and society's understanding of the police, then the public may look elsewhere for their information. The dominant ideology constantly works to recoup oppositional forces and so in times, such as the early 1970s, when there is a change in the public's perception of the police, the mythic (in Barthes's sense) structures at work must alter. Genres powerfully articulate these myths because, within them, they can offer both the past (same) *and* the present (the difference). They can readily evolve to help create a new consensus. After *The Sweeney*, which undoubtedly influenced the public's perception of the police (and, of course, cop series which followed), the public could see it was *necessary* that the law be broken otherwise criminals would never be caught. 'Don't worry,' was the message, 'you know you can trust the "down-to-earth" cockneys Regan and Carter.'

It is highly likely that *The Sweeney* was popular *because* it offered a 'modern' representation of the police while remaining reassuring:

> For Fiske... texts are popular precisely because they obviate that uncertainty about the adequacy of the discourses we use to understand the world. The text is believable – and also confirms our social experience as believable – 'because its discourses are part of the ideology of common sense'. (ibid., pp. 76–7)

It is far more comfortable for an audience to believe 'all is well with world', and that 'happy ever after' is attainable, than to realise that corruption, and evil, are rife. Ironically, it is possibly easier to focus on the ideology influencing a text in non-realistic genres because the text is obviously divorced, at least to an extent, from reality.

5.7 Non-realistic genres – horror

We have seen how the TV cop genre and reality interact resulting in the evolution of the genre and, arguably, hegemonic consent from the audience. However, some genres do not appear to have a direct relationship with reality, for example science fiction, musicals and horror texts. Clearly these genres also evolve, as society changes, and this evolution, like that of the TV cop genre, will be governed by ideological changes. In this section we shall consider how the horror genre articulates the ideological concerns of society.

As noted in Chapter 1, a consideration of Propp's 'spheres of action' can show a text's ideological basis through what the hero and villain represent. In horror texts, the narrative disruption is often caused by a non-human villain: monster, zombie, vampire, werewolf and so on. This disruption is characterised by violence and the resolution, therefore, will be the cessation of violence, usually with the destruction of the 'fiend'. The binary opposition mobilised in the narrative is human:non-human.

> The monster, and the disorder it initiates and concretises, is always that which disrupts and challenges the definitions and categories of the 'human' and the 'natural'. Generally speaking, it is the monster's body which focuses the disruption. Either disfigured, or marked by a hetero-geneity of human and animal features, or marked only by a 'non-human' gaze, the body is always in some way signalled as 'other', signalled, precisely, as monstrous. (Neale, 1980, p. 21)

Horror texts are ideal for articulating what is repressed, the Other, in the human psyche. Society necessitates the repression of certain instincts, what Freud characterised as the 'id'. In the Victorian Gothic novel, for instance, we can see an expression of sexuality which was forbidden in 'polite society'. Modern horror often deals with particularly male fears about gender roles:

> Whenever male bodies are represented as monstrous in the horror film they assume characteristics usually associated with the female body: they experience a blood cycle, change shape, bleed, give birth, become penetrable, are castrated. (Creed, 1993, p. 118)

We can relate this to Neale's description, above, about how the narrative disruption is inscribed upon the monster's body. Related to gender, we can deduce that the male body is defined as the norm ('human') and therefore opposed by the female body; women's bodies represent the Other (as they can be in SF films – see Chapter 4) and are therefore a threat to masculinity. Carol Clover (1992) has linked together a number of killers, in the genre, by their sexual inadequacy starting with Hitchcock's *Psycho* (1960, remade in 1998) and including the *Friday the Thirteenth* series and Buffalo Bill in *The Silence of the Lambs* (1991).

> In a male-dominated culture, where power, money, law, social institutions are controlled by past, present and future patriarchs, woman as the Other assumes particular significance. The dominant images of women in our culture are entirely male-created and male-controlled. Woman's autonomy and independence are denied; onto women men project their own innate, repressed femininity in order to disown it as inferior. (Wood, 1985, p. 199)

Horror films often 'disown' femininity by destroying it; in *Dressed to Kill* (1980) the opening sequence shows a sexually desperate wife first masturbating and then having sex with a stranger, twice:

> On leaving his place in the evening, she is suddenly attacked and killed in the elevator. The cause-and-effect relationship between (illicit) sex and death could hardly more clearly drawn. (Clover, 1992, p. 34)

Sexually transgressive women, which in patriarchal terms means those who are active rather than passive, are punished for their behaviour. One of the more subversive of contemporary filmmakers, David Cronenberg, has inverted this view of the female body as monstrous:

> The protagonists of *Dead Ringers* and *The Fly* suffer from *womb envy*, a feeling of impotence clearly stemming from their jealousy of female reproductive power. (Robbins, 1993, p. 135)

Of the two, *The Fly* (1986) is more obviously a horror movie. Scientist Seth Brundle (Jeff Goldblum) creates a teleportation device but, after trying it out, finds himself genetically combined with a fly. He then undergoes a metamorphosis and becomes Brundlefly. The basis of his transformation is scientific and so *The Fly* is science fiction but the gruesome images that litter the film also place it firmly within the horror genre. Before Seth realises what is happening to him, he peers at himself in a mirror and examines his peculiar fingernails:

> The image is overloaded with visual *double entendre*, suggesting simultaneously the two furtive adolescent rites of masturbation (the finger's phallic shape) and pimple squeezing (the splat of goo that Brundle wipes off the mirror with a tissue). Here the unsettling visceral effects for which Cronenberg is famous are wrapped in a familiar context, substantiating theories that much of the horror genre's chilling impact derives from its allowing its audience to experience the return of the repressed in disguised forms. (ibid., p. 140)

Brundle is characterised as sexually naive and is initiated into the 'pleasures of the flesh' by Ronnie (Geena Davis). Up to this point he had only been able to teleport inanimate matter; after having had sex he realises that he has to programme the computer with an appreciation of the flesh. Brundle fatally teleports himself in a drunken, jealous fit when he mistakenly believes Ronnie is visiting another lover:

> Her behavior motivates the male characters' excessive disturbance at the site of reproductive certitude, exposing their failure to accept the biological reality of the brief, merely speculative role of the male individual in procreation. (ibid., p. 137)

Brundle feels threatened by Ronnie's independence which emphasises his lack of control over the 'female Other'. Men can never be sure that it is they who have impregnated their partner and, in this, the whole of the 'patriarchal project' – which attempts to control women – is threatened.

> Seth's teleportation pods, with their frankly uterine shape and vulviform glass doors, are clear womb simulacra; the lingering shots of his naked fetal crouch in the transmitter pod and his triumphant naked emergence from the receiver pod figure his teleportation project as an attempt to give birth to himself. (ibid.)

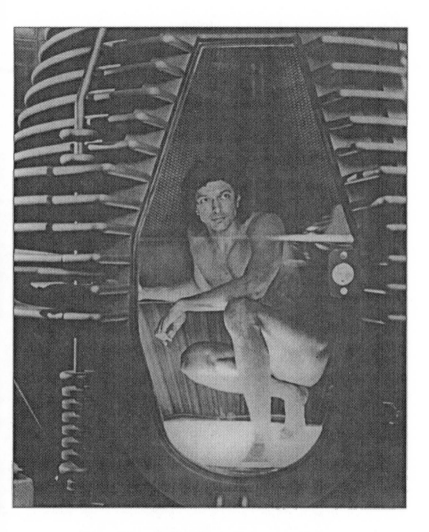

Figure 5.1 Seth's teleportation pods, with their
frankly uterine shape and vulviform glass doors

At the film's climax Brundlefly attempts to fuse himself with the pregnant Ronnie. In doing this he *will* control female sexuality for he will be able to give birth to his own child and hence live out the myth of total male control.

This reading of *The Fly* relies heavily upon Freudian ideas about the primacy of sexual motivation in behaviour. The horror genre, in dealing with the non-human, the monstrous part of our psyche, is ideal fodder for Freudian theory. There are other discourses that try to explain the attraction of horror; for instance the 1950s cycle of nuclear bomb generated mutants (for example *Them!*, 1954) articulated fears prompted by the Cold War and the arms race. Zombie films, particularly those directed by George Romero, can be seen as critiques of consumerism: the zombies wander around a shopping mall very like normal shoppers. Insecurities within the nuclear family, the prime social unit of bourgeois ideology, have manifested themselves in thrillers such as *Fatal Attraction* (1987) and *Sleeping With the Enemy* (1991).

Despite the non-realistic basis of the horror genre, its subject matter can still be related to contemporary society; we can unpick this relationship through an examination of ideology. Many horror texts deal with the male anxiety engendered by the sexually assertive woman who is threatening their traditionally dominant role. It has been suggested, in Chapter 4, that the *femme fatale* of neo *film noir* is also an example of increasingly powerful women in western society.

5.8 Genre and semiotics

In semiotic, or structuralist, terms genre can be considered to be *la langue* and individual texts *parole*. A genre's repertoire of elements, the rules of the sign system and generic texts articulate those rules. Iconography is also a sign system and can therefore be defined semiotically while the repertoire of elements are paradigms combined by genre in a syntagmatic fashion.

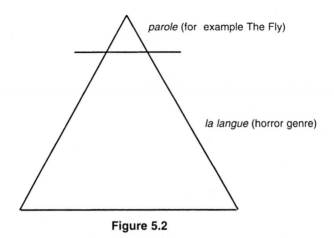

parole (for example The Fly)

la langue (horror genre)

Figure 5.2

Iconography

Clearly, because we recognise iconography as belonging to a particular genre, we are not perceiving the iconographic sign at the first level of signification, it exists at the second (or possibly a third) level, that of connotation.

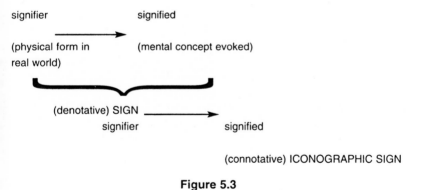

signifier   signified

(physical form in   (mental concept evoked)
real world)

(denotative) SIGN
    signifier   signified

                    (connotative) ICONOGRAPHIC SIGN

Figure 5.3

Iconography can connote, in conjunction with the other generic paradigms, a particular genre; for instance, while a crucifix will usually signify Christianity, it will only signify the horror genre in combination with other generic paradigms such as a vampire character. These paradigms are the repertoire of elements so a syntagmatic combination of, for example, a crucifix and a 'Gothic castle in stormy weather' setting is likely to signify the horror genre. Iconography evokes certain generic connotations which simultaneously define the genre and mobilise the discourses of that genre.

Exercise 5.3

Using the horror iconography of blood, crucifix, creaking doors, virginal victims and screams, note down the connotations you have of each of the signs *within the context of the horror genre*. (This instruction is important because if you simply consider the connotation of 'blood' you may think 'cut'.)

Some suggestions

Blood: connotes death because blood is necessary for life. If we can see blood then it has been spilt and a central opposition is established: lifeblood and death. Many teen horror movies celebrate an excess of gore; young teenage males, in particular, seem to be fascinated with the visceral detail of decapitation. Why should this obsession with bodily fluids be particularly pronounced at this age?

Crucifix: horror deals with the supernatural and so does religion. In addition, the important opposition of good:evil is often derived from religious imagery: a burning Hell beneath the Earth; the corruption of innocence; the defiance of the 'natural order'.

Creaking doors: associated with old houses or castles. Old buildings have a history (usually someone has died violently in the location or it is the residence of a certain Count Dracula) and the sound helps generate tension either as an enigma code (who is entering?) or through suggesting the protagonist can be heard as she or he enters.

Virginal victims: the good:evil opposition is often articulated by the natural:unnatural dichotomy. Nature is characterised by purity and the patriarchal ideology has defined virginal females as 'pure' (this is surely a response to male feelings of sexual inadequacy as it does not matter how fumbling a male is with a virgin because she will not know any better). Virgins also feature as a convenient princess for the hero to save and/or an opportunity to display naked female flesh.

Screams: out-of-control and usually female. The latest successful horror cycle was started by a film named after this iconography. The desperate edge to the 'scream', it is not a 'cry', suggests powerful forces and desperation; and again the female-as-victim is signified.

Genre as a syntagmatic system

As mentioned above, in semiotic terms, genre texts are a combination of the paradigms, or 'repertoire of elements': characters, setting, iconography, narrative and style of the text. A traditional genre text, for example gangster movies, exist as a combination of the following paradigms.

Table 5.3

Characters	Setting	Iconography	Narrative	Style of the text
gangsters	city	machine guns	gang warfare	fast moving
Mafia types	Chicago	fast cars	police v. gangs	action
moll	1920s	suits	rise and fall of 'hero'	chiaroscuro lighting
Mr Big	seedy areas	cigars		extreme violence
Mr Fixit	nightclub	lapel flowers		
		police technology		and so on

Postmodern genre texts, however, use another set of paradigms: they use, among other things, the genres themselves. *Pulp Fiction* (directed by Tarantino, 1994) is a postmodern movie; that is, we can best make sense of it with reference to other texts. I have considered elsewhere (Lacey, 1996a) how this film can be seen as the summation of Hollywood's history. In this context, we are interested in how it uses different genres in order to make meaning.

Pulp Fiction draws on the following genres and thereby draws upon these genres' repertoire of elements.

Table 5.4

Gangster movies	Film noir	Boxing movies	War movies
Mia as a gangster's moll; Mr Big (Marcellus Wallace); Mr Fixit (the 'Wolf')	Mia as a *femme fatale*; the briefcase is a reference to *Kiss Me Deadly*	the gold watch episode; Butch decides not to 'throw' the fight (as in *Body and Soul*)	Butch's dad's friend, played by Christopher Walken, tells a parody of a typical 'buddy' tale

This combination is what postmodernists call a bricolage. It is an eclectic mix of paradigms which intensifies a text's signification by 'its exploitation of signifiers from (a broad)... range of genres' (Philips, 1996, p. 136). However, *Pulp Fiction* draws on more than a number of genres, it also refers to the French *nouvelle vague*, a kitsch 1950s, the 1977 hit movie *Saturday Night Fever* and 1972's *Deliverance*.

Table 5.5

Nouvelle vague	Kitsch 1950s	Saturday Night Fever	Deliverance
Mia Wallace draws a rectangle* on screen instead of saying the word 'square'	the restaurant, Jackrabbit Slim's, is peopled by lookalikes of 1950s icons	a disco movie which starred John Travolta, who plays Vince; here, in contrast to the earlier film, his dancing is pathetic	Marsellus Wallace is raped by southern rednecks; this also occurred in *Deliverance*

*Presumably the fact Mia draws a rectangle, rather than a square, is also postmodern playfulness.

Tarantino is quite clearly a movie 'buff' (or nerd if you like). *Pulp Fiction* was a 'smash' hit (over $100 million at the North American box office) and it is highly unlikely that most of this audience were familiar with all of the paradigms Tarantino drew upon. Clearly this ignorance did not matter for many and audiences are entitled to ask 'so what?' Postmodernism does not, is not intended to, mean anything. (Those who are keen to investigate a structural theory of genre further are directed to Rick Altman's *Film/Genre*, 1999.)

5.9 Ideology and genre criticism

We have seen how ideology operates in genre texts but, inevitably, genre itself is an ideological construct. Chapter 5 of *Image and Representation* considered, briefly, the *'auteur* theory' of cinema which conceptualised the director as the film's author. While this had originally been a polemic attempting to give film the status of an art form, it had rapidly become a limited, and limiting, perspective with which to analyse cinema. 'Genre studies', a response to the *auteur* position, was generated in the late 1960s and early 70s by Film Studies to fulfil two complementary functions:

> First, it was to challenge and displace the dominant notions of cinema installed and defended on the basis of the assumed excellence of the 'taste' of a few journalists and reviewers, appealing to the 'age-old canons and principles' of Art in general...
>
> Secondly, in the wake of the realisation that any form of artistic production is a rule-bound activity firmly embedded in social history, the theory of cinema set about discovering the structures which underpinned groups of films and gave them their social grounding. (Willemen, 1980, p. 1)

These 'functions', or projects, were ideological in the sense that they attempted to create a new way of understanding, or aesthetics of, film texts. This in itself may seem to be a harmless activity, however, at the time, its subversiveness was more apparent. Much of this reappraisal of film culture was taking place in the British Film Institute's education department which had:

> become the intellectual centre of debate about the cinema in Britain, but the terms we used (*auteur*, genre, structuralism, semiology) antagonised the wider film culture to an extent that would hardly be credible now. The BFI itself mounted a governors' committee of inquiry into the activities of the department and in essence recommended that it stop being interested in ideas. (McArthur, 1992, p. 37)

Many of the 'leading lights' in the department resigned in protest; clearly the 'ideas' they were dealing with touched an Establishment nerve. The general thrust of these ideas was a redefinition of what constituted art and attacked, just as the original *auteur* theory had done, to an extent, the distinction between art and popular culture. Richard Dyer has described the conventional distinction between 'art' and 'entertainment', a distinction that also applies to 'art' and 'genre'.

Table 5.6

Art	Entertainment (genre)
edifying	hedonistic
elitist	democratic
refined	vulgar
difficult	easy

Source: Dyer, 1992, p. 12

As we have seen, genre texts are 'easy' for an audience because they offer familiar structures that can be read without much difficulty. Genre texts are democratic in that they are, at least in their time, popular culture texts. Their function is usually to give pleasure which they often do in a melodramatic fashion; that is to say, vulgarly. To an extent we are conflating entertainment and genre here; but the important point is that art and genre can be considered as opposites.

In the days before the *auteur* theory, European art cinema was often contrasted, favourably, with Hollywood's generic cinema. The former was supposed to deal with the universal themes of existence while the latter pandered, with formulaic fiction, to the lowest common denominator in the audience. However, Andrew Tudor suggests that art cinema *is* a genre:

> Deliberately an obviously intellectual... with extremely visible individual stylistic characteristics. Bergman's silhouettes, puritan obsessiveness, and grunting Dark Age meals; Antonioni's minimal dialogue, grey photography, and carefully bleak compositions; and Fellini's self-indulgent surrealistic imagery. (Tudor, 1976, p. 123)

This categorisation is clearly at odds with the idea of a repertoire of elements, but Tudor's point does show a certain amount of hypocrisy in the elitist assumption that art is better than genre: 'art films' were, and are, also characterised by expectation. A similar thing happens when critics, and publishers, attempt to categorise a new writer. Novelists who do not readily lend themselves to genre categorisation find themselves being described as being similar to other writers. For example, Oonya Kempadoo was described in a catalogue as 'the new Arundhati Roy'.

In the late 1990s, genre criticism is well established in 'academia' and so the battle appears to have been won; that is, until the next new way of considering texts appears.

5.10 Genres and scheduling

This book has been, primarily, concerned with how a text signifies itself as belonging to a genre. However, extra-textual variables can also affect how an audience defines a text as a particular genre. For example:

> When CBS scheduled *Cagney and Lacey* after *Magnum* on a Thursday evening, it rated poorly. But when rescheduled on a Monday... known as 'women's night'...(it topped the ratings). Because *Cagney and Lacey* shows a particularly even mix of generic characteristics, its prime genre was in some doubt, and so scheduling was able to tip the balance away from masculine cop show towards soap opera or woman's show. (Fiske, 1987, p. 113)

Exercise 5.4

Consider the listings in Figure 5.4 and 'move' five programmes to different times or onto different channels; what difference does the change make to audience expectation? For example, what sort of text would audiences expect Three Colours Red to be if it was broadcast at 8.00pm on ITV?

The consideration of scheduling does show how much when and where a programme is broadcast affects our *expectations* of such programmes. Clearly, in most instances, rescheduling would not change the genre of a piece; it is only with generically ambiguous texts, like *Cagney and Lacey*, that it can make that much difference. It is notable that minority texts, such as the art film *Three Colours Red*, are consigned not only to Channel 4 but also to the 'small' hours of the morning.

MONDAY 7 JULY

OTHER REGIONS

BBC SCOTLAND
BBC1 6.30–7.00pm Reporting Scotland
BBC2 7.15am as BBC2 England **8.35** Upfor it **9.35** Great Myths and Mysteries of the 20th Century: The Hindenburg Crash Mystery **10.00** as BBC2 England

ANGLIA
6.00am as Yorkshire/North East **12.55pm** A Country Practice **1.25** Home and Away **1.50** Up Elect **2.20** Blue Heelers **3.20** as Yorkshire/North East **5.10** Shortland Street **5.40** as Yorkshire/North East **6.00** Home and Away **6.25** Anglia News **7.00** as Yorkshire/North East **10.40** Crime Question **11.40** Highlander **12.40am** Film: The Ordeal of Bill Carney: drama based on a true story starring Richard Crenna and Ray Sharkey **2.35** Rockmania: music magazine **3.35** God's Gift **4.35** World in Action **5.00** Coronation Street **5.30** as Yorkshire/North East

BORDER
6.00am as Yorkshire/North East **12.20pm** Breakaways: holiday destinations **12.25** Border News **12.30** as Yorkshire/North East **12.55** Shortland Street **1.25** Home and Away **1.50** Dr Quinn: Medicine Woman: frontier medical drama **2.50** Gardener's Diary: tips **3.20** as Yorks/North East **5.10** Dinosaurs: familyfun **5.40** as Yorkshire/North East **6.00** Lookaround: Regional Weather **6.30** Home and Away **7.00** as Yorkshire/North East **10.40** Hooked on Scotland **11.10** The Rock and Goal Years: music and soccer action **11.40** Emmerdale **12.40am** War of the Worlds: sci-fi drama **1.35** Late and Loud: studio debate **2.40** Real Stories of the Highway Patrol **3.00** Film: Rage on Ice: drama about a young ice hockey player **4.35** World in Action **5.00** The Time ... the Place: studio debate **5.30** as Yorkshire/North East

CENTRAL
6.00am as Yorkshire/North East **12.55pm** A Country Practice **1.25** Home and Away **1.50** Blue Heelers **2.50** High Road **3.20** as Yorkshire/North East **5.10** Shortland Street **5.40** as Yorkshire/North East **6.00** Home and Away **6.25** Central News **7.00** as Yorks/North East **10.40** Film: The Killing Mind: thriller starring Stephanie Zimbalist **12.40am** War of the Worlds: sci-fi drama **1.35** Late and Loud: studio debate **2.40** Real Stories of the Highway Patrol **3.00** Film: Rage on Ice: drama about a young ice hockey player **4.35** Jobfinder **5.25** Asian Eye **5.30** as Yorkshire/North East

GRANADA
6.00am as Yorkshire/North East **12.55pm** Shortland Street **1.25** Home and Away **1.50** Dr Quinn: Medicine Woman **2.50** Gardener's Diary **3.20** as Yorkshire/North East **6.00** Granada Tonight **6.30** On the Ball: sports quiz **7.00** as Yorkshire/North East **10.40** Funny Business **11.10** The Rock and Goal Years **11.40** Emmerdale **12.40am** War of the Worlds: sci-fi drama **1.35** Late and Loud: studio debate **2.40** Real Stories of the Highway Patrol **3.00** Film: Rage on Ice: drama about a young ice hockey player **4.35** World in Action **5.00** The Time ... the Place: studio debate **5.30** as Yorkshire/North East

1 BBC1

9.30pm Goodbye Dalestrace: times are a changing for Sharon, Tracey and Garth, but are they for the good?

6.00pm Six O'Clock News
Martyn Lewis and Moira Stuart.
Weather Suzanne Charlton
Subtitled 991

6.30–7.00 Leeds
Look North
Mike McCarthy and Clare Frisby with a roundup of the day's news from across Yorkshire and Lincolnshire. With sports news from Damian Johnson and weather from Darren Bett.
Editor John Lilley Subtitled 571

6.30–7.00 Newcastle
Look North
News from the North East and Cumbria, with Carol Malia, Chris Jackson, John Lawrence. Sports news from Steve Sutton......... 571
REGIONAL PROGRAMMES

7.00 Big Break
Jim Davidson hosts the popular snooker game show. Tonight's programme features Steve Davis, Martin Clark and Mark Davis. With referee John Virgo.
Director Phil Chilvers; Producer John Burrowes Stereo Subtitled 8993

7.30 Mastermind
Tonight's edition comes from the Cambridge Union Society. The contenders are Ann Kelly, Akintunde Akinkunmi, Leo Stevenson, and Susan Long. Their chosen subjects are the life and music of Buddy Holly, the Nuremberg Trials, Dutch Art 1620–72 and Olave, Lady Baden-Powell. Introduced by Magnus Magnusson.
Director/Producer David Mitchell Stereo Subtitled 755

8.00 EastEnders
Ian wrestles with the residents. There's a clash involving the men in Peggy's life.
Repeated on Tuesday Stereo Subtitled 2939

8.30 The Peter Principle
Last in the new comedy series about an inept bank manager. *Bank Holiday.* When Susan is asked to apply for the job of manager at a different branch of C and P Bank, Peter decides he should have a go himself.
Peter .... JIM BROADBENT
Susan .... CLAIRE SKINNER
Geoffrey .... STEPHEN MOORE
Bradley .... DAVID SCHNEIDER
David .... DANIEL FLYNN
Brenda .... TRACY KEATING
Iris .... JANETTE LEGGE
Written by Mark Burton, John O'Farrell and Dan Patterson; Director Nick Wood; Producer Dan Patterson
Stereo Subtitled 7674

9.00 Nine O'Clock News
With John Humphrys. Subtitled
Regional News
Weather Suzanne Charlton
Subtitled 3026

9.30 Birds of a Feather
Three Up, Two Down. With their finances in ruins, Sharon and Tracey take drastic action to prepare for a more secure future. But Garth has his own ideas, and Dorien has men on her mind.
See today's choices.
Sharon .... PAULINE QUIRKE
Tracey .... LINDA ROBSON
Dorien .... LESLEY JOSEPH
Garth .... MATTHEW SAVAGE
Jonathan .... ROBIN KERMODE
Kimberley .... KIRSTIE SENIOR
Waiter .... ASHOK KUMAR
Letting agent .... LLOYD MAGUIRE
Jerry .... ROBERT HARLEY
Japanese family .... YOSHINORI YAMAMOTO, KUMI NARITA, AKIRA NARITA
Episode written by Gary Lawson and John Phelps; Director Baz Taylor; Producer Tony Charles
Stereo Subtitled 87858

10.00 Panorama
Another in depth look at a major topical story from home or abroad.
Editor Steve Hewlett Subtitled 873129

10.45 Omnibus
Dame Henrietta's Dream
Hampstead Garden Suburb was founded at the turn of the century by Dame Henrietta Barnett, a Victorian philanthropist who dreamed of rehousing east London's poor in an area without class divisions. Tonight's programme looks at life in the suburb, highlighting the controversy surrounding the proposal to erect an eruv, an artificial boundary that must not be crossed by orthodox Jews on the Sabbath.
See today's choices.
Producer Sharon Maguire; Editor Nigel Williams
Stereo Subtitled 594587
◆ See John Peel: page 9

11.40 A Dry White Season
Drama starring **Donald Sutherland** **Janet Suzman** and featuring **Marlon Brando**
South Africa, 1976: Afrikaner Ben du Toit's eyes are finally opened to the full horror of apartheid when Gordon, his gardener for 15 years, is arrested and tortured to death. Increasingly ostracised by his friends and family, Ben begins a dangerous crusade to uncover the truth and expose a corrupt and brutal regime.
Ben du Toit .... DONALD SUTHERLAND
Susan du Toit .... JANET SUZMAN
Stanley Makhaya .... ZAKES MOKAE
Captain Stolz .... JURGEN PROCHNOW
Melanie Bruwer .... SUSAN SARANDON
Ian McKenzie .... MARLON BRANDO
Gordon Ngubene .... WINSTON NTSHONA
Emily .... THOKO NTSHINGA
Bruwer .... LEONARD MAGUIRE
Colonel Viljoen .... GERARD THOOLEN
Director Euzhan Palcy (1989, 15)
Subtitled 455620
◆ See Films: pages 52–59 ★★★
◆ Ten things every Susan Sarandon fan ought to know: p 50

1.25–1.30am Weather

2 BBC2

8.30pm The *Travel Show* team seek value for money on a long weekend break in the Portuguese city of Lisbon

6.30pm Athletics
Live coverage from tonight's IAAF Grand Prix in Stockholm. The men's 100 metres should provide one of the evening's highlights with Trinidad's Ato Boldon likely to defend the title he won at last year's meeting. Triple-jumper Jonathan Edwards was Britain's only winner in Stockholm 12 months ago, but with the world championships just over three weeks away, a large British contingent is expected to be in action tonight. Commentary is provided by David Coleman, Paul Dickenson, Stuart Storey and Christina Boxer. Introduced by Helen Rollason with Brendan Foster.
Producer Martin Webster; Editor Andrew Clement Stereo 35113

8.00 Motormonth
Tonight, there's coverage of the continuing battle for the British Rally championship with action from the Scottish International, staged through the forests around Dumfries. After three events, Alister McRae leads the championship by a single point. There's also a report from the Le Mans 24-hour race on the challenge mounted by the McLaren F1 GTR car driven by former touring car ace Steve Soper and ex-Formula One stars JJ Lehto and Nelson Piquet. Plus, a look at the remarkable array of racing cars on show at the Goodwood Festival of Speed. Presented by Steve Rider.
Producer Ken Burton; Series producer Mark Wilkin Stereo Subtitled 3281

8.30 The Travel Show
This week, Juliet Morris takes a fly-drive package holiday along the border that links Texas with Mexico. Picking up her hire car at San Antonio airport, she discovers an alternative Grand Canyon in Big Bend National Park, and calls into the small Mexican town of Ciudadacuna for breakfast. In *A Tale of Two Travellers*, Fi Glover and Simon Calder spend a long weekend in the Portuguese city of Lisbon where they find the difference in their budgets (Fi has £550 to spend, Simon just £300) contributes to their separate experiences in a city reputed to be the nightlife capital of Europe.
Series producer Andrea Michell; Editor Liz Warner Stereo 8216

9.00 The Vicar of Dibley
Another episode from the first series of the comedy.
The Window and the Weather. Replacing a window in the church proves to be a problem.
Geraldine Granger .... DAWN FRENCH
David Horton .... GARY WALDHORN
Hugo Horton .... JAMES FLEET
Alice Tinker .... EMMA CHAMBERS
Letitia Cropley .... LIZ SMITH
Frank Pickle .... JOHN BLUTHAL
Jim Trott .... TREVOR PEACOCK
Owen Newitt .... ROGER LLOYD PACK
Daniel Frobisher .... NICHOLAS LE PROVOST
Written by Richard Curtis; Director Dewi Humphreys; Producer Jon Plowman
Repeat Stereo Subtitled 3
Postponed from 23 June

9.30 United Kingdom!
A season of programmes following the lives of people from all four corners of the nation.
I Just Wanna Be Joe Public
Having spent most of the last years in prison, 35-year-old Tony, from Bolton, has reached a crossroads. Abused by his father as a child, violence has featured prominently in Tony's life but now, with his latest prison sentence nearing completion, he has decided to go straight and set an example to his five children. This film follows Tony's efforts to start a new life. (*Tottering Bipeds* is tomorrow at 7.10pm).
Director Colin Luke; Producer Allan Neuroder Stereo Subtitled 1

10.00 Athletics
Highlights from tonight's IAAF Grand Prix meeting in Stockholm including action from the men's 5,000 metres. Stereo 66
Followed by **UK Image** Another humorous film reflecting part of the British shared experience with photographer Martin Parr

10.30 Newsnight
With Kirsty Wark. Subtitled 93

11.15 Cricket: Third Test
Highlights from the final day's play at Old Trafford. Introduced by Richie Benaud. Stereo 594
Followed by **Weatherview**

12.00 The Midnight Hour
Late-night political chat. With Bernard Ingham.
Editor Alexandra Henderson
Stereo 78
CEEFAX page 622

12.30–7.15am
The Learning Zone
OPEN UNIVERSITY
12.30 Ensembles in Performance Rpt Subtitled 88241 **1.00** The Newtonians Rpt 36779 **1.30** Ernst and the Surrealist Revolution Rpt 75108
SUMMER NIGHTS
2.00 Great Outdoors Collection: Tracks 12206
BBC FOCUS
4.00 Italia 2000 Rpt 86008 **4.3** Royal Institution Discourse Rpt 80002 **5.30** RCN Nursing Update Unit 72 78011
OPEN UNIVERSITY
6.00 The University of Salamanca Rpt 7262136 **6.25** Ferrara Rpt 7241663 **6.50–7.15am** Religion and Society in Victorian Bristol Rpt 6472717
LEARNING ZONE GUIDE (0181) 746 1

ITV YORKSHIRE/C3 NORTH EAST

THE WORLD

8.30pm Anthea Turner's travels are mapped out, but will viewers identify this week's destination?

5.55–7.00pm Yorkshire
5.55 Calendar Regional news magazine, with Christa Ackroyd and Mike Morris.
Subtitled 735200
Followed by **Regional Weather**
6.30–7.00 Tonight A topical weekday regional magazine, presented by Christine Talbot.
Editor Simon Schofield *Stereo Subtitled* 839

5.55–7.00pm North East
5.55 Regional Weather 324007
6.00–7.00pm North East Tonight
Magazine and news programme, presented by Mike Neville, with Pam Royle and Andrew Friend in Newcastle and Dawn Thewlis and Andy Kluz on Teesside. Plus reports from Melanie Abbott in Sunderland and Wendy Homewood in York. There's also sports news and weather reports.
Editor Graeme Thompson
Subtitled 97281

7.00 Wheel of Fortune
More contestants try to solve word puzzles as they compete for a car or a cash prize of £20,000. Hosted by Bradley Walsh and Jenny Powell.
Director Chris Fox Producer Kevin Moon
Stereo Subtitled 4587

7.30 Coronation Street
Steve moves in on Maxine. Les Battersby tries to interest Roy in some merchandise.
Episode written by John Stevenson
For cast see Wednesday, Repeated Saturday at 1.20am Subtitled ...823

8.00 World in Action
Tonight a programme exposes a scam which is exploiting charitable causes and conning them large amounts of money. It reveals how the unsuspecting charities are being conned into authorising collections on their behalf – only to discover that they receive a fraction of the money collected, with the operators keeping the rest. Amazingly, it is all legal.
Producer Jackie Finch Editor
Stewart Prebble Repeated on 4.30am
Stereo Subtitled 7007
NOTE: this Material Advice is topical. its subject matter may change

8.30 Turner round the World
Soul singer Alexander O'Neal is tonight's special guest as the live game show hosted by

Anthea Turner, in which viewers compete for a prize of a round-the-world trip for two. Pre-recorded segments show Anthea in a mystery city. If viewers identify the location they can ring 0891 333333 (calls charged at 25p per minute). Last in the series.
Director Stuart McDonald, Producer
Richard Woolfe *Stereo* 9842

9.00 Bramwell
CHOICE Medical drama set in Victorian London. On the eve of his wedding to Alice, Robert withdraws his support for Eleanor's work at the Thrift. Last in the series.
See today's choices.

Eleanor Bramwell	JEMMA REDGRAVE
Robert Bramwell	DAVID CALDER
Joe Marsham	MAUREEN BEATTIE
Joe Marsham	KEVIN MCMONAGLE
Nurse Carr	RUTH SHEEN
Oliver Colt	BERWICK KALER
Bart Loonis	TOM CHADBON
Kate	KEELEY HAWKES
Sidney Bentley	BEN HULAER

Written by Lucy Gannon. Producers
Harriet Davison, Tim Whitby. Director
David Tucker *Stereo Subtitled* 5738

10.00 News at Ten
With Trevor McDonald *Subtitled*
Weather Martyn Davies 80649
10.30 Regional News
Weather 323736
10.40 New Voices
The series featuring writers new to TV drama.
Dance for a Stranger
A suicidal solicitor plans to die, but a secretary intervenes.
Jane	EMILY WOLLF
Mr Jackson	JOHN THOMPSON
Writer John Martin Jenson
Producer Christine Benson
Director Debbie Isitt 834991

11.10 Baywatch Nights
Heatwave. Members of a band are mysteriously killed off. *Stereo* 738649

12.05am Blue Bayou
CHOICE Crime drama starring Alfre Woodard. A Los Angeles district attorney moves to New Orleans with her wayward son and joins the investigation into a socialite's murder.
Ansonia Pitre	ALFRE WOODARD
Nora Pitre	KEITH WILLIAMS
Lily Pitre	MARIO VAN PEEBLES
Lolly Forrest	ELIZABETH ASHLEY
Benny Forrest	JOY THOMAS
Dennis Forrest Serrata	PAMELA GIDLEY
Director Karen Arthur (1990)
Stereo 837408
♦ *See Films: pages 52–59* ★★

1.50 Not Fade Away
Former Herman's Hermits lead singer Peter Noone chooses his favourite music.
Showcased Thursday 9595408

2.50 The Chart Show
Shown on Saturday at 11.30am
Stereo 4995601

**3.50 New series
Cybernet**
The latest computer games.
Repeated Friday 2.30am ..859517936

4.20 Jobfinder
Job news. *Stereo* 6203175

**5.30–6.00am
Morning News** 73137

4 CHANNEL 4

10.55pm Far Eastern fashion: Chinese designers are moving towards more daring creations

6.00pm Tour de France
The cyclists face one of the longest stages of the race today, the 262km ride from St Valéry-en-Caux to Vire.
Repeated at 4.55am Stereo 129

6.30 Hollyoaks
Jude faces her father. Mandy gives Cindy an ultimatum.
Jude Cunningham	DAVINA TAYLOR
Lewis Richardson	BEN HULL
Cindy Cunningham	STEPHANIE WARING
Maddie Parker	YASMIN BANNERMAN
Mandy Richardson	SARAH DUNN
Lucy Benson	ALanna TAYLOR
Tony	TONY SAWYER
Tony Hutchinson	NICK PICKARD
Jennifer Bolton	WILLIAM MELLOR
Lisa Bolton	ISABELLE MURPHY
Jake Bolton	JOSHUA SAUNDERS
Emily Bolton	BETH McDONALD
Ian Bolton	STEPHEN MACKENNA
Dawn Cunningham	LISA WILLIAMSON
Carol Groves	NATHALIE CASEY
Julie Matthews	JULIE BUCKFIELD
Kathleen O'Neill	EMMA RIGBY
Hollyoaks Director David Andrews
Omnibus next Tuesday
Stereo Subtitled 281

7.00 Channel 4 News
With Jon Snow.
Weather *Stereo Subtitled* 632587

**7.50 New series
Chester Mystery Plays**
First in a series of five daily short plays telling a tale from the Bible, as performed by the people of Chester every five years since 1422. Today, how God created the world.
Subtitled 481007

8.00 Dosh
The guide to making the most of your money. This week covers CVs and successful job interview techniques, advice on buying a personal computer and how to deal with cowboy contractors.
With Adam Faith.
Series editor Deborah Attwell
Stereo Subtitled 5649

8.30 Absolutely Animals
Wendy Turner encounters a dog trained to warn his epileptic owner of impending attacks. Quite how dogs can do this is a medical mystery, but more animals are now being taught to use their special ability. There's a report on a new wave of deer poaching in Devon, and Mark Evans shows how to keep a tropical fish tank clean.
Executive producer Nick Cheatham
Series editor Barbara Altounyan
Stereo Subtitled 7484

4 CHANNEL 4 (continued)

9.00 Secret History
Breaking the Sound Barrier
CHOICE Britain was a leading contender to produce the first plane to break the speed of sound until the top secret project was cancelled in the forties. Tonight's film probes the reasons behind Britain's sudden withdrawal from the race, won by the Americans on 14 October 1947.
See today's choices.
Director, Producer Tony Stark
Executive producer Andy Fontialba
Subtitled 3378

10.00 NYPD Blue
Where's Swaldo? An African-American activist, once the victim of a racial slur from Sipowicz, is murdered.
Bobby Simone	JIMMY SMITS
Andy Sipowicz	DENNIS FRANZ
Arthur Fancy	JAMES MCDANIEL
James Martinez	NICHOLAS TURTURRO
Sylvia Costas	SHARON LAWRENCE
Greg Medavoy	GORDON CLAPP
Diane Russell	KIM DELANEY
Stereo Subtitled	801216

10.55 Mao's New Suit
For decades Chinese people followed the example of Chairman Mao in fashion, wearing simple outfits in blue or grey. But things are changing. This film follows two young Chinese designers as they break away from tradition and parade bold new ideas at their first fashion show, held in the booming city of Shanghai.
Director, Producer Sally Ingleton
Stereo Subtitled 2700674

12.00 Canto Fever
Three Manchester university students, all of Chinese origin, speak about Cantonese pop music. 6544137

**12.15–4.55am
Century of Cinema**
12.15 Three Colours Red
CHOICE Drama starring Irène Jacob, Jean-Louis Trintignant. When a fashion model runs over a dog and returns it to the owner, a retired judge, an unlikely relationship develops between them. In French with English subtitles.
(1994, 15) 848514
♦ *See Films: pp 52–59* ★★★★★
2.05 Polish Cinema
Documentary by director Paweł Łoziński, exploring the power of film images. 9772963
3.20 A Short Film about Love
CHOICE Drama. A shy 19-year-old man becomes infatuated with an older woman, in Polish with English subtitles.
(1988, 18) 601872
♦ *See Films: pages 52–59* ★★★
4.55 Tour de France
A repeat of today's action.
Stereo Subtitled 4004750
5.30–6.00am Backdate
Retrospective quiz.
Repeat Stereo Subtitled 71779

5 CHANNEL 5

9.00pm Suburban blues: Dan Aykroyd upsets the life of John Belushi when he moves next door

6.00pm Move On Up
Quiz with Richard Morton.
Director/Producer Mike Mansfield
Stereo Subtitled 7833858

6.30 Family Affairs
Jack's lover is revealed.
This week's episodes written by Stuart Morris, Maureen Gold, Veronica Henry, Dave Collins. Producer Morag Bain
Director Brita Leslie Lyon. Repeated tomorrow at 12.30pm. For cast see Tuesday. Omnibus next Sunday
Stereo Subtitled 7744930

7.00 Tell the Truth
Kirsty Young conducts a live debate into the future of hunting with representatives from the pro-hunting lobby and those in favour of a ban. Both parties present their arguments and face questions from a studio audience.
Director Stuart McDonald, Producer
Claudia Joseph 9938484

8.00 Hot Property
A middle-aged couple whose children have left home look for a property in Sussex.
Producers Jennifer Gordon, Cas Peacock.
Executive producers Fenton Bailey and Randy Barbato. Repeated tomorrow at 10.30am *Stereo Subtitled* 8029387

8.30 5 News
With a *First on Five* report.
Stereo Subtitled 6008804

9.00 Neighbors
Comedy starring John Belushi, Dan Aykroyd. Earl and Enid Keese enjoy a contented suburban life, but then their world is turned upside down by the arrival of a raucous couple next door.
Earl Keese	JOHN BELUSHI
Vic	DAN AYKROYD
Enid Keese	KATHRYN WALKER
Ramona	CATHY MORIARTY
Director John G Avildsen
(1981, 18) 60805200
♦ *See Films: pages 52–59* ★★★

10.50 The Jack Docherty Show
The first of five chat show compilations. *Stereo* ...1557468

11.35 Prisoner: Cell Block H
Paul baits Tony. *Repeat* 5853723

12.35am Live and Dangerous
With extreme sports action in San Diego. *Stereo* 85781311

**5.30–6.00am
100 Per Cent**
Shown at 5.30pm Stereo ..3004446

Figure 5.4

247

5.11 Conclusion: narrative and genre

Narrative and genre are metalanguages, they 'suggest' to an audience how to read a text. Although the concepts are closely related, this relationship is not on equal terms. At the bottom of the pile are 'generic and narrative' texts; above them is genre; on top is narrative. This suggests that, in a sense, all 'narrative genres' can offer are, simply, a variation on narrative form; for instance, another way of resolving a disruption using a different sets of characters, settings and so on. Similarly, all generic *texts* can offer are variations on the genre form.

Narrative

Narrative genres, for example horror

Narrative and generic texts, for example *The Fly*

Figure 5.5

We have seen, in this book, that narrative is endemic (*homo narrans*) and, although not all genres are narrative in their construction (for example, lifestyle magazines), genre is only slightly less influential. So maybe we are *homo narrans de generibus* (tellers of generic tales).

APPENDIX 1

The purpose of the appendix is to elaborate on narrative detail for those who wish to know more about films referred to in the text.

Basic Instinct (Paul Verhoeven, 1992)

This film generated much publicity through its use of 'explicit' sex scenes. It is a *film noir* (see Chapter 4) which suggests that the *femme fatale* (Catherine Tramell played by Sharon Stone) character is the 'ice-pick' murderer until the closing scenes when the 'real' killer is revealed. However, there is much ambiguity about this point; in the final scene of the film, the hero – Nick (Michael Douglas) – is having sex with Catherine when she reaches for an ice pick but does not pick it up:

> the film tries to have it both ways, depending on whether one follows its narrative, which established Beth Gamer as the killer, or its *mise-en-scène*, which, as Verhoeven claims, identifies Catherine Tramell as the culprit through her metonymic association with the deadly ice pick in the final shot. (Cohan, 1998, pp. 267-8)

We might be inclined to argue here that Verhoeven is an unreliable sender as it is unlikely that both versions are true. However, it is arguable that the film is coherent in the narrative it presents as it is possible that Tramell framed Beth Gamer.

Nora Prentiss (Vincent Sherman, 1947)

Although Nora discourages Richard Talbot's infatuation he decides to fake his death as he cannot bring himself to ask for a divorce. He takes on a new identity but after being facially scarred, beyond recognition, he ends up in court charged with the murder of himself. Even when he's found guilty he cannot reveal the truth because he would forced, shamefully, to face his family. Parting from Nora, who has supported him throughout, he ends the film on death row.

Psycho (Alfred Hitchcock, 1960)

Later in the film, after Marion has been murdered, the camera roams around her room and focuses on the stolen money reminding the audience that if she had not sinned then she would have lived and Norman Bates's crime was one of lust not avarice.

The Searchers (John Ford, 1956)

Edwards does get an opportunity to kill Debbie but, in one of the most famous scenes in cinema, he picks her up (in the same way he had done at the film's beginning). Edwards' hate has gone, coinciding with the shift from him being the hero to becoming the helper. Edwards has visibly aged by the film's ending suggesting the time for racial hatred is over.

Strange Days (Kathryn Bigelow, 1995)

The total budget of the film was $42m and it grossed only $7.919m at the North American box office (source: IMDB).

North America is heading for a conflagration until, at the last moment, in an almost *deus ex machina*, the chief of police says 'arrest that man': the villain is captured (they were rogue cops and not LAPD death squads) and the explosion of racial violence never happens. This 'happy ending' sits very awkwardly with the subversive view of North American society offered up until this point. The ending seems forced, as if without it finance would not have been forthcoming. This is characteristic of Hollywood; in the 1930s gangster-movie cycle the hero was the gangster (obviously a villain in society's terms); the principal character, therefore, had to be punished – usually by death – at the narrative's resolution.

The Usual Suspects (Bryan Singer, 1995)

After a convoluted opening it becomes clear that the narrator is Verbal Kint (played by Kevin Spacey) who is being interrogated by a customs officer. Much of the tale is taken up with questioning the identity of Keyzer Soze who, we find at the end, is (probably) Kint and that much (all?) of the details in the narration where taken from words on a noticeboard in the interrogation room. This suggests that the whole tale was made up.

Appendix 2: Popular Culture Genres

Television

The top ten programmes on British television (source: Barb/RSMB) for the week 26 May–1 June 1997 were:

1. *EastEnders*
2. *Coronation Street*
3. *Emmerdale*
4. *Birds of a Feather*
5. *Touching Evil*
6. *Neighbours*
7. *The Bill*
8. *Lenny's Big Amazon Adventure*
9. *A Royal Gala*
10. *National Lottery Live*

Five of the top ten programmes (six if we include *The Bill*) are soap operas which, although narratively unconventional, do, as we have seen, fulfil both Propp's and Todorov's ideas.

In 1977 the top ten were (source: *Radio Times* 28 June–4 July, 1997):

1. *Coronation Street*
2. *Sale of the Century*
3. *General Hospital*
4. *What's On Next*
5. *Man About the House*
6. *Dawson and Friends*
7. *Crossroads*
8. *News at Ten*

9. *Get Some In*
10. *Winner Takes All*

My vague memories of 1977 suggest that at least three of these programmes were soap operas and two others sitcoms; the latter, too, conforms to conventional narrative structure except, as a series, their resolution returns the situation to exactly the same as situation A1.

Movies

In 1996 the top ten box-office films (source: *Screen International* 24–30 January, 1997) in North America were:

1. *Independence Day*
2. *Twister*
3. *Mission: Impossible*
4. *The Rock*
5. *Ransom*
6. *101 Dalmatians*
7. *The Nutty Professor*
8. *The Birdcage*
9. *A Time To Kill*
10. *The First Wives Club*

Early in 1997 the trade journal *Screen International* listed the 'US All-Time Highest Grossers' ($m) adjusted to the then current dollar value:

1. *Gone With The Wind* (1939) ($1,250.6)
2. *Snow White and the Seven Dwarfs* (1937) ($955.9)
3. *ET – The Extraterrestrial* (1982) ($698.2)
4. *Star Wars* (1977) ($648.4)
5. *One Hundred and One Dalmatians* (1961) ($632.0)
6. *Bambi* (1942) ($621.9)
7. *Jaws* (1975) ($568.2)
8. *The Sound of Music* (1965) ($544.6)
9. *The Ten Commandments* (1956) ($527.1)
10. *Mary Poppins* (1964) ($498.0)

In popular film, at least, I think it is fair to say that the fairy-tale structure is evident; although, famously, *Gone with the Wind* ends with the hero rejecting the 'princess' with, 'Frankly my dear, I don't give a damn'. *Titanic* (1997), the box-office phenomenon of 1998 – it was released on Christmas Day 1997 which explains its absence from the above chart – managed the 'trick' of creating tension with a conventionally structured narrative despite the fact that, almost certainly, everybody who saw the film knew the ship sank.

Video

To take a week at random, the top ten video rentals in Australia for the week ending 16 October 1998 were (source: *Screen International*, 30 October, 1998):

1. *Good Will Hunting*
2. *Titanic*
3. *Sphere*
4. *Hard Rain*
5. *MouseHunt*
6. *The Fallen*
7. *For Richer For Poorer*
8. *Scream 2*
9. *The Jackal*
10. *The Man in the Iron Mask*

These are all North American texts and, no doubt, all reflect conventional narrative structure. It could be argued that this is simply a result of the dominance of Hollywood at the expense of local product. However, the contrary is also true: one of the reasons Hollywood dominates is that it emulates 'fairy-tale' structure so successfully. Even if we consider a nation with considerable cultural differences to North America, Japan, we find the list – video rentals in the week before the Australian list – dominated by conventionally constructed texts:

1. *Good Will Hunting*
2. *The Princess Mononoke*
3. *Face/Off*
4. *Ring*
5. *Rasen*

6. *The Devil's Advocate*
7. *Men In Black*
8. *Copland*
9. *I Know What You Did Last Summer*
10. *Men In Black* (dubbed version)

The only non-USA text here is *The Princess Mononoke*, which broke Japanese box-office records durings its theatrical release. Although I have not seen this animated feature, the fact that it was released in North America – dubbed by American actors – suggests it too has an essentially conventional structure.

Books

The top ten best-selling books in Britain in 1996 were (source: Hamilton, 1997):

1. *The Green Mile* (Stephen King)
2. *The Rainmaker* (John Grisham)
3. *The Horse Whisperer* (Nicholas Evans)
4. *Highway Code* (Department of Transport)
5. *The Seventh Scroll* (Wilbur Smith)
6. *Sophie's World* (Jostein Gaarder)
7. *A Ruthless Need* (Catherine Cookson)
8. *Come to Grief* (Dick Francis)
9. *Coming Home* (Rosamund Pilcher)
10. *From Potter's Field* (Patricia Cornwell)

With the exception of the *Highway Code*, I would be very surprised if any of these texts did not fit comfortably within Propp's and Todorov's schemata. Although I may be wrong, the fact that I can state this with some confidence is a reflection of the universality, in the west at least, of the narrative structures described.

BIBLIOGRAPHY

Aeschylus (1961) (introduction Philip Vellacott) *Prometheus Bound* (London: Penguin).
Aldiss, B. (1973) *Billion Year Spree* (London: Weidenfeld & Nicolson).
Alexander, M. (1973) *Beowulf* (Harmondsworth: Penguin).
Altman, R. (1999) *Film/Genre* (London: British Film Institute).
Andrew, G. (1998) *The 'Three Colours' Trilogy* (London: British Film Institute).
Ang, I. (1985) *Watching Dallas* (London: Methuen).
Aristotle (1965) translated by T.S. Dorsch, *On the Art of Poetry/Classical Literary Criticism* (Harmondsworth: Penguin).
Arroyo, J. (1997) 'Kiss Kiss Bang Bang' (*Sight and Sound*, March, **7**(3)).
Asa Berger, A. (1992) *Popular Culture Genres* (Newbury Park: Sage).
Asa Berger, A. (1997) *Narratives in Popular Culture, Media, and Everyday Life* (London, Thousand Oaks, New Delhi: Sage).
Asimov, I. (1958) *The Caves of Steel* (St Albans: Panther).
Asimov, I. (1968) *I, Robot* (London: Grafton).
Auerbach, E. (1968) *Mimesis* (Princeton: Princeton University Press).
Auster, P. (1987) *The New York Trilogy* (London: Faber and Faber).
Ballard, J.G. (1965) *The Drowned World* (Harmondsworth: Penguin).
Ballard, J.G. (1973) *Crash* (London: Jonathan Cape).
Ballard, J.G. (1977) *Image – Music – Text* (Glasgow: Fontana).
Barthes, R. (1990) *S/Z* (Oxford: Blackwell).
Basinger, J. (1994) *A Woman's View* (London: Chatto & Windus).
Beckett, S. (1956) *Waiting for Godot* (London: Faber and Faber).
Bettelheim, B. (1976) *The Uses of Enchantment* (New York: Knopf).
Blade Runner (http//kzsu.stanford.edu.uwi/br/off-world.html).
Billson, A. (1997) *The Thing* (London: British Film Institute).
Booth, W.C. (1961) *The Rhetoric of Fiction* (Chicago: University of Chicago Press).
Bordwell, D. (1988) 'ApProppriations and ImPropprieties' (*Cinema Journal* **27**(3)).
Bordwell, D. and Thompson, K. (1993) *Film Art*, 4th edn (New York: McGraw-Hill).
Bowker, J. (ed.) (1991) *Secondary Media Education* (London: British Film Institute).
Branigan, E. (1992) *Narrative Comprehension and Film* (London and New York: Routledge).
Bratchell, D.F. (ed.) (1990) *Shakespearean Tragedy* (London: Routledge).
Britton, A. (1994) 'Detour', in Cameron, I. (ed.) *The Movie Book of Film Noir* (London: Studio Vista).

Broeshe, P. (1998) 'Beware the serial killers are back' (*Guardian* 17 October).

Brontë, E. (1978) *Wuthering Heights* (London: J.M. Dent).

Brown, F. (1977) *The Best of Frederic Brown* (New York: Del Rey).

Brown, M.E. (1987) 'The Politics of Soaps' (*Australian Journal of Cultural Studies* 4(2)).

Bruno, G. (1990) 'Ramble City: Postmodernism and *Blade Runner*', in Kuhn, A. (ed.) *Alien Zone* (London and New York: Verso).

Brunsdon, C. (1998) 'Structure of anxiety: recent British televsion crime fiction' (*Screen* 39(3)).

Bukatman, S. (1997) *Blade Runner* (London: British Film Institute).

Burch, N. (1980/81) 'How we got into pictures' (*Afterimage* Nos 8/9, Winter).

Cain, J.M. (1985) *The Five Great Novels of James M. Cain* (London: Pan).

Cameron, I. (ed.) (1994) *The Movie Book of Film Noir* (London: Studio Vista).

Carr, T. (ed.) (1977) *Best Science Fiction of the Year 5* (London: Book Club Associates).

Cawleti, J.G. (1976) *Adventure, Mystery, and Romance* (Chicago and London: University of Chicago Press).

Chambers Dictionary of World History 1994 (Edinburgh: Chambers).

Chandler, R. (1975) *The Raymond Chandler Omnibus* (London: Book Club Associates).

Chatman, S. (1978) *Story and Discourse* (Ithaca, NY: Cornell University Press).

Chaucer, G. (1989) *The Canterbury Tales* (New York and London: W.W. Norton).

Clarke, A. (1986) 'This is not the boy scouts', in Bennett, T., Mercer, C. and Woollacott, J. (eds) *Popular Culture and Social Relations* (Milton Keynes: Open University).

Clover, C. (1992) *Men, Women and Chainsaws* (London: British Film Institute).

Clute, J. and Nicholls, P. (eds) (1993) *The Encyclopedia of Science Fiction* (Griffin, NY: St Martin's).

Cohan, S. (1998) 'Censorship and narrative indeterminacy in "Basic Instinct"', in Neale, S. and Smith, M. (eds) *Contemporary Hollywood Cinema* (London and New York: Routledge).

Cohan, S. and Hark, I.R. (eds) (1993) *Screening the Male* (London: Routledge).

Cook, P. (ed.) (1985) *The Cinema Book* (London: British Film Institute).

Creed, B. (1990) 'Alien and the Monstrous-Feminine', in Kuhn, A. (ed.) *Alien Zone* (London and New York: Verso).

Creed, B. (1993) 'Dark Desires', in Cohan, S. and Hark, I.R. (eds) *Screening the Male* (London: Routledge).

Daiches, D. (ed.) (1971) *Companion to Literature* vol. 1 (Harmondsworth: Penguin).

Dargis, M. (1997) 'N for Noir' (*Sight and Sound* 7(7), July).

Defoe, D. (1985) *Robinson Crusoe* (London and Harmondsworth: Penguin).

Dick, P.K. (1978) *The Three Stigmata of Palmer Eldritch* (St Albans: Triad/Panther).

Dickens, C. (1969) *Hard Times* (Harmondsworth: Penguin).

Dos Passos, J. (1996) *USA* (Harmondsworth: Penguin).

Dugdale, J. (1998) 'Peek viewing for the girls' (*Guardian* 30 June 1998).

Dundes, A. (1968) 'Introduction to the Second Edition' in Propp, V. *Morphology of the Russian Folktale* (Austin: University of Texas).

Dyer, R. (1982) 'Don't Look Now – the Male pin-up' (*Screen* 23(3–4)).

Dyer, R. (1992) *Only Entertainment* (London: Routledge).

Dyer, R. (1993) *The Matter of Images* (London: Routledge).

Dyer, R. (1996) 'There's nothing I can do! Nothing!': femininity, seriality and whiteness in 'The Jewel in the Crown' (*Screen* 37(3)).

Dyer, R. (1997) 'Kill and Kill Again' (*Sight and Sound* 7(9)).

Dyer, R. (1999) *Se7en* (London: British Film Institute).

Dyer, R. (1999a) 'Kill and Kill Again – The Fascination of Serial Killing' (London: British Film Institute, Media Studies Conference).

Eagleton, T. (1983) *Literary Theory* (Oxford: Blackwell).

Early, G. (1997) 'Ali's Rumble' (*Sight and Sound*, **7**(5)).

Eco, Umberto (1985) 'Innovation and repetition' (*Daedelus*, Fall).

Eco, Umberto (1987) OU Foundation course narrative (Hard Times 4 Narrative).

Eldridge, J. (ed.) (1993) *News Content, Language and Visuals* (London: Routledge).

Eliot, T.S. (1974) *Collected Poems 1909–1962* (London: Faber and Faber).

Ellis, J. (1992) *Visible Fictions*, rev. edn (London: Routledge).

Ellroy, J. (1994) *The Big Nowhere* (London: Arrow).

Elsaesser, T. (1985) 'Tales of Sound and Fury', in Nichols, W. (ed.) *Movies and Methods* vol. 2 (Berkeley and Los Angeles: University of California Press).

Epic of Gilgamesh, The (1960) (trans. N.K. Sanders) (London: Penguin).

Evans, I. (1976) *A Short History of English Literature*, 4th edn (Harmondsworth: Penguin).

Faulkner, W. (1930/1963) *As I Lay Dying* (Harmondsworth: Penguin).

Feuer, J. (1984) 'Melodrama, Serial Form and Television' (*Screen* **225**(1)).

Fiske, J. (1987) *Television Culture* (London: Routledge).

Fiske, J. and Hartley, J. (1978) *Reading Television* (London: Methuen).

Fowles, J. (1977) *The French Lieutenant's Woman* (Triad/Granada).

French, S. (1996) *The Terminator* (London: British Film Institute).

Geraghty, C. (1991) *Women and Soap Opera* (Cambridge: Polity).

Ginsberg, A. (1956) *Howl* (San Francisco: City Lights Books).

Gledhill, C. (1980) 'Klute 1: a contemporary film noir & feminist criticism', in Kaplan E.A. (ed.) *Women in Film Noir*, rev. edn (London: British Film Institute).

Gledhill, C. (ed.) (1987) *Home is Where the Heart Is* (London: British Film Institute).

Gledhill, C. (1987a) 'The Melodramatic Field – An Investigation' in Gledhill, C. (ed.) *Home is Where the Heart Is* (London: British Film Institute).

Glover, D. (1989) 'The stuff that dreams are made of: Masculinity, femininity and the thriller', in Longhurst, D. (ed.) *Gender, Genre & Narrative Pleasure* (London: Unwin Hyman).

Griffith, R. (1976) 'Cycles and Genres' in Nichols, W. (ed.) *Movies and Methods* (Berkeley and Los Angeles: University of California Press).

Gross, L. (1995) 'Big and Loud' (*Sight and Sound* **5**(8)).

Hamilton, A. (1997) 'Fastsellers of 1996' (*Guardian* 9 January).

Hammett, D. (1982) *The Four Great Novels* (London: Pan).

Hanscombe, G. (1986) Penguin Passnotes: William Golding *The Lord of the Flies* (London: Penguin).

Hawkes, T. (1977) *Structuralism and Semiotics* (London: Methuen).

Hayward, P. and Wollen, T. (eds) (1993) *Future Visions* (London: British Film Institute).

Heath, S. (1981) *Questions of Cinema* (Basingstoke and London: Macmillan).

Henderson, B. (1985) 'The Searchers: An American Dilemma', in Nichols, W. (ed.) *Movies and Methods* vol. 2 (Berkeley and Los Angeles: University of California Press).

Henderson, J.L. (1964) '*Ancient Myths and Modern Man*' in Jung, C.G. (ed.) *Man and His Symbols* (London: Aldus).

Heyward, S. (1996) *Key Concepts in Cinema Studies* (London: Routledge).

Hoberman, J. (1994) 'Paranoia and the Pods' (*Sight and Sound* **4**(5)).

Hobson, D. (1990) 'Women, audiences and the workplace', in Brown, M.E. (ed.) *Television and Women's Culture* (London, Thousand Oaks, New Delhi: Sage).

Hobson, D. (1991) 'Soap operas at work', in Seiter, E., Borchers, H., Kreutzner, G. and Warth, E. (eds) *Remote Control* (London: Routledge).

Hodge, J. (1996) *Trainspotting* – The Screenplay (London: Faber and Faber).

Holland, P. (1997) *The Television Handbook* (London: Routledge).

Hunter, L. (1994) *Screenwriting* (London: Robert Hale).

Hurd, G. (1976) '*The Sweeney* – contradictons and coherence' (*Screen Education* No. 20).

Hurd, G. (1981) 'The Television Presentation of the Police', in Bennett, T., Boyd-Bowman, S., Mercer, C. and Woollacott, J. (eds) *Popular Film and Television* (London: British Film Institute).

Interactive Movie Database website (IMDB) (http://us.imdb.com/).

Jackson, R. (1981) *Fantasy: The Literature of Subversion* (London: Methuen).

Jaggi, M. (1998) 'The impure norm' (*Guardian* 2 May).

Jameson, F. (1992) *The Geopolitical Aesthetic* (Bloomington and London: Indiana University Press and British Film Institute).

Jung, C.G. (1964) *Man and His Symbols* (London: Aldus).

Kafka, F. (1977) (trans. Douglas Scott & Chris Waller) *The Trial* (London: Picador).

Kaplan E.A. (ed.) (1980) *Women in Film Noir*, rev. edn (London: British Film Institute).

Keats, J. (1966) *Selected Poems and Letters of Keats* (Oxford: Heinemann Educational Books).

Keeble, R. (1994) *The Newspapers Handbook* (London: Routledge).

Keeping, C. and Crossly-Holland, K. (1982) *Beowulf* (Oxford: Oxford University Press).

Kennedy, D. (1998) 'Mr Skint strikes it rich' (*The Times* 10 January).

Kerr, P. (1979) 'Out of what past? Notes on the B film noir' (*Screen Education*, nos.32–33).

Kerr, P. (1993) *A Philosophical Investigation* (London: Arrow).

King, S. (1977) *The Shining* (Sevenoaks: New English Library).

Kitses, J. (1969) *Horizons West* (London: Secker and Warburg/British Film Institute).

Kitses, J. (1996) *Gun Crazy* (London: British Film Institute).

Krutnik, F. (1991) *In a Lonely Street* (London: Routledge).

Kuhn, A. (1982) *Women's Pictures* (London, Boston, Melbourne and Henley: Routledge & Kegan Paul).

Kuhn, A. (1985) *History of Narrative Codes*, in Cook, P. (ed.) *The Cinema Book* (London: British Film Institute).

Kuhn, A. (ed.) (1990) *Alien Zone* (London and New York: Verso).

Lacey, N. (1996) 'Gender and SF: What Does the Future Hold?' (Science Fiction Genre Project, Stafford).

Lacey, N. (1996a) 'Pulp Fiction – Back to the Future' (in the picture *Film Reader 1*, 36 Hospital Rd, Keighley, BD20 5EU).

Lacey, N. (1998) *Image and Representation* (Basingstoke: Macmillan).

Lacey, N. (1998a) *Media Studies* – Exam Success Guide (Deddington: Philip Allan).

Lacey, N. (1998b) 'On Me 'Ed Girl!' (in the picture, number 34, autumn itp, 36 Hospital Rd, Keighley, BD20 5EU).

Lawley, P. (1985) 'Top Girls', in Berney, K.A. (ed.) *Contemporary British Dramatists* (London, Detroit, Washington DC: St James Press).

LeGuin, U. (1969) *The Left Hand of Darkness* (St Albans: Panther).

LeGuin, U. (1977) 'The Word for World is Forest', in Ellison, H. (ed.) *Again, Dangerous Visions 1* (London: Pan).

Lem, S. (1961/1973) *Solaris* (London: Arrow).

Lem, S. (1976) *The Star Diaries* (London: Futura).

Lemon, L.T. and Reis M.J. (eds) (1965) *Russian Formalist Criticism* (Lincoln: University of Nebraska Press).

Lesage, J. (1985) 'S/Z and The Rules of the Game', in Nichols, W. (ed.) *Movies and Methods* vol. 2 (Berkeley and Los Angeles: University of California Press).

Levi-Strauss, C. (1968) *Structural Anthropology* (Harmondsworth: Penguin).

Longhurst, D. (ed.) (1989) *Gender, Genre & Narrative Pleasure* (London: Unwin Hyman).

Longhurst, D. (1989a) 'Science fiction: The dreams of men', in Longhurst, D. (ed.) *Gender, Genre & Narrative Pleasure* (London: Unwin Hyman).

Luthi, M. (1984) *The Fairytale as Art Form and Portrait of Man* (Chicago: University of Chicago Press).

MacArthur, T. (ed.) (1992) *The Oxford Companion to the English Language* (London: Quality Paperbacks Direct).

MacCabe, C. (1980) *Godard: Images, Sounds, Politics* (Basingstoke and London: Macmillan).

MacCabe, C. (1981) 'Pierrot le fou' (*The Movie* (72)).

MacCabe, C. (1992) Preface to 'The Geopolitical Aesthetic' (Frederic Jameson (1992)).

MacCabe, C. (1999) 'Bayonets in Paradise' (*Sight and Sound* 9(9)).

Making Music (1997) September (138).

Malory, T. (1969) *The Death of Arthur* (Harmondsworth: Penguin).

Marketing of a Film – Judge Dredd – A Case Study 95 Film Education.

Masterman, L. (1985) *Teaching the Media* (London and New York: Routledge.)

McArthur, C. (1972) *Underground USA* (London: Secker and Warburg/British Film Institute).

McArthur, C. (1992) *The Big Heat* (London: British Film Institute).

Metzger, B.M. and Coogan, M.D. (eds) (1993) *The Oxford Companion to the Bible* (New York and Oxford: Oxford University Press).

Modleski, T. (1982) *Loving With a Vengeance* (London: Methuen).

Monaco, J. (1976) *The New Wave* (London: Oxford University Press).

Monaco, J., Pallot, J. and Baseline (1992) *The Second Virgin Film Guide* (London: Virgin).

Moon, B. (1992) *Literary Terms: A Practical Glossary* (London: English & Media Centre).

Morley, D. (1992) *Television, Audiences and Cultural Studies* (London: Routledge).

Mosenzon, Y. (1996) 'Pretty Woman' – A Proppian Fairy Tale (in the picture *Film Reader 1*, 36 Hospital Road, Keighley, BD20 5EU).

Nash, M. (1976) 'Vampyr and the Fantastic' (*Screen* 17(3)).

Natriss, D. (1997) The UK Episode Guide to The X-Files (website).

Neale, S. (1980) *Genre* (London: British Film Institute).

New Encyclopedia Britannica, 15th edn (1989) (Chicago: University of Chicago).

Nichols, W. (1981) *Ideology and the Image* (Bloomington: Indiana University Press).

Nowell-Smith, G. (1981) 'The Television Presentation of the Police', in Bennett, T., Boyd-Bowman, S., Mercer, C. and Woollacott, J. (eds) *Popular Film and Television* (London: British Film Institute).

O'Keefe, B. (1996) 'The Language of *Trainspotting*' (*The English Review*, November).

O'Sullivan, T. and Jewkes, Y. (eds) (1997) *The Media Studies Reader* (London: Edward Arnold).

O'Sullivan, T., Hartley, J., Saunders, D., Montgomery, M. and Fiske, J. (1994) *Key Concepts in Communications and Cultural Studies*, 2nd edn (London: Routledge).

Orwell, G. (1954) *Nineteen Eighty-Four* (Harmondsworth: Penguin).

Panofsky, E. (1955) *Meaning in the Visual Arts* (New York: Anchor).
Paretsky, S. (1993) *V.I. Warshawski* (London: Penguin).
Parrinder, P. (1980) *Science Fiction: Its Criticism and Teaching* (London and New York: Methuen).
PatronSaints/Gibson (1998) infovillage.com/PatronSaints/Gibson.html
Peacock, T.L. (1969) *Nightmare Abbey/Crotchet Castle* (Harmondsworth: Penguin).
Penley, C. (1990) 'Time Travel, Primal Scene and the Critical Dystopia', in Kuhn, A. (ed.) (1990) *Alien Zone* (London and New York: Verso).
Phelps, G. (1979) *An Introduction to 50 British Novels 1600–1900*, (London: Pan).
Philips, P. (1996) 'Genre, star and auteur', in Nelmes, J. (ed.) *An Introduction to Film Studies* (London: Routledge).
Pirie, D. (1996) 'Wave Theory' (*Sight and Sound*, 6(6)).
Place, J.A. and Peterson, L.S. (1976) 'Some Visual Mofits of Film Noir', in Nichols, W. (ed.) *Movies and Methods* (Berkeley and Los Angeles: University of California Press).
Place, J. (1980) 'Women in film noir', in Kaplan E.A. (ed.) *Women in Film Noir*, rev. edn (London: British Film Institute).
Poe, E.A. (1967) *Selected Writings* (Harmondsworth: Penguin).
Poe, E.A. (1976) *The Science Fiction of Edgar Allan Poe* (Harmondsworth: Penguin).
Poole, S. (1998) 'Eat pixels, sucker' (*Guardian* 22 May).
Pope, R. (1995) *Textual Intervention* (London: Routledge).
Propp, V. (1968) *Morphology of the Russian Folktale* (Austin: University of Texas).
Pye, D. (1994) 'Film Noir and Suppressive Narrative', in Cameron, I. (ed.) *The Movie Book of Film Noir* (London: Studio Vista).
Rayns, A. (1994) 'Sono otoko, kyobo ni tsuki (*Violent Cop*)' (*Sight and Sound* 4(1)).
Rich, B.R. (1995) 'Dumb Lugs and Femmes Fatales' (*Sight and Sound* 5(11)).
Ridley, M.R. (1989) *Othello* (London: Routledge).
Robbins, H.W. (1993) 'More Human Than I Am Alone', in Cohan, S. and Hark, I.R. (eds) *Screening the Male* (London: Routledge).
Rogin, M. (1998) *Independence Day* (London: British Film Institute).
Romney, J. (1998) 'They're out to get you' (*Guardian*, 19 October).
Rosen, C. (1971) *The Classical Style* (London: Faber & Faber).
Ross, A. (1987) 'Miami Vice: selling in' (*Communication 9*).
Rushing, J. Hocker and Frentz, T.S. (1995) *Projecting the Shadow* (Chicago and London: University of Chicago Press).
Russell, M.D. (1997) *The Sparrow* (London: Black Swan).
Ryall, T. (1975) 'Teaching Through Genre' (*Screen Education* 17).
Scholes, R. and Rabkin, E.S. (1977) *Science Fiction: History Science Vision* (New York: Oxford University Press).
Schrader, P. (1972) 'Notes of film noir' (*Film Comment* 8(1)).
Shelley, M. (1968) *Frankenstein in Three Gothic Novels* (Harmondsworth: Penguin).
Slotkin, R. (1973) *Regeneration Through Violence* (Middletown: Wesleyan University Press).
Sontag, S. (1979) 'The Imagination of Disaster', in Mast, G. and Cohen, M. (eds) *Film Theory and Criticism*, 2nd edn (Oxford: Oxford University Press).
Sophocles (1947) (trans. E.F. Watling) *The Theban Plays* (Harmondsworth: Penguin).
Stafford, R (1997) Youth Pictures Project (itp, 36 Hospital Rd, Keighley, BD20 5EU).
Stafford, R. (1998) Melodrama and Genre Project (itp, 36 Hospital Rd, Keighley, BD20 5EU).

Stafford, R. (1996) Science Fiction Genre Project (in the picture 36 Hospital Road, Keighley, BD20 5EU).

Stam, R., Burgoyne, R. and Flitterman-Lewis, S. (1992) *New Vocabularies in Film Semiotics* (London: Routledge).

Sterne, L. (1967) *The Life and Opinions of Tristram Shandy* (Harmondsworth: Penguin).

Storr, A. (1992) *Music and Mind* (London: HarperCollins).

Strange, O. (1961) *Sudden* (London: Corgi).

Strinati, D. (1997) 'Postmodernism and Popular Culture' in O'Sullivan, T. and Jewkes, Y. (eds) *The Media Studies Reader* (London: Edward Arnold).(

Sutcliff, R. (1961) *Dragonslayer* (Oxford: Heinemann Educational).

Taubin, A. (1996) 'The Allure of Decay' (*Sight and Sound* 6(1)).

Thomson, D. (1981) 'Pizza (or Pasta) Westerns' (*The Movie* (71)).

Thomson, D. (revised 1995) *The Biographical Dictionary of Film* (London: Andre Deutsch).

Thwaites, T., Davis, L. and Mules, W. (1994) *Tools for Cultural Studies* (South Melbourne: Macmillan).

Tilley, A. (1991) 'Narrative', in Lusted, D. (ed.) *The Media Studies Book* (London: Routledge).

Todorov, T. (1975) *The Fantastic* (Ithaca, NY: Cornell University Press).

Todorov, T. (1988) 'The typology of detective fiction', in Lodge, D. (ed.) *Modern Criticism and Theory: a Reader* (New York: Longman White Plains).

Tolson, A. (1996) *Mediations* (London and New York: Edward Arnold).

Trinta, A.R. (1998) 'News from Home: A Study of Realism and Melodrama', in Geraghty, C. and Lusted, D. (eds) *The Television Studies Book* (London: Routledge).

Trumbell, D. (1995) 'Escape From Gravity' (*Sight and Sound* 5(5)).

Tudor, A. (1976) 'Genre and Critical Methodology', in Nichols, W. (ed.) *Movies and Methods* (Berkeley and Los Angeles: University of California Press).

Tulloch, J. (1990) *Television Drama: Agency, Audience and Myth* (London: Routledge).

Turner, G. (1993) *Film As Social Practice*, 2nd edn (London: Routledge).

Vogler, C. (1999) *A Winter's Journey*, 2nd edn (London: Michael Wiese Productions).

Walker, M. (1982) 'Melodrama and the American Cinema' (*Movie* Nos. 29/30).

Walker, M. (1994) 'Film Noir: Introduction', in Cameron, I. (ed.) *The Movie Book of Film Noir* (London: Studio Vista).

Ward, A.C. (1975) *Longman Companion to 20th Century Literature*, 2nd edn (London: Book Club Associates).

Warshow, R. (1970) *The Immediate Experience* (New York: Atheneum Books).

Watson, J. (1998) *Media Communication* (Basingstoke: Macmillan).

Watson, J. and Hill, A. (1993) *A Dictionary of Communication & Media Studies*, 3rd edn (London: Edward Arnold).

Watt, I. (1972) *The Rise of the Novel* (Harmondsworth: Pelican).

Weiten, W. (1986) *Psychology Applied to Modern Life*, 2nd edn (Pacific Grove: Brooks/Cole).

Welsh, I. (1993) *Trainspotting* (London: Minerva).

Wentworth, S. (1994) *One Night of Love* (Richmond: Mills & Boon).

White, T.H. (1962) *The Once and Future King* (Glasgow: Fontana).

Widdicombe, R. (1994) 'Discovering legends in his own lifetime' (*The Sunday Times, The Culture* 4 September).

Willemen, P. (1980) Introduction, in Neale, S. (ed) *Genre* (London: British Film Institute).

Williams, R. (1977) *Marxism and Literature* (Oxford: Oxford University Press).

Winder, D. (1994) *Internet Jargon A–Z* (Bath: Future Publishing).

Winnington, R. (1946) 'Critic's Prologue' (Penguin *Film Review* no. 1, August).

Withall, K. (1996) 'Into the Labyrinth – The Serial Killer Cycle' (In the picture *Film Reader 1*, 36 Hospital Road, Keighley, BD20 5EU).

Wittstock, M. (1998) 'For those watching in black and white...' (*Guardian* 2 March).

Wollen, P. (1976) 'North By North-West: a morphological analysis' (*Film Form* 1(1)).

Wollen, P. (1985) 'Godard and Counter Cinema: Vent d'Est', in Nichols, W. (ed.) *Movies and Methods* vol. 2 (Berkeley and Los Angeles: University of California Press).

Wood, R. (1981) *Howard Hawks*, rev. edn (London: British Film Institute).

Wood, R. (1985) 'An Introduction to the American Horror Film', in Nichols, W. (ed.) *Movies and Methods* vol. 2 (Berkeley and Los Angeles: University of California Press).

Wordsworth, W. (1970) *The Prelude* (Oxford: Oxford University Press).

Wright, W. (1975) *Sixguns and Society* (Berkeley: University of California Press).

Zoonen, L. van (1994) *Feminist Media Studies* (London, Thousand Oaks and New Delhi: Sage).

INDEX